BANNED BOOKS

BANNED BOOKS
387 B.C. to 1978 A.D.

Fourth Edition
of
Banned Books: Informal Notes . . .

By Anne Lyon Haight
Updated and Enlarged
By Chandler B. Grannis

With an Opening Essay by Charles Rembar, Esq.

R. R. BOWKER COMPANY
New York & London, 1978

Published by R. R. Bowker Company
1180 Avenue of the Americas, New York, N.Y. 10036
Copyright © 1978 by Xerox Corporation
Censorship in America: The Legal Picture © Charles Rembar 1978
Printed and bound in the United States of America
Library of Congress Cataloging in Publication Data
Haight, Anne Lyon.
  Banned books, 387 B.C. to 1978 A.D.

  First-3d published under title: Banned books.
  Bibliography: p.
  Includes index.
  1. Condemned books—Bibliography.   2. Prohibited
books—Bibliography.   I. Grannis, Chandler B.
II. Title.
Z1019.H15 1978   098′.1   78-9720
ISBN 0-8352-1078-2

Contents

Preface

The number of people who want to prevent other people from reading or seeing certain things is truly amazing; amazing, that is, unless we admit that there is a censorious impulse, latent or overt, in most of us. Power gives the impulse free rein, but people without power are also tempted by the wish to censor, partly to obtain some measure of influence over others, and partly to strike out against something they fear.

Censorship by religious, kingly, and parliamentary authorities was familiar in the past. Actual or attempted repression by governmental authorities at every level is all too familiar in the present. This is true even in the relatively free societies. Britain has its severe Official Secrets Act; the United States, with some difficulty, escaped having one passed in 1976. Both nations experience localized efforts to restrict freedom.

In the United States, changes in public attitudes have been continuous, especially in the past couple of decades. Looking back, one sees what may have been a relatively simple picture in 1935 when Bowker's *Banned Books* appeared in its first form as the record of an exhibition by the Junior League of New York City. The situation was more serious both in 1955, when the second edition cited the ravages of McCarthyism, and in 1970, at the time of the third edition, when new court decisions were being digested and political and sexual issues were being angrily debated.

Since 1970, questions about undue governmental secrecy have taken on immensely increased importance, and decisions regarding obscenity, far from settling that issue, have been followed by wide confusion.

Issues of the freedom to write and publish material about public affairs have come repeatedly into focus in connection with the Vietnam War and its final stages, the "Pentagon Papers" case, the Watergate revelations, and the disclosures of wrongdoing in the Federal Bureau of Investigation and the Central Intelligence Agency. Access to materials formerly classified or suppressed has been opened by court decisions and freedom-of-information laws. Debate has sharpened over the application of rights to privacy and of the public's "right to know."

Other issues involving the freedom to publish and to read relate to changes in personal and social attitudes. The defiance of some former values—about sex, family, use of language, patterns of living—was shocking or highly disturbing in the 1960s; it had become commonplace by the late 1970s. But it remained upsetting to some and therefore led to continuing attempts at censorship, especially in relatively conservative communities.

The U.S. Supreme Court decisions of June 1973 seemed to give renewed regulatory authority to local and state bodies, and this was welcomed especially by those who wished to shield not only young children but high school and college students and adults from materials presumably offensive to community standards—whatever "community" was taken to mean.

All these trends are necessarily reflected in this new edition of *Banned Books*.

To bring the legal picture up-to-date, in fact up to early May 1978, Charles Rembar has written a provocative, deeply informed opening essay for this book, challenging not only to all-out conservatives, but also to fervent libertarians. Mr. Rembar was the successful defender of *Lady Chatterley's Lover*, *Tropic of Cancer*, and *Memoirs of a Woman of Pleasure* (*Fanny Hill*), and has given a lively account of these cases in state and federal courts and the U.S. Supreme Court in his book *The End of Obscenity* (Random House, Bantam Books).

This edition of *Banned Books* presents, for the most part, examples of actual or attempted book bannings over the centuries, worldwide, but with emphasis on recent U.S. episodes. Many of the older notes have been revised, some considerably expanded, and about 60 new entries are added. Appendix 1, "Trends in Censorship," has been greatly revised and expanded. Appendixes 2 and 3, respectively, present quotations from famous statements on censorship and from some significant court decisions—both modestly expanded.

Appendix 4, an added feature, is an extensive set of excerpts from *The Report of the Commission on Obscenity and Pornography*, a U.S. government document that has received far less attention than it deserves. Though issued in 1970 in editions from the Government Printing Office and from Random House and Bantam Books, it remains the only comprehensive study of the subject. Established by Congress, with members appointed by President Johnson, the Commission recommended among many other points (a minority dissenting) that sex education, discussion, and research should be promoted; that laws restricting sexual materials for adults should be repealed; but that restrictions on access by children be retained, along with restrictions on public displays and mailings unwanted by those subjected to them. The report's "permissive" recommendations were repudiated by President Nixon and the majority of commissioners were vilified by him and others. Nevertheless, the document should be recognized as recording some of the most careful research and thought yet available in connection with sexually oriented materials.

Appendix 5 is a selection of federal statutes and Customs and postal regulations bearing on questions of censorship. In preparing this guide, up-to-date as of May 1978, Henry R. Kaufman, vice president and general counsel of the Association of American Publishers, has done a valuable service for the book world and the related communications industries.

The materials that publishers, booksellers, librarians, educators, writers—and readers, too—must defend in the everyday business of disseminating literature are more open, frank, and challenging than ever before. I hope that this edition of *Banned Books* will lead readers further into the issues it raises. The old basic areas of censorship remain— doctrine, sex, secrecy, security. The points of conflict keep shifting. The methods of censorship are various, and are imposed not only by bureaucracy, but also by the social climate; not only by official suppression, but by the writer's or editor's expurgation. (For a broad review of expurgation see Noel Perrin's entertaining *Dr. Bowdler's Legacy* [Atheneum, 1969].)

Many books that will reward the reader are named in "Selected Readings and References" at the end of this volume. Still other studies are awaited. In the international area of human rights, particularly the rights of silenced or otherwise persecuted writers, the P.E.N. American Center has begun issuing country-by-country studies. Amnesty International publishes periodic reports. In the area of claimed needs for secrecy and confidentiality, the issues are by no means clear-cut; they are at this writing being debated in the courts and in public media. All these areas call for careful, book-length analysis.

For the opportunity to work on the 4th edition of *Banned Books*, I am grateful to the R. R. Bowker Company and the heirs of Anne Lyon Haight, creator of the book, a woman of lively intellect and devotion to freedom in the classic American sense. I am grateful, equally, to the staff of Bowker's Frederic G. Melcher Library—Jean R. Peters, Librarian, and Iris Anderson, Asst. Librarian; the custodians of the *Publishers Weekly* reference files—Jean Norrington and her successor Miriam E. Phelps; and the staff of the Book Editorial Department at Bowker.

Some Notes on Organization and Style

Entries in the main portion of this book are arranged according to the birth dates of the authors. Where two or more authors were born in the same year, arrangement is alphabetical based on surname. In cases where the author's birth date is not known, each entry is placed according to the year of the event cited. The same is true of entries headed not with authors' names but with titles or place names.

Years of first publication are given, where known, after the titles listed below the author's name.

In several entries, the term *Index* appears. This refers to the Vatican's now terminated list of prohibited books, *Index Librorum Prohibitorum.*

Chandler B. Grannis

New York, N. Y.
May 1978

Censorship in America:
The Legal Picture

by Charles Rembar

One of the interesting aspects of this volume, *Banned Books*, is that none of the books it names is banned. That is, at present, in the United States. And under the current state of the law none could be. I use the word "banned" in its ordinary sense: suppressed, suppressed by government. The word "book" too is used in its principal sense—the printed word in volume form.*

In the past, book banning has happened in two main ways. Books have been censored at the start and never seen the light of print. This was the method employed in England prior to the eighteenth century. Or their publication or sale or transportation has been made a crime, so that their distribution is perilous and their reading generally sneaky. This was the method in England from 1720 on, and in this country from early in the nineteenth century until 1966.

There have also been partial interferences. The closest to suppression is injunction, a curious hybrid that amounts to post-prior-censorship: the book comes out and then, if the government wins, further publication ceases, while copies already circulating keep right on circulating. There is the barrier to importation that Customs has interposed from time to time, which does not necessarily affect domestic publication. And exclusion from the mails, which does not necessarily foreclose delivery by other means of transportation. Injunction requires action by a court, as do the efforts of postal and customs officials if challenged. Finally, there is extrajudicial suppression, when police or other officials threaten prosecu-

---

*Books have had their publication stopped or altered at the suit or threat of suit by a private party for copyright infringement, for libel or privacy, or for breach of contract. This is quite different from government suppression, although recently we have had the odd example of the government, in the CIA cases, taking the role of private party and suing to restrain publication for breach of contract where the author has made a contract with the government not to disclose the information he puts in the book.
© Charles Rembar 1978

tion. Whenever resisted, this last has been held unlawful, and the police know better today.*

We still have conflict about the acceptability of books in libraries, school and public. Typically, it arises when trustees or school boards seek to expel a book that the librarian would keep. This is significant conflict, but it is far from the total suppression that banning by law imposes. The book remains available everywhere except on the particular shelves. Moreover, the question is complicated by the fact that the library, limited by its budget, cannot possibly contain more than a small fraction of all books that are published. Books are chosen or rejected according to the judgment of some group or individual, and the factors that can justly form the judgment are several: the reputation of the author, the significance of the subject, the merit of the particular book, the effect the book may have on the education (in the broadest sense) of those who use the library. Except where irrational or badly motivated decisions are made, it can be argued, on behalf of the boards, that what we have here is not a question of censorship but a question of selection, that choices must be made as to how their meager funds should be used, and that it is undemocratic to lodge the power of decision in bureaucratic employees (librarians) rather than in representatives elected by communities. In the abstract, the argument is fine. In fact, bureaucratic employees usually have their hearts in the right place—and, even more important, their heads—while the elected officials are usually giving vent to political or moral bias.

But despite our continuing proper concern with other First Amendment problems, there is no longer banning of books in the ordinary sense of those words, indeed the only sense in which the words were understood when the first edition of *Banned Books* was published.

One day in the early 1960s, I had lunch with Samuel Roth, a man with a scholarly air. He had recently come out of prison. Roth said, among other things, that people did not read enough; it was important they read more. Unfortunately (his word), there were very many people who would read only the sort of books he published.

Note the emphasis on reading. The most famous name in the indices of obscenity decisions was talking about the printed word. That was what the law of obscenity until a very recent date was all about—literary censorship. It was called literary censorship to distinguish it from the other principal forms of censorship—political and religious. Even the word "pornog-

---

*When President Eisenhower's Postmaster General excluded *Lady Chatterley's Lover* from the mails, and before the General's decision was overruled by the courts, the publisher, Grove Press, on its lawyer's advice, shipped copies by truck. This, of course, could have resulted in criminal prosecution if the case had been lost; the federal antiobscenity law covers any kind of transport in interstate commerce. But the postal order did not in itself control other kinds of interstate shipment, and the publisher was willing to take the risk.

raphy," which now mostly refers to pictures, until then denoted literature; etymologically, it means "writing about harlots." Not photographs, not films, not radio, not television, not the theater. Writing. That would be the main field of the First Amendment battles of the 1960s. The question was: should any books be banned, and, if so, which?

The question has been answered. The answer, theoretically, is: Only a very few, those that fail at every tier of the celebrated triple test—prurient appeal, patent offensiveness, and lack of value. The answer, practically, is: None. This, again, is the United States. Things are different elsewhere in the world. In countries where four-fifths of all humans live, disapproved books do not appear, or if they happen to appear they are savagely suppressed.

Hence, the present edition of this work is not so much current events as history. This does not negate its significance. We need this list to remind us how poisonous censorship is, and how powerful, and how recently things were different. The victory is but lately won. The forces on the other side have not vanished; they can regroup and fight again. As recently as the 1930s, one of the most respected courts in America, the Supreme Judicial Court of Massachusetts, affirmed the criminal conviction of a bookseller for selling one of America's most respected novels—Theodore Dreiser's *An American Tragedy*. Ditto Lillian Smith's *Strange Fruit* in the 1940s. Still later, the U.S. Supreme Court let stand a New York banning of Edmund Wilson's *Memoirs of Hecate County*. And, in the mid-1950s, the decade before the last one, Norman Mailer's *The Naked and the Dead* was still being investigated by the Georgia State Library Commission. A change so radical and fresh—with anti-intellect, antifreedom urges still strong among us (it is hardly necessary to name the other issues on which they make their presence felt)—surely has an interest more than antiquarian.

The illumination offered by this volume may help avoid stupidity. The First Amendment, which in my opinion protects every book, does not protect every attempt to communicate, nor can it. This obvious truth eludes too many advocates. Examples of what the Amendment does not protect are easy to find. Take just one of many, one which no good liberal will dispute. The Securities and Exchange Commission can silence a swindler who would make false statements in the sale of stocks and bonds. (Note to flailing libertarians: here we even have "prior restraint," Great Sacred Cow that confuses First Amendment thought.)

There are too many people, on both sides, who fail or refuse to understand the nature of the First Amendment. The danger from the authoritarians who would control expression is sufficiently familiar. What is less obvious is the danger from authoritarians who wave the banner of freedom. Their efforts would turn the free-speech guarantee into a garbage

xiv   CENSORSHIP IN AMERICA

van, which is made to carry such things as topless-bottomless bars and advertising by lawyers (two things not so very different). The courts, as much the slaves of fashion as the rest of us, meekly go along. Where once they held the First Amendment in much too narrow a compass, now, having overlearned their lesson, they bloat it unhealthily. A few days ago, a majority of our Supreme Court made corporate political power a special pet of the First Amendment.

In the obscenity field two caveats that the most libertarian of our Justices, Hugo Black and William Douglas, time and again expressed tend to be ignored. One is that those who claim protection of the Amendment must not intrude on those who wish to be let alone. A subway ad for a paperback book contains a picture that one might reasonably consider offensive or disturbing to children. The sight of subway ads cannot be avoided by subway riders. Children ride the subways. The ad is removed, and the publisher hollers "Censorship." Wrong. He is bullying a captive audience.

The other caveat is that the First Amendment protects not action but expression. Yet we hear the Amendment cited by lawyers for massage parlors. Wrong again. Whether the parlors are a good thing or a bad thing, their operation has to do with conduct, which is, unquestionably, subject to government control, not with speech or writing—with action, not expression. Indeed, the control of conduct is what government is all about.*

Why can we not rest easy? Why is it important that the caveats be observed, that the true aims of the guarantees be properly understood? It is important because the ultimate fate of the Amendment lies in how it is seen by citizens. Citizens can be led; the courts were far ahead of them in the 1960s. But the excesses of those who would use the guarantees for their own purposes—for purposes the First Amendment was not designed to protect—can lead the citizen to turn against the Amendment. It is the sort of turn that has ample antecedent in other aspects of our history, and freedom will be the loser. In pursuit of private interests, we can, in Milton's marvelous phrase, become blind mouths. The exercise of reading this book may help improve our vision.

*At a joint lecture on obscenity censorship before the New York City Bar Association, attended by a rather large group (large because the subject is one that usually draws and because admission was free), I mentioned the distinction in trying to answer a question from the floor. One of my colleagues, a very good lawyer, attacked the answer and the distinction. Suppose, he said, a play is presented in a public theater, and the play consists entirely of acts of sexual intercourse. The play, he added, is not advertised, this to avoid the possible complication of the Ginzburg "pandering" decision. Would you, he asked, call this play "action" or "expression"?

You say there is no advertising, I said. Suppose I want to see the play and don't know where to find it. Luckily, I meet a friend who has already seen it. What's my question to my friend? Do I ask: "Where's the expression?"

How did the writing and publishing of books free themselves of their shackles? To answer this, we need to go back a bit.

First let me try to clear away a common misconception. We speak of the banning of books, or of other forms of expression, as though the courts were creating the ban. Newspapers and news magazines and radio and television all report judicial decisions as though the motive power for censorship came from the judiciary. It does not. It comes from us, the people. In the United States (Britain at one time was different), the courts have no power to censor or to punish publication, except as some legislative assembly has declared the publishing unlawful. Congress, or a state legislature, or a municipal government, must first enact a statute or an ordinance declaring certain defined expression illegal.

All our laws, of course, are enforced through the courts. But no American court will ever act against a book except on the authority of a statute. On the contrary, the most significant function of the courts in this regard since 1959 has been to hack away at the statutes, to permit the publication of books despite the legislative declarations. Our elected representatives have ordered that some kinds of books be banned, and the courts, citing the First Amendment, have countermanded their orders. When a court decides a case in favor of the prosecution—as courts used to do with books and still occasionally do where other media are concerned—it is allowing the statute to operate. Except for the existence of the statute, the court would not act at all. So our courts are not, and have never been, the burners of our books. We the people are.

Many of the books mentioned in this volume were banned for obscenity. Banning has three principal targets—sedition, heresy, and obscenity. That is to say, speech and writing that goes against the government, against established religion, and against sexual convention. If we consider them separately, obscenity censorship is the least important of the three. But they cannot really be separated, not in practice or in theory, not in their history or their essence.

Seditious utterance and heresy had always been subject to punishment, the most horrid forms of punishment. Obscenity did not become a problem until large numbers of people were reading, and that, of course, did not occur until after printing was invented. Literary censorship is an elitist notion; obscenity is something, it was thought, from which the masses should be shielded. I never heard a prosecutor or a condemning judge announce that his moral fiber had been injured by the book in question. It was always someone else's moral fiber for which anxiety was felt. It was "they" who would be damaged. In the seventeenth century, "they" began to read; literacy was no longer confined to the clergy and the upper class. And it is in the seventeenth century that we first hear about censorship for obscenity.

It was easy in that century. The printing of books was licensed by the government. You could no more publish a book without a license than now you can run a saloon. Licensing of printing disappeared from Britain at the end of the seventeenth century, about the time of the Glorious Revolution. The connection is not so strong as is generally assumed; the event owes as much to administrative difficulty as to Lockean liberality. But before very long the publication of obscenity became a crime, without benefit of legislation. It happened in a case that demonstrates the inseparability of the various forms of suppression. It is called *Curll's Case.**

Curll was prosecuted in 1720 for publishing a book alleged to be obscene. There was no statute that made such publishing a crime. The king's attorney general, however, made this argument:

> What I insist upon is that this is an offense at common law, as it tends to corrupt the morals of the King's subjects, and is against the peace of the King. Peace includes good order and government, and that peace may be broken in many instances without an actual force. (1) If it be an act against the constitution or civil government; (2) If it be against religion; and (3) If against morality.
>
> (1) Under the first head fall all the cases of seditious words or writings. . . .
>
> (2) It is a libel if it reflects upon religion, that great basis of civil government and society; and it may be both a spiritual and temporal offense. . . .
>
> (3) As to morality. Destroying that is destroying the peace of the government, for government is no more than publick order, which is morality. My Lord Chief Justice Hale used to say, Christianity is part of the law and why not morality too? . . .

Obscenity prosecution thus had its genesis in an attitude that goes beyond obscenity and takes in political and religious dissidence. The same spirit that would have the government stamp out obscene books would also have the government stamp out seditious speech and heresy. The argument prevailed. The court decided that the publication of obscenity was a crime at common law. The common law is in theory law that comes from immemorial custom and tradition—law so old, as judges used to put it, "that memory runneth not to the contrary." This particular tradition must have lain around unnoticed for a thousand years or more.

---

*Curll—his name is variously spelled with one "l" and with two—had a colorful career, which included a great feud with Alexander Pope (see also p. 26 of this book). The ancient antagonists were united in death by our Citizens for Decent Literature, who relied heavily on *Curll's Case* in their Supreme Court brief on *Fanny Hill.* The brief cited, along with *Curll,* Pope's quatrain advising that vice should not be "seen too oft"—an observation with which a reader of the book might agree, though not necessarily for Pope's, or the Citizens', reasons.

By the end of the century, our Constitution had explicitly rejected the ideas that prevailed in *Curll's Case* so far as the new federal government was concerned. Or seemed to. Despite the First Amendment, the Alien and Sedition Laws were soon afterward enacted and judicially upheld, by a judge who had been prominent in the drafting of the Constitution. To a large part of the citizenry, perhaps to most, the Bill of Rights, which at the present moment looms larger than the body of the Constitution, was at the time an insignificant appendage—something like the boilerplate that follows the main provisions of a contract.*

The government of this country has never punished anyone for writing a heretical book. But the notion that it might punish the author of a seditious book lasted a long time, and that it might punish the author of an obscene book lasted even longer. In the 1950s, the Supreme Court recognized that books could not be suppressed on the ground that they urged sedition. Despite the pressures of the McCarthy era and some deplorable judicial writing (the product of a conflict between those pressures and the Justices' good instincts), the law actually moved in the direction of political freedom. In the course of the litigation in which the Communist party leaders were prosecuted and most of them convicted, the Court made it plain that the government could not, under the Constitution, suppress a book that advocated the hated Communist doctrine.

It took another decade before we were willing to extend the First Amendment to the third of the linked breaches of the king's peace. It was not until *Fanny Hill* that the Supreme Court confirmed the rejection by our Constitution of the whole of the argument made by the king's attorney general.

Meanwhile the law of obscenity had flourished. From the time of *Curll's Case* forward, the threat of prosecution was enough to drive a book underground. Neither the author nor the original publisher of *Fanny Hill* was brought to court, but the book disappeared from public view. (Twelve years after its publication, a dealer named Drybutter was put in the pillory for selling the book.) The cases that did go to court contributed little to legal thought. A criminal case does not ordinarily carry a judicial opinion unless there is an appeal, and in obscenity prosecutions there were very few appeals until well into the nineteenth century.

Nothing is criminal in the United States unless a statute says so; we have no common law crime. But at the start there was some confusion. In 1815, in Philadelphia, there was a conviction of certain entrepreneurs who

---

*In the last half century, the Supreme Court has applied the guarantees of the First Amendment not only to the federal government, but also to the states. This was accomplished by way of an expansive interpretation of the due process clause of the Fourteenth Amendment.

exhibited a painting "representing a man in an obscene, impudent and indecent posture with a woman." The first reported decision on literary censorship came six years after the case of the impudent posture. It came in Boston, and it involved, appropriately, that prima ballerina of the law of obscenity, *Fanny Hill*. Two booksellers were convicted. On their appeal, the upper court dismissed a number of points raised by the defense, but said nothing about whether the book was obscene. Apparently the answer was obvious.*

Twenty years later, in its customary xenophobic mood, Congress moved to guard against infection from abroad; in passing a tariff act, it gave Customs power to confiscate. But this was rather limited, and we still had no definition of obscenity.

England sent us one. It came in the form of judicial interpretation of a statute. Parliament, in 1857, enacted the first major piece of antiobscenity legislation, Lord Campbell's Act. When people get morally indignant, they are apt to pass laws against things that are already illegal. Lord Campbell's Act was an example.†

The Act had to do with procedures for stamping out the crime, not with saying what it was. Definition came 11 years later, in the case of *Queen* v. *Hicklin*. The case involved an anti-Catholic pamphlet, more libelous than obscene, published by the Protestant Electoral Union. The Lord Chief Justice formulated a test of obscenity that had an enduring and baleful influence in both Great Britain and the United States. He said: "I think the test of obscenity is this, whether the tendency of the matter charged as obscenity is to deprave and corrupt those whose minds are open to such immoral influences, and into whose hands a publication of this sort may fall."

Meanwhile, things had been stirred up in the United States. Most of the stirring was done by Anthony Comstock. Remembered as an old bluenose, Comstock was in fact a young bluenose. In his early twenties he had made his reputation as a crusader against vice. In 1873, at the age of 28, he set a standard for all future lobbyists to shoot at: single-handed, he got Congress to pass the archetype of American antiobscenity legislation. There are very few Acts of Congress that bear the name of anyone other than a senator or representative: the mark of the man is that this statute is known as the Comstock Act. On the day of its passage, its author made a

---

*One of them was named Holmes, and considering the population of Boston in the early nineteenth century, we may speculate on the degree of consanguinity between the convict and the celebrated physician-litterateur and that great man of law, his son.

† Another, in the Vietnam period, was the congressional tautology declaring it a crime to burn a draft card, when it was already a crime to be without one's draft card. Lord Campbell's Act at least affected the procedures for punishing obscene publication; the card burning statute made no change in the penalties that already existed, which would apply whether one burned one's card, threw it out the window, or chewed it up and swallowed it.

diary entry: "Oh how can I express the joy of my Soul or speak the mercy of God!"

This rich vein of repressive legislation—sometimes referred to as the Comstock Load—provided the model for most American antiobscenity statutes, and occupied the entire stage until a short time ago. In the decade just past, members of Congress and state legislatures, apprised of the existence of the First Amendment and deeply alarmed by it, began to fashion new statutes in an effort to overcome the decisions of the 1960s.

They had no problem with earlier decisions. American courts had eagerly adopted the *Hicklin* test, and used it to define obscenity in applying both the Comstock Act and the similar statutes that every state but one eventually enacted. Both the Comstock Act and the typical state statute referred to material "obscene, lewd and lascivious." Congress, in a magnificent afterthought, enacted a statute in 1909 in order to add the word "filthy." "Lustful," however, became the favorite of the courts. To "lustful," the judges often added a set of alliterative synonyms—"lewd," "lascivious," "lubricious," "libidinous," "licentious." The words suggest a certain ambivalence on the part of the condemning judges. The musical "l"s are surely more romantic than the scornful "f" and the hostile "k."

While we are on the subject of legislation, we may note that at the moment Congress is dealing with the subject as part of an attempt to overhaul the entire federal Criminal Code. A bill has passed the Senate and is now before the House. So far as the substance of the law is concerned, the proposed legislation, with one small exception, in effect says this: Everything is obscene that the Supreme Court in its 1973 decisions has said can constitutionally be held to be obscene. Put another way, the bill codifies the standards set by the Supreme Court. Since the present legislation—the old Comstock Act—is restricted in its scope by the First Amendment decisions, Congress, in this part of its revision of federal criminal law, is essentially doing nothing. If Congress attempted to take in more than those decisions allow, the excess would be unconstitutional.

In two respects the *Hicklin* rule was modified after a time. It had focused on "matter" rather than on books. This permitted prosecutors to proceed against selected pages or paragraphs, and permitted courts to condemn a work though neither judge nor jury had read it through. By the end of the 1940s, however, many courts had held that a book should be judged as a whole, not on the basis of isolated passages. The other change had to do with *Hicklin's* solicitude for the susceptible. It was gradually realized that what was published for the world at large should not be constricted by rules designed for minors; adult reading could not be reduced to the level of a child's bookshelf.

These modifications were sensible but peripheral. In its essence—"the tendency of the matter to deprave or corrupt"—*Hicklin* survived and flourished. Courts decided whether publication was permissible by deciding whether a book was "lustful." If it was, it was obscene, and its author and publisher criminals. As to how provocative a book must be to rate as lustful, the answer, of course, was subjective. Somewhat more charitable answers were given as time went on. But while the law of obscenity dropped a few gables and dormers as the memory of Campbell's queen and Comstock's congress began to fade, the underlying idea of *Hicklin* was not relinquished until a moment ago.

The famous *Ulysses* case, in 1934, made more of an impression on commentators than on the law. Apart from the support it gave to proponents of the whole-book rule, the decision actually confirmed the *Hicklin* test. Both the trial court and the appellate court were able to conclude that *Ulysses* was not really lustful. The "erotic passages," said the upper court, "are submerged in the book as a whole and have little resultant effect." And the more publicized decision of the district court depended on its finding that the sex in the book repelled rather than attracted. It was, in Judge Woolsey's words, "emetic, not aphrodisiac," the judge thus elevating into legal principle the proposition that nausea is not immoral.

The censors were hardly checked. Shortly before the *Ulysses* case, there had been the conviction of the bookseller who sold *An American Tragedy*, and, in the 1940s, condemnation of *Strange Fruit* and *Memoirs of Hecate County*. Such decisions are hardly comprehensible to the present college generation, yet they are little older than those who find them so astonishing.

Early in 1957, the Supreme Court struck down a Michigan statute that defined obscenity as material having a "deleterious influence upon youth." "Surely," said Justice Frankfurter, "this is to burn the house to roast the pig." But the effect of the decisions was simply to make one of the *Hicklin* modifications, acknowledged in many states, compulsory in all. A few months later, in the famous *Roth* case, the Supreme Court held that state and federal antiobscenity laws that spoke in general terms were valid. Affirming a pair of criminal convictions, the Court sustained both the Comstock Law and one of its statehouse nephews, an act of the California legislature. The second paring down of *Hicklin* was given sanction: judgments could not rest on isolated passages. With these familiar footnotes, however, a solid majority ruled that antiobscenity statutes could stand firm against the First Amendment guarantees.

The Court set out a definition of obscenity that incorporated the limits upon *Hicklin*, suggested that frames of reference may change in time, and substituted "prurient" for "lustful" as the key word. The court added that it was merely confirming the existing judicial view of the subject. One of its other statements was to become important, but at the time it drew no attention.

The *Roth* case was hailed as a victory for those bent on suppression. The majority opinion was widely accepted as one that gave constitutional approval to the established law of obscenity. There had been attacks on the Comstock Act and a typical state law, and the attacks had been repulsed. The favorite arguments of those who opposed censorship—that obscenity was impossible to define and that there was no demonstrable connection between exposure to it and antisocial behavior—had been explicitly rejected. There was some stately language about the importance of the First Amendment guarantees, but obscenity, the Court held, lay outside those guarantees.

Obscenity was given an elaborate definition, the prurient-interest formula, which the opinion said was only a summary of what most courts had already been saying. The two unpalatable elements of the *Hicklin* rule were no longer accepted. But otherwise the old law remained intact. Indeed, it could fairly be said that *Roth* had strengthened it: the idea that antiobscenity law was unconstitutional had been rejected.

Banned Books was quite right when, at the time, it viewed the *Roth* case not as a victory for freedom but as a defeat. There is a remarkable current misapprehension on this point, aggravated by another on what the Supreme Court said. Time and again we see mention of the "social value test of the *Roth* case" or of its "triple test." It is remarkable because it is found not merely in hurried journalism, where legal errors can be expected, but in the statements of lawyers and judges, who certainly ought to know better. No one, at the time, suggested that the *Roth* opinion stood for anything more than its two main propositions: (1) antiobscenity statutes are not unconstitutional, and (2) the test of obscenity is whether there is appeal to prurient interest, judging the book by its effect on the average person in the light of community standards. The first suggestion that *Roth* meant something more came two years later, in the *Lady Chatterley* case. It came without judicial sanction; it was only an argument of counsel.

The argument was based on a rather absentminded statement in the *Roth* opinion. In the course of declaring that obscenity lay outside the protection of the First Amendment, the Supreme Court opinion had added the disparaging statement that obscenity was "utterly without redeeming social importance." Counsel for *Lady Chatterley* argued that this offhand remark was the most important part of the opinion. A book, he said, is purely "press" within the meaning of the First Amendment. Hence there had to be some strong reason for excluding it from the Amendment's shelter. The reasons the *Roth* majority had given were not good. One was that the Supreme Court "had always assumed that obscenity is not protected." Assumptions, however, are not law; certain older courts had always assumed that heresy required burning. Another was a group of earlier judicial statements on obscenity, but these were gleaned from cases that had nothing to do with obscenity. They were *obiter dicta,* tossed off when obscenity was not in issue. *Dicta* so *obiter* cannot constitute precedent. Finally, the *Roth* majority had called on constitutional history. But there is no specific evidence of the attitude toward obscenity of those who framed the First Amendment. The Court's historical argument was all inference, and the inference was unwarranted.

However, the *Chatterley* argument continued, the *Roth* opinion had mentioned that obscenity was utterly without social importance. When one focused on the goals of free expression, this utter absence of importance might justify permitting legislatures to deal with obscenity unhampered by the First Amendment. But this was the only thing in the *Roth* opinion that might justify exclusion of a book from the guarantee of freedom of the press. Hence it was only material utterly devoid of social importance that, in law, one could call "obscene." The argument, in effect, was that the *Roth* statement had to be read in reverse: those things that had utterly no social importance—and those alone—could be labeled obscenity and deprived of the First Amendment's protection.

The argument appeared to influence the decision in *Lady Chatterley*, though the opinions did not give it explicit statement. Then, in the welter of the Henry Miller litigation that followed, and in the three trials of *Fanny Hill*, it gained express judicial acceptance. Meanwhile, the Supreme Court had added the test of "patent offensiveness." Finally, in 1966, the Supreme Court, reversing the ban on *Fanny Hill*, made it clear that a book could not be suppressed unless it failed by all three criteria—prurient appeal, patent offensiveness, and lack of social value. "Value" had in the course of the cases been gradually substituted for "importance."*

A case argued on the same day as *Fanny Hill*, and two in the years that followed, attracted a degree of attention not matched by their significance. The first was the Supreme Court's affirmance of Ralph Ginzburg's conviction, in which the majority opinion set forth the celebrated "pandering" doctrine. That doctrine, about which so much has been written, simply and rudely amounted to this: "If you promote what you sell by claiming it is obscene, we'll take you at your word." The precedent was rather special, and hardly any use to prosecutors. Late in 1967 came the *Redrup* case, which involved some magazines. It was hailed by libertarians, but in fact the opinions did no more than summarize the various views the various justices had already stated in other cases. *Stanley* v. *Georgia*, decided in 1969, was another case in which more was seen than it had to offer. The Court held that a man could not be convicted for possessing films for his personal use in the privacy of his home. From this,

---

*During this period an editor in a house that published original paperbacks told me of a negotiation with a literary agent who was offering a novel devoted principally to sex. The editor said it was not a very good book. The agent protested that it really had quality, that it was a book of social value. "Don't worry," said the editor. "We can work around it."

hopeful libertarians argued that if one had the right to own the films (or anything else that might be deemed obscenity), filmmakers, distributors, and sellers must have the right to make it possible for one to do so. The argument was specious and was never accepted by the Court. It was specious because privacy was involved, and because there is a difference between selling and using. Consider drugs, or liquor during Prohibition.

In June of 1973 the Court handed down a group of decisions that caused libertarians much dismay. Too much dismay, I thought. They were five-to-four decisions, the four Nixon appointees together with Justice White making up the majority in each case. The majority opinions were written by Chief Justice Burger. On the question whether the "community standards" of the *Roth* case were national or local—a question that *Roth* had left open and hadn't been closed in 16 years—they decided in favor of "local standards." (Still leaving an open question, since the opinions didn't say what "local" meant. State, city, county, neighborhood? Are the standards of Seventy-second Street and Park Avenue the standards of Forty-second Street and Eighth Avenue?) On the value test, they substituted, for *Fanny Hill*'s "not utterly without redeeming social value," a requirement that there be some "serious value." The majority also said that antiobscenity statutes had to define what they prohibited with specificity (and at the same time announced that the thoroughly unspecific Comstock Act was sufficiently specific).

Justices Douglas, Brennan, Stewart, and Marshall dissented. The last three took the position that there should be no antiobscenity regulation except where children are concerned or where the medium is obtrusive, while Justice Douglas adhered to his long-held position that expression should be subject to no restriction whatever for obscenity.

Most people who opposed censorship regarded these decisions as a huge step backwards. "Most people" included nearly everybody who wrote about the decisions—lawyers and nonlawyers—and very many people wrote about them. For months, the papers and magazines were full of articles deploring the event. I disagreed; I thought the 1973 decisions left the law essentially unchanged.

It was the third of the *Fanny Hill* tests—the so-called "social value" test—that had been the most significant, both theoretically and practically. It was through that test that the First Amendment had its greatest impact. "Prurient interest" and "patent offensiveness" contributed little. They are finally only a way of confusing the question of desirable-versus-undesirable with the question of constitutional-versus-unconstitutional. The vociferous antagonists of the pornography-is-bad-for-you school and the pornography-is-good-for-you school are both, so far as the Constitution is concerned, beside the point. The question is not whether the material in issue is harmful or salutary, but whether it is "speech" or "press" within the meaning of the First Amendment. The social value argument, in essence, is that a book that has some value—it needn't be much—is naturally part of the press, whatever the evil (or good) that may flow from it. Hence it cannot, under the Constitution, be forbidden simply because it may stimulate a sexual response (whether a positive reponse, the pleasant excitement felt by some readers of *Lady Chatterley* or *Fanny Hill*, or a negative response, the abraded sensibilities suffered by some readers of Henry Miller).

"Prurient interest" and "patent offensiveness" are entirely subjective, and as standards they could give no solid protection. "Social value," in contrast, is a reasonably objective test. If qualified critics and scholars were willing to come to court and testify to the value of a book—not to assert it was not obscene, or not prurient or not offensive, but to tell why in their opinion it had merit and to make some sense when cross-examined—their testimony answered the question of value. It was ultimately a question for the court, and if the court found such evidence of value, it didn't matter that the jury thought the book was a dirty book nobody ought to read.

It had worked. Writers began to use language and deal with scenes and subjects they had never tried before. The law stopped looking over the author's shoulder; every author felt the difference.

How was the state of the law affected by the decisions of 1973? So far as prurient interest and patent offensiveness are concerned, does it matter greatly that there are local standards? These are tests on which the courts have been quick to accept a negative verdict from the jury. When a jury decides such matters, you almost surely get the jurors' own notions of what is prurient and what is offensive. It doesn't make much difference whether the judge instructs them that the legal standards are national or local; the operative standards are in their own heads.

The most important question, then, is whether the value test survives. Is that brake on jury prejudices (and on the prejudices of lower-court judges) still functioning, and to what extent? The 1973 opinions put the issue in terms of the presence of "serious value," rather than utter absence of value, and they do not say whether value too must be weighed by local standards. But it is important that the opinions do not say. When that open question comes before the Court—assuming it is properly argued—the Court will hold that the new statement of the value test, like its predecessor, presents a constitutional question, which must ultimately be decided by the Court itself. Any other conclusion would conflict with too many precedents and deny the reality of the matter. The value of a book exists apart from the manners or habits of any single state or town or city. Even if a jury should declare a book prurient and patently offensive and lacking in all value, it remains the obligation of the higher courts to decide whether, on the record, the book has the requisite value. Making predictions about what the Supreme Court will do is, of course, a risky business, but nothing in the

1973 opinions excludes this view, and the logic of the la\
(There is considerable logic in the law, though there is als\
else.)

If this is so, then the principal change that occurred i\
obscenity in June 1973 was a change in the value formula—f
without" to "a lack of serious." But here again there was in fact no change.
"Utterly without" was a judicial overstatement—a useful one, but one that
could not be taken literally. A speck of value of some sort can always be
found, in any book or magazine or film. "Serious value" is probably a
closer verbalization of the test that the courts are, and have been, willing to
apply than "utterly without." The new formula does not, and should not,
and will not—again, if the matter is well argued—demand any great
measure of value.

Moving from the conceptual to the empirical, the plain fact is that there
has been no suppression of books since the 1973 decisions—no ban, no
successful prosecution. Hence the statement at the outset of this
introduction. But that does not mean there cannot be, nor that there never
will be.

We sorely need the reminder the present volume gives us of where we
have been, and where, if we don't watch out, we will return. "Constant
vigilance," the Supreme Court has told us, is required if we are to preserve
our First Amendment freedoms. Told us, incidentally, in a case in which
the Court upheld antiobscenity laws and sent defendants to jail. This
volume will help us keep our vigil.

May 2, 1978

Banned Books

Homer (c.850 B.C.)

The Odyssey

387 B.C. Greece: Plato suggested expurgating Homer for immature readers.

A.D. 35. Rome: Caligula tried to suppress *The Odyssey* because it expressed Greek ideals of freedom—dangerous in autocratic Rome.

Confucius (551–478 B.C.)

Analects (Sayings of Confucius and His Disciples)

c.250 B.C. China: The first ruler of the Chin dynasty, wishing to abolish the feudal system, consigned to the flames all books relating to the teachings of Confucius; he also buried alive hundreds of his disciples.

213 B.C. The Emperor Shih Huang Ti disapproved of the traditional culture of China, considered it moribund, and persecuted the literati who were its apostles. He burned the *Analects* and all extant books except practical works on medicine, divinations and husbandry, but preserved those in the Imperial Library.

Socrates (c.470–399 B.C.)

399 B.C. Socrates accused "firstly, of denying the gods recognized by the state and introducing new divinities, and, secondly of corrupting the young." Found guilty, he was condemned to death. Accounts of the events are in Xenephon's *Memorabilia* and Plato's *Apology*. Western history of censorship begins here. Although Socrates left no writings, his forthrightness as teacher and philosopher exposed him to the punishments of the state.

Aristophanes (c.448–c.380 B.C.)

The Clouds, 423 B.C.

The Birds, 414 B.C.

Lysistrata, c.411 B.C.

423 B.C. Greece–Athens: *The Clouds* was a play in which Socrates was pilloried as a typical representative of impious and destructive speculations.

A.D. 66 His comedies were considered obscene by Plutarch.

1930 United States: Customs ban lifted on *Lysistrata*. During the period of prohibition the book was published and sold for as little as thirty-five cents; and the drama was played in New York and Philadelphia, as adapted by Gilbert Seldes.

1942 Greece–Athens: Performance of classic Greek plays banned by Nazi occupation authorities.

1954 United States: Post Office officials seized a copy of the 1926 translation of *Lysistrata*, by Jack Lindsay, addressed by Fanfrolico Press, England, to Harry A. Levinson, Beverly Hills bookseller. The Post Office quickly reversed itself and delivered the book, but only because it was "not for general distribution."

1955 United States: In a successful challenge of the Comstock Act of 1873 which empowered the Postmaster General to rule on obscenity of literature sent through the mail, *Lysistrata* was declared mailable.

1967 Greece–Athens: The military clique then controlling the country banned a number of classic plays, including those named above, presumably because of their independent and antiwar themes.

Ovid (Publius Ovidius Naso) (43 B.C.–c. A.D. 17)

Ars Amatoria (*The Art of Love*), c.1 B.C.

Elegies, B.C.

A.D. 8 Rome: The Emperor Augustus banished Ovid for writing *Ars Amatoria* and for an unknown act of folly. He was sent to the Greek town of Tomi, near the mouth of the Danube, where he died in exile eight years later.

1497 Florence: The works of Ovid were cast, with those of Dante and his friend Propertius, into the great bonfire of Savonarola, as erotic, impious, and tending to corrupt.

1599 The Archbishop of Canterbury and the Bishop of London ordered the burning of, among other works, Christopher Marlowe's translation of Ovid's *Elegies*—apparently less because of their content than because of the work with which they were bound, Sir John Davies' *Epigrammes*, which satirized contemporary authorities.

1928 United States: The Customs still barred *Ars Amatoria*, although inexpensive editions were sold freely within U.S. borders.

1929 United States–San Francisco: *Ars Amatoria* banned.

1957 United States: *The Art of Love* and related poems, in the Rolfe

Humphrey translation, became the first best-seller of the University of Indiana Press.

Petronius, Gaius (d.c. A.D. 66)

Satyricon, before A.D. 66

1934 England–London: This comic satire on Roman life in the time of Nero, under whom Petronius served as consul and "arbiter" of public entertainment, survives as a fragment. According to one authority (Donald Thomas, *A Long Time Burning*), the first English translation to get in trouble was a modern one, ordered destroyed by the police court of the City of Westminster in London.

Apuleius, Lucius (c. A.D. 125–)

De Asino Aureo (*The Golden Ass*)

1931 United States: Import ban raised on this book, which had been freely circulated since 1928.

Arius (c. A.D. 256–336)

Thaleia

A.D. 325 Arius, presbyter of Alexandria, was excommunicated in 321 for heretical teachings about the nature of Christ, and in 325 the Council of Nicaea exiled him and condemned his *Thaleia*, the collection of popular verses expressing his ideas. This was the first writing banned by the Catholic Church. (See *Index Librorum Prohibitorum*.)

The Bible

553 Italy–Rome: Emperor Justinian issued a decree commanding exclusive use of the Greek and Latin versions of the *Bible* and forbidding the *Midrash*, but accepting the Hebrew exposition of the *Old Testament*.

1409 England: The Synod of Canterbury at St. Paul's, London, issued a decree forbidding the translation of the Scripture from one tongue to another, and the reading of a translation later than that of John Wycliffe under penalty of excommunication, unless special license be obtained.

1525–1526 The *New Testament*, partially translated by William Tyndale, was printed at Cologne, as it was violently opposed by the clergy in England. He fled to Worms where he continued to publish clandestinely. The sheets of 6,000 copies of the *Testament* were smuggled into England where they were publicly burned by the dignitaries of the Church, thus becoming the first printed book to be banned in England.

1535 The *Old* and *New Testaments* translated by Miles Coverdale were the first complete *Bible* to be printed in English. Not being licensed by Church or State, it had to be printed on the Continent.

1538 France–Paris: Regnault, famous printer of English books, was seized by the Inquisition and imprisoned while printing the "great" *Bible* for Cromwell, the sheets of which were destroyed.

1551 Spain: *The Inquisitorial Index of Valentia* (supplement) forbade *Bibles* in Spanish or any other vernacular.

1554 *The Inquisitorial Index of Valladolid* listed 103 editions of the *Bible* condemned because of errors and heresies to suppression, correction or cancellation.

1555 England: A proclamation by Queen Mary commanded "that no manner of persons presume to bring into this realm any mss., books, papers, etc. in the name of Martin Luther, John Calvin, Miles Coverdale, Erasmus, Tyndale, etc. or any like books containing false doctrines against the Catholic faith."

1560 Switzerland: The Geneva or *"Breeches Bible"* went into 140 editions between 1560 and 1644, although it was forbidden in the churches.

1611 England: Copyright in the King James Version rests perpetually in the Crown. Permission to reprint has been given to Oxford, Cambridge, Eyre & Spottiswoode and William Collins. Because of Crown copyright, no authorized *Bible* in English was printed in what is now the United States until after the Revolution.

1624 Germany: The *Bible* translated by Martin Luther in 1534 which had been the most widely read book in the country was condemned to the flames by Papal authority.

1631 England: In the edition of 1,000 copies of the *Bible* printed by R. Barker and assigns of Peter Bill the word "not" was omitted from the seventh commandment. The printers were heavily fined and the edition so vigorously suppressed that few copies have survived. It was named the *"Wicked Bible."*

1782 United States–Philadelphia, Pa.: Robert Aitken printed what is generally considered the first *Bible* in English in the United States, although there is now accepted evidence that a *Bible* was secretly printed in Boston about 1752.

1900 Italy–Rome: Pope Leo XIII decreed that translations of the *Bible* in the vernacular were permitted only if approved by the Holy See.

1926 Soviet Union: Official directions to libraries stated: "The section on religion must contain solely anti-religious books. Religiously dogmatic books such as the *Gospel*, the *Koran*, the *Talmud*, etc. must be left in the large libraries, but removed from the smaller ones." Import of the *Bible* is not permitted.

1952 United States: The *Revised Standard Version* was attacked by a Fundamentalist minister because of changes in terminology.

1953 North Carolina: A leaf of the same edition was burned in protest by a Baptist minister.

1956 Soviet Union: The *Bible* published after a lapse of 38 years.

The Talmud

4th–6th cent.: Compiled between these dates and with the *Old Testament* became the *Bible* of the Jews.

1190 Egypt–Cairo: With his *Guide for the Perplexed*, Maimonides, the Jewish philosopher, aroused the Christians' resentment, which culminated in the first official burning of Hebrew books by orders of Dominicans, Franciscans, and others.

1244 France–Paris: *Talmud* burned on charges of blasphemy and immorality. The book was persecuted in various places for another 100 years.

1264 Italy–Rome: Pope Clement IV appointed a committee of censors who expunged all passages that appeared derogatory to Christianity. (Talmudic references to ancient paganism were widely misrepresented as criticism of the Church.)

1490 Spain–Salamanca: In an auto-da-fé, thousands of Hebrew books including biblical texts were burned by order of the Inquisition.

1926 Soviet Union: Reported that the *Talmud* and other religiously dogmatic books were left in the large libraries, but removed from the small ones; virtually no printing of the work provided since then.

The Koran (Seventh Century)

1542 Switzerland: Protestant authorities at Basel confiscated the entire edition published by Oporinus, who promptly appealed to the scholars. Exonerated by Luther, the edition was released.

1790 Spain: Ban lifted by the *Index*. Every version had been prohibited, especially the Twelfth Century Latin Translation by Peter of Cluny "cum refutationibus variorum."

1926 Soviet Union: Restricted to students of history.

1953 United States: Published in a paperbound edition.

Abélard, Pierre (1079–1142)

Introductio ad Theologiam, 1120
Lettres d'Hélöise et Abélard

1120 France–Soissons: A provincial synod charged Abélard with religious heresy, forced him to burn his *Introductio ad Theologiam*, and imprisoned him in the convent of St. Médard.

1140 Italy–Rome: All works banned by the Council at Sens and ordered burned by Pope Innocent III. St. Bernard called Abélard "an infernal dragon and the precursor of the anti-Christ."

1559 and 1564 Italy–Rome: All writings placed on the *Index*.

1930 United States: Customs ban lifted on *Love Letters*.

Bacon, Roger (c.1214–c.1292)

Opus Maius, 1268

Opus Minus, 1268

Opus Tertium, 1268

1257 England: Bonaventura, General of the Franciscan order, suspicious of Bacon's supposed dealings in the black arts, interdicted his lectures at Oxford, and placed him under the superintendence of the order in Paris, where he remained for ten years under injunction not to write for publication.

1278 Italy–Rome: After the death of his protector, Clement IV, his books were condemned by Jerome de Ascoli, General of the Franciscans, afterwards Pope Nicholas IV, and Bacon was put into prison for 14 years.

Dante Alighieri (1265–1321)

La Divina Commedia, 1302–1321

De Monarchia, 1310–1313

1318 France–Lombardy: *De Monarchia* was publicly burned.

1497 Italy–Florence: Works burned by Savonarola in the "bonfire of the vanities."

1559 Italy–Rome: *De Monarchia* banned by Pope Paul IV and the *Index of Trent* for asserting that the authority of kings was derived from God, not through God's Vicar on earth, the Pope.

1581 Portugal–Lisbon: *La Divina Commedia* prohibited by Church authorities until all copies were delivered to the Inquisition for correction.

Boccaccio, Giovanni (1313–1375)

Il Decamerone, 1353

1497 Italy–Florence: Manuscripts and printed parts were thrown into Savonarola's "bonfire of the vanities."

1559 Italy–Rome: Prohibited by the *Index* of Pope Paul IV, unless expurgated. The revisers retained the episodes, but transformed the erring nuns into noble women, the lascivious monks into conjurors, the Abbess into a Countess (21st story), the Archangel Gabriel into the "King of the Fairies"; and the Pope authorized the edition.

c.1600 France: Censured by the Sorbonne and condemned by Parliament.

1922 United States: The Post Office authorities of Cincinnati seized an expurgated edition, and the district judge fined the importing bookseller $1,000.

1926 Banned by the Treasury Department.

1927 The Customs Department mutilated a copy printed by the Ashendene Press, and returned it to Maggs Bros., London, with the text missing. C. H. St. John Hornby wrote a protest to the London *Times*.

1931 Ban lifted by the Customs.

1932 United States–Minnesota: Ban lifted.

1933 Australia: Cheap editions banned.

1934 United States–Detroit, Mich.: Seized by the police as salacious.

1935 United States–Boston, Mass.: Still banned by the New England Watch and Ward Society.

1953 England: On list published in *Newsagent Bookseller Stationer* of nearly 700 titles named for destruction by local magistrates.

1954 England–Swindon: Copies ordered destroyed as "obscene" by magistrate's court, but an appeal court reversed the decision.
United States: On blacklist of the National Organization of Decent Literature.

Wycliffe, John (c.1320–1384)

De Civili Dominio, 1376

1377 England: Pope Gregory XI issued five bulls on May 22, attacking Wycliffe's doctrines as expounded in his treatise on civil lordship (*De civili dominio*) which had been read to his students at Oxford in the previous year.

1409 Bohemia–Prague: Pope Alexander V's bull ordering the surrender of all of Wycliffe's books was carried out under the instructions of Archbishop Sbynko of Prague, who burned 200 volumes of Wycliffe's writings in the palace courtyard, and at the same time excommunicated Jan Hus (below) who sympathized with the English theologian.

Hus, Jan (c.1373–1415)

De Ecclesia, 1413

1413–1415 Bohemia–Prague: Hus, whose criticism of the church and whose sympathy with the teachings of John Wycliffe had led him into deep trouble with church authorities, was summoned to Constance in Switzerland and then tried in nearby Gottlieben on the Rhine for teaching false doctrine. Refusing to recant his propositions, he was condemned and burned at the stake.

Schedel, Hartmann (1410–1485)

Nuremberg Chronicle, 1493

1493 Italy–Rome: This great illustrated history of the world includes (plate CLXIX), a picture of the female Pope Joan and her baby, here said to have succeeded as "John VIII" on the death of Leo IV, who died in 855. She is here said to have been of English origin, though born in Mainz; to have disguised herself as a man and gone to Athens with a learned lover; and later in Rome to have become so famous for knowledge of the Scriptures that she was finally elected Pope by general consent. She seemed to justify this choice until, during a procession to the Lateran Basilica, she suddenly broke down, gave birth to a son and died ignominiously. The earliest known mention of her is by Stephen de Bourbon, who died in 1261. In 1400 an image of her was included among the images of most of the Popes in Sienne Cathedral. In 1600, at the request of Pope Clement VI, her name was changed to Pope Zachary. In 1493 the legend was generally believed, but the earlier doubts became more general, and the picture and account of Joan were piously inked over or cut out of many copies of this and other books. There has been much controversy as to the truth of the legend, and it is now generally thought to be false.

Savonarola, Girolamo (1452–1498)

Writings

1497 Italy–Florence: Savonarola, Dominican monk and spiritual reformer, attempted to turn the pleasure-loving Florentines from their "pagan" ways and turned the annual carnival into a "burning of the vanities," including works by Ovid, Propertius, and Boccaccio.

1498 He was forced by tortures on the rack to confess his heresy in demanding church reforms, and in denouncing papal corruptions. After the ceremonial of degradation, he was hung on a cross and burned with all his writings, sermons, essays, and pamphlets.

Erasmus, Desiderius (c.1466–1536)

De Conscribendis Epistolis Opus, c.1495

Moriae Encomium, 1512

Greek Testament, 1516

1512 England: *Moriae Encomium* (*Praise of Folly*), in which kings, bishops, popes, and all manner of people, were impiously shown to be subject to folly, delighted the Pope, but was prohibited in the Universities of Paris, Louvain, Oxford, and Cambridge. It was written in the house of Thomas More.

1516 Switzerland–Basel: Erasmus dedicated his most important work, the *Greek Testament*, to Pope Leo X who lauded him for "exceptional service to the study of sacred theology and to the maintenance of the true faith."

England: His powerful Catholic friends, including Cardinal Wolsey, Charles V, and Henry VIII, urged Erasmus to declare against Luther. He refused, but engaged in a sharp argument with the reformers, and continued to attack the abuses of the church, while remaining loyally within its folds. While Erasmus continued to look at the religious question in a sane, rational, and objective way, the Lutherans and Calvinists calumniated him as a traitor to their cause, and Rome denounced him for heresy.

1524 France–Paris: The Sorbonne forbade the sale or perusal of *Colloquia*.

1550 Spain: The *Spanish Index* condemned all Erasmus' works.

1555 Scotland: Mary, Queen of Scots, forbade the reading of Erasmus.

1557 Italy–Rome: *De Conscribendis Epistolis Opus* forced to be corrected to conform with the Inquisition.

1559 The *Index* condemned all Erasmus' works more harshly than the works of Luther or Calvin.

1576 Pope Gregory XIII authorized an anonymously expurgated edition, published anonymously.

1612 Spain: *Spanish Index* devoted 59 folio pages in double columns to damning Erasmus.

1930 Italy–Rome: Erasmus was not specifically mentioned in the latest edition of the *Index*.

Machiavelli, Niccolò (1469–1527)

Discorsi, 1503

Il Principe, 1513

1555 Italy–Rome: Although Machiavelli had been the ambassador and advisor of Popes and Cardinals in his day, Pope Paul IV placed his works in the severest category of the *Index*, and Clement VIII made a fresh prohibition of a Lausanne edition of his *Discorsi*.

1576 France: Selected maxims from *Il Principe* translated into French, were attacked by the Huguenot Gentillet for their political views. Cesare Borgia was supposed to have been the "Prince." The author contended that "if all rulers were good, you ought to keep your word, but since they are dishonest and do not keep faith with you, you, in return, need not keep faith with them."

1602 England: The Elizabethans derived from Gentillet their idea of and hostility for *Il Principe*.

1935 Italy: In Fascist thinking, *Il Principe* demonstrated disjointed Italy's need for an all-powerful dictator supported by a national army. Mussolini paid Machiavelli tribute by encouraging the distribution of *Il Principe* in thousands of cheap copies.

Licensing

1501 Rome: Pope Alexander VI issued a bull against unlicensed printing.

1535 France: Francis I issued an edict prohibiting under penalty of death the printing of books.

1585 England: The Star Chamber assumed the power to confine all printing to London, Oxford and Cambridge, to limit the number of printers, to prohibit all unlicensed publications and to enter houses in search of unlicensed presses or books.

1637 Prohibition of the importation into England of books deemed injurious to religion, the Church or the government.

1643 Licensing act passed by the Long Parliament, provoking John Milton's *Areopagitica*.

1660 Reaffirmation of the edicts of 1637.

1679 Licensing act expired, to be renewed for an additional seven years in 1685.

1695 Licensing ended in England.

1765 Search for and seizure of authors for libel declared illegal.

1967 Press censorship against obscenity ended in Denmark. One result, it was later claimed in surveys, was that interest in pornography was being shown more by foreign visitors than by Danes.

Vergil, Polydore (c.1470–1555)

De Rerum Inventoribus, 1499

1671 Italy–Rome: Although the author had been enthroned Bishop of Bath in 1504, this work was placed on the *Index* because of a passage which suggests that the Church's discovery of Purgatory stimulated a market for indulgences. The volume, treating of the origin of all things, ecclesiastical and lay, was so well liked that it was translated into French, German, English and Spanish.

1756 All editions appeared on the *Index*, except those following the text sanctioned by Pope Gregory XIII.

Michelangelo (Michelangelo Buonarroti) (1475–1564)

The Sistine Chapel

1933 United States: Plate 40 of this volume reproduces a copy of *The Last Judgment*, made by Venusti from the original fresco in the Sistine Chapel, before the addition of clothing to the nude figures by Daniele Volterra, by order of Pope Paul IV, and with the permission of Michelangelo. This book was ordered from Europe by the Weyhe Gallery and Book Shop. They received the following official letter from an assistant collector of customs who, apparently, had never heard of the great painter.

> Sirs:—There is being detained . . . 2 packages addressed to you, containing obscene photo books, 'Ceiling Sistine Chapel,' Filles–Michael Angelo, the importation of which is held to be prohibited under the provisions of the Tariff Act. The package will therefore be seized and disposed of in due course as provided by law. You may however avail yourself of the privilege of applying to the Secretary of the Treasury . . . for mitigation of the penalty of forfeiture with permission to export, or please execute the Assent to forfeiture below, returning same . . . Respectfully, H. C. Stuart, Asst. Collector.

After being ridiculed by the newspapers, the Treasury Department realized the ignorant mistake and relinquished the book.

Luther, Martin (1483–1546)

Works

Address to the German Nobility, 1520

1517 Germany–Wittenberg: Luther nailed 95 theses, criticizing the use of indulgences, to the door of the Castle Church at the University. The Theological faculties of Louvain and Cologne ordered copies of the theses to be burned on grounds of heresy. Defending them in debate in 1519, Luther was forced to declare his differences with the Church.

1521 France: The theological faculties of the University of Paris ordered the *Theses* burned.
Italy–Rome: A Papal bull by Leo X excommunicated Luther, and forbade printing, selling, reading, or quoting, his *Works*, thereby creating a passionate interest in them. (In three months 4,000 copies of *Address to the German Nobility*, in which Luther stated the causes of social discontent, were sold; in five days 5,000 copies of the vernacular edition of the *New Testament* were sold.) He also ordered a formal burning of Luther's effigy and books.
Germany: Charles V, on his own authority, issued an edict against

Luther, and ordered his books seized. At the same time he sent him a safe conduct to appear before the diet of Worms. The diet issued an edict against him, and threatened to exterminate his followers.
Strassburg: A contemporary comment was: "Lutheran books are for sale in the marketplace immediately beneath the edicts of the Emperor and the Pope who declared them to be prohibited."

1525 Luther became the virtual leader of the German nation. He invoked a censorship of the "pernicious doctrines" of Anabaptists, Calvin and Zwingli.

1532 Luther turned the tables and demanded the suppression of the translation of the *New Testament* by Einser, a Catholic priest.

1930 Italy–Rome: The works of Luther omitted by the *Index*.

1953 Canada: The Quebec Censorship Board banned the motion picture *Martin Luther* on the ground that it would antagonize the people of the predominately Roman Catholic province.

Agrippa, Henry Cornelius (1486–1535)

De Incertitudine et Vanitate Scientiarum et Artium, 1530
De Occulta Philosophia, 1531

1509 France–Dôle: Charged with heresy for his lectures at the University, Agrippa was forced to take refuge with Maximilian in the Netherlands.

1531 Netherlands: *De Incertitudine*, a sarcastic attack on existing sciences and on the pretensions of learned men, was banned as heretical.
Belgium: The author was imprisoned at Brussels for satires written on the scholasticism of the professors.

1533 Italy–Rome: Charges of magic and conjury were brought against the author by the Inquisition for *De Occulta Philosophia*, Book 1.

Tyndale, William (c.1492–1536)

The New Testament of Our Lord and Savior Jesus Christ, 1525–1526
Practyse of Prelates, 1530

1525–1526 England: The *New Testament*, translated by Tyndale in part, was printed at Cologne, as it was violently opposed by the clergy who damned it as "pernicious merchandise." He continued the work at Worms and the sheets of 6,000 copies were smuggled into England where they were publicly burned by the dignitaries of the church; consequently only one complete copy has survived which is in the library of the Baptist College at Bristol. Cardinal Wolsey ordered Tyndale to be seized at Worms, but he took refuge with Philip of Hesse at Marburg.

1530 Germany–Marburg: Church and State authorities banned *Practyse of Prelates*, a treatise condemning the Catholic clergy and the divorce of Henry VIII.

1536 Belgium–Vilvorde Castle: Tyndale was imprisoned, strangled and burned at the stake with his translations of the *Bible*, although about 50,000 copies in seven editions were in circulation.

1546 England: Tyndale's books were ordered delivered to the Archbishop to be burned, because he had called church functionaries "horse-leeches, maggots and caterpillers in a kingdom."

1555 His books fell under the ban of Queen Mary's proclamation, and were forbidden in the realm for containing false doctrines against the Catholic faith.

1939 The Royal Society of Literature made a reprint of Tyndale's *New Testament* to celebrate the 400th anniversary of the man who made the first partial English translation.

Aretino, Pietro (1492–1556)

Works

Sonnetti Lussuriosi, 1524

1527 Italy–Rome: The Pope condemned a book containing these verses and the erotic engravings that accompanied them, made by Marcantonio Raimondi from pictures by Guilio Romano. The edition became known in England as *Aretino's Postures* and served as a sub rosa *Joy of Sex* for many generations. John Donne, however, observed that it left out some "postures" mentioned by Greek and Roman writers.

1545 The Council of Trent condemned Aretino's works; many of them were derisive towards authority.

Rabelais, François (c.1494–1553)

Pantagruel, 1533

Gargantua, 1535

1533 France: The first two parts of *Pantagruel*, published without the knowledge of the author, were listed on the *Index* of the Sorbonne, and on the official blacklist of Parliament.

1535 Italy–Rome: A Papal bull absolved Rabelais from ecclesiastical censure.

1546 France: The third book of *Pantagruel* was published under the author's name "avec privilège du Roi."

1552 Taking advantage of the King's absence from Paris, the divines of the Sorbonne censored the fourth book on publication.

1554 Cardinal de Chatillion persuaded Henry II to raise the ban on the works of Rabelais.

1564 Italy–Rome: The *Index* listed Rabelais in its severe first class as "Rebelisius."

c.1900 France: An imaginative Frenchman, Robertet, refined the coarse language of these books in an adaptation for children. The story of Pantagruel, the giant, son of Gargantua, the giant, their feasts, their wars, and adventures, told with a satiric humor had the same appeal to the imagination as Swift's *Gulliver's Travels*.

1930 United States: The Customs Department lifted the ban on all editions with the exception of those with so-called obscene illustrations, specifically Frank C. Pape's drawings for an edition of the Motteux translation.

1938 South Africa–Johannesburg: All works banned.

1953 The 400th anniversary of the death of Rabelais was celebrated in the literary world.

Calvin, John (1509–1564)

Civil and Canonical Law, 1542

1542 France: *Civil and Canonical Law* forbidden by the Sorbonne.

1555 England: Queen Mary's proclamation required "that no manner of persons presume to bring into this realm any mss., books, papers, by John Calvin . . . containing false doctrine against the Catholic faith."

1559 and 1564 Italy–Rome: All works listed for heresy in the first class prohibition of the *Index*.

Servetus, Michael (Villanovanus Michael) (1511–1553)

Christianismi Restitutio, 1553

1553 France: The author's theological tracts, recast as *Christianismi Restitutio*, were secretly printed at Vienne, in Dauphine, France, by Balthazar Arnoullet. Imprisoned by the Inquisition, he escaped, was recaptured and burned at the stake with his books.

Ponce De Leon, Luis (1527–1591)

1571 Spain: Denounced to the Inquisition for translating the *Song of Solomon* and for criticizing the text of the *Vulgate Bible*, Leon was imprisoned for nearly five years at Valladolid.

Montaigne, Michel de (1533–1592)

Les Essaies, 1580–1588

1595 France–Lyons: Certain sections of the unexpurgated edition were banned for being tolerant of an easy morality (fifth chapter of third book, etc.).

1676 Italy–Rome: Listed in the *Index*.

Scot, Reginald (c.1538–1599)

A Discoverie of Witchcraft, 1584

1584 England–London: The author held that the prosecution of those accused of witchcraft was contrary to the dictates of reason as well as of religion, and he placed the responsibility at the door of the Roman Church. All obtainable copies were burned on the accession of James I in 1603 and those remaining are now rare.

1586 A decree of the Star Chamber greatly tightened the censorship laws.

Stubbs, John (c.1543–1591)

The discoverie of a gaping gulf where into England is likely to be swallowed by another French marriage, 1579

1579 England–London: A virulent attack on the proposed marriage between Queen Elizabeth and the Duke of Anjou. The copies of the book were burned in the kitchen stove of Stationer's Hall and the author was condemned to have his right hand cut off by means of a cleaver driven through the wrist by a mallet. Stubbs thereupon raised his hat with his left hand and cried, "God save the Queen."

Tasso, Torquato (1544–1595)

Gerusalemme Liberata, 1575–1592

1595 France: Suppressed by Parliament as containing ideas subversive to the authority of kings. This lyric epic was written and published in 1592 in a revision excluding the suppressed material.

Parsons, Robert (1546–1610)

A Conference about the Next Succession to the Crowne of Ingland, 1594

1603 England–London: The intention of the book was to support the title of the Infanta against that of James I, after the death of Queen Elizabeth. The authors were Parsons the Jesuit, Cardinal Allen, and Sir Francis Englefield. The book was rigorously suppressed by Parliament, which enacted that "whosoever should be found to have it in their house should be guilty of high treason." The printer is said to have been hanged, drawn, and quartered.

1683 Oxford: Condemned by the university and burned in the quadrangle, particularly because of a passage which says "Birthright and proximity of blood do give no title to rule or government."

Cervantes Saavedra, Miguel de (1547–1616)

The Life and Exploits of the Ingenious Gentleman Don Quixote De La Mancha, first part, 1605; second part, 1615

1624 Portugal–Lisbon: A few paragraphs were proscribed by the Spanish *Index.*

1640 Spain–Madrid: Placed on the *Index* for one sentence: "Works of charity negligently performed are of no worth."

Raleigh, Sir Walter (1552–1618)

The History of the World, 1614

1614 England: Suppressed by James I "for divers exceptions, but especially for being too saucy in censuring Princes."

Thomas, William (d.1554)

The Historie of Italie, 1549

1554 England–London: This book gave great offense to Queen Mary because of its criticism of the Italian clergy. The book was burned by the common hangman, and the author was hanged and quartered at Tyburn. A royal proclamation had been issued in 1538 by which no one was allowed to print any book unless he had received license from some member of the Privy Council or from a person appointed by the King, thus establishing the first regular censorship in England.

Index Librorum Prohibitorum

1559–1966 Following earlier condemnations of books judged heretical, the Congregation of the Inquisition (or Holy Office) of the Roman Catholic Church published in 1559 the first list of banned and recommended books to use the name *Index.* Other editions followed until 1948, with a supplement a little later. In 1966 the Congregation for the Doctrine of the Faith (successor to the Holy Office) under Pope Paul VI terminated publication; the *Index* thus became no longer a list of works that Catholics were forbidden to read because of possible corruption of faith and morals, but rather a historic document. However, the Vatican reserves the right to regulate the use of books by the faithful, and to prohibit their reading of books inherently forbidden by canon law.

Books named in the *Index* were condemned mostly for doctrinal reasons or for criticizing or seeming to criticize the Papacy and the Church, or for moral reasons. Among the many important writers included (along with many more who were obscure or not long remembered), and important titles, were: *The Book of Common Prayer*, Montaigne's *Essays*, works of Balzac, Spinoza, Oliver Goldsmith's *History of England*, Samuel Richardson, Jean-Jacques Rousseau, George Sand, Lawrence Sterne, Voltaire, Andrew Marvell, Victor Hugo, Stendhal, D'Annunzio, Emile Zola, Abbé Ernest Dimnet, André Gide, Jean-Paul Sartre, Alberto Moravia—a bewildering mixture.

Bacon, Francis, Baron of Verulam and Viscount St. Albans (1561–1626)

Advancement of Learning, 1605

1640 Spain: All works banned by the Inquisition and placed on Sotomayor's *Index*.

1668 Italy–Rome: Book IX of *Advancement of Learning*, dedicated to the King, was placed on the *Index, donec corrigetur* (until it is corrected) where it remained in the 1948 edition of the list.

Galilei, Galileo (1564–1642)

Dialogo sopra i due Massimi Sistemi del Mondo, 1632

1616 Italy–Rome: Galileo was reprimanded by Pope Paul IV, and told not to "hold, teach or defend" the condemned doctrine of Copernicus, whose theory he had tried to reconcile with religion.

1633 *Dialogo* banned by Pope Urban VIII for heresy and breach of good faith. The author was examined by the Inquisition under threat of torture and sentenced to incarceration at the pleasure of the Tribunal. Galileo, although a white-haired old man of 70, was compelled to kneel, clothed in sackcloth, and deny that which he knew to be true. He promised "that he would never again in words or writing spread this damnable heresy." He is said to have murmured as he rose from his knees: "Nevertheless it does move." By way of penance he was enjoined to recite once a week for three years the seven penitential psalms, although he felt "that Holy Writ was intended to teach men how to go to Heaven, not how the heavens go."

1642 On Galileo's death, his common-law wife submitted his manuscripts on telescopic and pendulum inventions to her confessor who subsequently destroyed them as heretical.

1954 United States: *Dialogo* translated into English for the first time since 1661; an event for scholars, as the book is extremely rare due to the almost total destruction of copies in the great fire of London in 1666.

Hayward, Sir John (c.1564–1627)

First Part of the Life and Raigne of King Henrie IV, 1599

1600 England: At Whitsuntide, when 1,500 copies were ready for distribution, they were taken by the wardens of the Stationer's Company and delivered to the Bishop of London, in whose house they were burned. The book contained a dedication to Essex in terms of extravagant laudation and included a description of the deposition of Richard II. Essex's enemies at court easily excited the suspicion of the Queen that Hayward, under guise of an historical treatise, was criticizing her own policy and hinting at what might possibly befall her in the future.

Marlowe, Christopher (1564–1593). *See* Ovid (Publius Ovidius Naso) (43 B.C.–C. A.D. 17)

Shakespeare, William (1564–1616)

The Tragedie of King Richard the Second, 1597
The Merchant of Venice, 1600
King Lear, 1608

1597 England: The original edition of *Richard the Second* contained a scene in which the King was deposed, and it so infuriated Queen Elizabeth that she ordered it eliminated from all copies. It was not reinserted until after her death, in the edition of 1608. Elizabeth complained that the play had been acted forty times in streets and houses "for the encouragement of disaffection."

1601 Sir Gilly Merrick paid players 40 shillings to revive the play on the afternoon when the Earl of Essex sought to rouse London against the Queen.

1788 *King Lear* was prohibited on the English stage until 1820, probably out of respect to King George III's acknowledged insanity, when the royal duties were transferred to a Regent.

1815 Coleridge said: "Shakespeare's words are too indecent to be translated . . . His gentlefolk's talk is full of coarse allusions such as nowadays you could hear only in the meanest taverns."

1818 Thomas Bowdler, M.D., published the *Family Shakespeare* omitting "those words and expressions which cannot with propriety be read aloud in the family." "Bowdlerize" thereupon became synonymous with "expurgate."

1931 United States: *The Merchant of Venice* was eliminated from the high school curricula of Buffalo and Manchester, New York. Jewish organizations believed that it fostered intolerance.

1953 Minority groups still felt that Shylock was depicted as an unfortu-
nate characterization of a Jew and sought the suppression of the
play.

Leighton, Alexander (1568–1649)

An Appeal to the Parliament: or Sion's Plea against the Prelacie,
1628

1630 England–London: The book was a virulent attack on prelacy and
an appeal to political Presbyterianism, to take the sword in hand.
Condemned by the authorities, the author was seized and dragged to
Newgate, where he was clapped in irons, and cast into a loathsome
and ruinous doghole full of rats and mice. Tried by the Star Chamber
Court, he was sentenced to a fine, to be degraded from holy orders,
whipped at the Westminster pillory and have one ear cut off, his nose
split, and to be branded with S.S. for "sower of sedition." This not
being enough, he was returned to prison, whipped, lost his other ear,
and was imprisoned for life. The suppression of this book led to even
stricter censorship laws by the Star Chamber.

Jonson, Ben (1573–1637)

Eastward Ho, 1605

1608 England–London: Jonson was imprisoned for collaborating with
Marston and Chapman on the comedy, *Eastward Ho,* which was
derogatory to the Scots. Released by the intervention of powerful
friends, he was given a feast in celebration, at which Jonson's mother
revealed that she had planned to give him poison if his prison
sentence had been carried out.

Marston, John (c.1575–1634)

The Metamorphosis of Pigmalion's Image, 1598

1598 England–London: The book is dedicated to the "World's mightie
monarch good opinion," and the purpose of the author was to
ridicule the immorality and evil tendency of a class of poems then
fashionable, and to which Shakespeare's *Venus and Adonis* be-
longed. Characterizing the book as licentious, the prelates Whitgift
and Bancroft ordered its suppression and destruction.

Holinshed, Raphael (d. c.1580)

Chronicles of England, Scotland and Ireland, 1577

1587 England: Upon publication of the second edition, Queen Elizabeth's
Privy Council ordered excised certain passages about the history of

Ireland, which were offensive to her. It was from this edition that Shakespeare drew material for *Macbeth, King Lear* and *Cymbeline*.

1723 Queen Elizabeth's excisions were published separately.

Pynchon, William (1590–1662)

The Meritorious Price of our Redemption, 1650

1650 Massachusetts Bay Colony–Boston, Mass.: Pynchon's book was the first work to be publicly burned in what is now the United States. The treatise was at variance with Puritan orthodoxy on several points of theology. In view of the rigid adherence to the established doctrines enforced by the clergy, it was not surprising that Pynchon's opinions should have aroused a storm of wrath and indignation. His book was read with horror by the members of the General Court and condemned to be burned in the marketplace by the common executioner. Pynchon, a prominent citizen of the colony, was one of the original grantees of the charter. Though publicly censured, he escaped prosecution and left soon after for England.

Descartes, René (1596–1650)

Les Méditations Métaphysiques, 1641

1633 Holland: Descartes, a devoted Catholic, abandoned his treatise on Copernican beliefs when he learned that Galileo's treatise had been suppressed in Rome for supporting Copernicus's hypothesis of the earth revolving around the sun.
Italy–Rome: Through the influence of Jesuits, this author's works containing Copernican theories were placed on the *Index*, and forbidden in many institutions of learning until corrected or expurgated.

1665 Italy–Rome: *Méditations* was placed on the *Index* until corrected, as the whole system was opposed to the whole system of Aristotle.

1772 Italy–Rome: This edition was forbidden by the *Index* unconditionally, probably because it contained matter written by others.

1926 Soviet Union: All philosophical works suppressed.

1948 Italy–Rome: *Méditations* and six other books still remained on the *Index*.

Prynne, William (1600–1669)

Histrio-Mastix. The Players Scourge or Actors Tragaedie, 1633

1633 England–London: This book, written with purity of conviction and moral earnestness, was brought to the attention of the King and Queen by Archbishop Laud. Prynne violently denounced all theatrical plays, including those at court, where they were frequently given, and he was therefore accused of a supposed attack on the Queen, who was fond of the drama. She and her ladies had unfortunately taken part in a performance of Walter Montagu's *Shepherd's Paradise*. The Star Chamber decreed that Prynne be fined, imprisoned, branded and have his ears cut off. His library was confiscated and his book was burned by the common hangman.

Later, when Laud was on trial for alleged offenses, and was sentenced to death, Prynne was one of the chief prosecutors.

Williams, Roger (c.1603–1683)

The Bloudy Tenent of Persecution, 1644

1635 Massachusetts Bay Colony: Denying that the state had authority over conscience, and being outspoken in civil matters, Williams was "enlarged" out of Massachusetts and went to Rhode Island, where he founded Providence.

1644 England–London: *The Bloudy Tenent* was ordered by the House of Commons to be publicly burned for the toleration of all sorts of religion. This book, written primarily as an attack on John Cotton, contained a dialogue on intellectual freedom in civil and ecclesiastical governments and an argument for democratic liberty and tolerance. Cotton replied with *The Bloudy Tenent Washed and Made White in the Bloud of the Lamb*, 1647. Williams retaliated in 1652 with *The Bloudy Tenent yet More Bloudy: by Mr. Cotton's Endeavour to Wash it White in the Bloud of the Lamb*.

1936 United States: The Massachusetts Legislature passed a bill revoking the 300-year-old sentence of expulsion.

Browne, Sir Thomas (1605–1682)

Religio Medici, 1642

1642 England: This famous work, written as a "private exercise to my-self," was printed without the knowledge of the author.

1645 Italy–Rome: The Latin translation was placed on the *Index* by Pope Leo XIII, although Browne professed to be absolutely free from heretical opinions. He insisted upon his right to be guided by his own reason when no specific guidance was proffered by Church or Scripture.

Milton, John (1608–1674)

Areopagitica, A Speech for the Liberty of Unlicenc'd Printing, to the Parliament of England, 1644

lastes, 1649

lo Anglicano Defensio, 1651

Lost, 1667

.. Papers, 1676

1476 England: Shortly after Caxton set up his press in Westminster, the crown forbade all printing except by Royal permission. This prelicensing continued for nearly 200 years, eventually calling forth the *Areopagitica*.

1644 This famed and eloquent plea for freedom of the pen was delivered before Parliament and was published without license in defiance of a restraining ordinance. *Areopagitica* was condemned by Cromwell and the Parliament of Protestant England for such sentences as this: "And yet on the other hand unlesse warinesse be us'd, as good almost kill a man as kill a good Book . . . who destroyes a good Booke, kills Reason itselfe, kills the Image of God as it were in the eye."

1652 France: *Pro Populo Anglicano Defensio*, written as a reply to the attack on the commonwealth of Salmasius, was burned for political reasons.

1660 England: *Pro Populo Anglicano Defensio* was publicly burned. *Eikonoklastes* was burned by the common hangman at the time of the Restoration for attacking the hypocrisy of the religion of Charles I, and for arguing against the divine right of kings. The author escaped the scaffold only through the influence of friends.

1694 Italy–Rome: *State Papers*, published posthumously and surreptitiously, was listed on the *Index*.

1695 England: Precensorship of the press abolished and never again enforced.

1758 Italy–Rome: *Paradise Lost*, translated into Italian by Paolo Rolli, listed on the *Index*.

L'Estrange, Sir Roger (1616–1704)

Considerations and Proposals in Order to the Regulation of the Press, 1663

1663 England–London: This extravagant denunciation of the liberty of the press was dedicated to Charles II, and recommended a stringent enforcement and extension of the licensing act of May 1662. Master printers, L'Estrange argued, should be reduced in number from 60 to 20, and all workshops ought to be subjected to the strictest supervision. Severe penalties should be uniformly exacted, and working printers guilty of taking part in the publication of offensive works should on conviction wear some ignominious badge. He was rewarded for his vehemence by his appointment to the office of "surveyor of the imprimery," or printing presses, in succession to Sir John Birkenhead. L'Estrange was repeatedly imprisoned for his political views and writings and for his religious pamphlets. At times he was forced to flee the country for protection.

La Fontaine, Jean de (1621–1695)

Contes et Nouvelles en Vers, 1665–1671

1675 France–Paris: Suppressed by the Lieutenant of Police for political satire.

1703 Italy–Rome: Placed on the *Index*.

1869 France: Publisher fined for producing the Fermiers–Généraux édition de luxe.

Molière (Jean-Baptiste Poquelin) (1622–1673)

Le Tartuffe ou l'Imposteur, 1664–1669

1664 France: *Tartuffe*, a satire on religious hypocrisy, banned from the public stage by Louis XIV who, nevertheless, read it aloud to an audience which included high dignitaries of the church. The first three acts were given repeatedly at court, but Molière could not get permission for a public performance. During these years the church called him "a demon in human flesh," closed his theater, and tore down his posters.

1667 While the King was away in Flanders, the play was given as *The Impostor*. The theater was ordered closed by the Chief of Police, and the Archbishop of Paris laid a ban of excommunication on all who might act in the play, read, or see it.

1669 Permission was granted by the King to perform the play in public.

Pascal, Blaise (1623–1662)

Lettres à un Provincial, 1656–1657
Pensées, 1670

1657 France: *Lettres* burned for being too free with the dignity of all secular authorities.

1660 Pascal having become converted to the Jansenist teaching, the *Lettres* aroused a storm of controversy because of their anti-Jesuit flavor. Louis XIV ordered that the book "be torn up and burned at the 'Croix du Tiroir' at the hands of the High Executioner, fulfillment of which is to be certified to his Majesty within the week; and that meanwhile all printers, booksellers, vendors and others, of whatever rank or station, are explicitly prohibited from printing, selling, and distributing, and even from having in their possession the said book . . . under pain of public (exemplary) punishment."

1789 Italy–Rome: *Pensées* placed on the *Index* "avec les notes de M. Voltaire."

Locke, John (1632–1704)

An Essay Concerning Human Understanding, 1690

1683 England: Locke's theory of civil, religious, and philosophical liberty was too radical, and he escaped to Holland, the asylum of exiles such as Descartes, Erasmus, Grotius, and Spinoza, in search of liberty of thought. There he hid for some time under the name of Dr. Van der Linden. King Charles II deprived him of his studentship at Oxford, thereby closing the university to him.

1700 Italy–Rome: The French translation of *An Essay Concerning Human Understanding* was placed on the *Index*.

1701 England–London: The Latin version was prohibited at Oxford with the express ruling "that no tutors were to read with their students" this essential investigation into the basis of knowledge.

Racine, Jean (1639–1699)

Athalie, 1691

c.1810 France: Under the imperial censorship of Napoleon, certain passages in *Athalie*, a religious tragedy alluding to tyranny, were canceled before a new edition was permitted.

Fénelon, François de Salignac de la Mothe (1651–1715)

Explication des Maximes des Saints, 1697
Les Aventures de Télémaque, Fils d'Ulysse. Imprimé par Ordre du Roi pour L'Education de Monsieur le Dauphin, 1699

1697 Italy–Rome: Although the author had been appointed Archbishop of Cambrai four years earlier, his *Explication des maximes des Saints* was condemned by Pope Innocent XII as being against Christianity.

1699 France–Paris: Mme. de Maintenon caused the author's banishment, pretending to believe *Télémaque* a satire on herself and the King. Actually she was punishing him for opposing her marriage to Louis XIV.

Defoe, Daniel (1660?–1731)

The Shortest Way with the Dissenters, 1702
The Life and Strange Surprising Adventures of Robinson Crusoe, of York, Mariner, 1719
Moll Flanders, 1721

Roxana, 1724

The Political History of the Devil, 1726

1703 England–London: *The Shortest Way with the Dissenters*, a satire recommending that all dissenters be killed, was at first taken seriously by the Church. When the sarcastic import was discovered the book was burned and the author fined, imprisoned and pilloried.

1713 Defoe was prosecuted by the Whigs for writing treasonable anti-Jacobite pamphlets and imprisoned.

1720 Spain: *Robinson Crusoe* placed on the Spanish *Index*.

1743 Italy–Rome: *The Political History of the Devil* was listed on the *Index*.

1930 United States: Customs raised its ban on *Moll Flanders* and *Roxana*.

Harbin, George (c.1666?– ?)

Hereditary Right of the Crown of England, 1713

1714 England–London: The book apparently implied that the Pretender, James, had the right to the throne. One Hilkaiah Bedford, who had delivered the manuscript to the printer, was tried because of its treasonable nature, was convicted, heavily fined, and died in prison.

Swift, Jonathan (1667–1745)

A Tale of a Tub Written for the Universal Improvement of Mankind, 1704

The Predictions for the Ensuing Year by Isaac Bickerstaff, 1708

Drapier Letters, 1724

Gulliver's Travels, 1726

1708 Ireland: The *Predictions for the Ensuing Year* was burned as "such uncanny prescience could not otherwise than signify collusion with the evil one himself."

1724 *Drapier Letters*. Printed anonymously, the letters protested the introduction of a half-penny coin into Ireland on the ground that heavy profits from the coinage would accrue to favorites at the English Court. The Irish nation was so aroused that all efforts by Robert Walpole to prosecute the printer or to identify Swift as the author were frustrated.

1726 Privately printed and published anonymously, *Gulliver's Travels*, a satire on courts, political parties, and statesmen, was denounced on all sides as wicked and obscene.

1734 Italy–Rome: *A Tale of a Tub*, charged with ridicule of papists and dissenters, was listed on the *Index*.

1841 Listed in the catalogue of Pope Gregory XVI.

1881 Ban lifted by Pope Leo XIII.

Curll, Edmund (1675–1747)

1716 England–London: Curll, a publisher and bookseller, appeared before the bar of the House of Lords for publishing matter relating to members of the House. He was called again in 1721.

1727 Perpetually in trouble with the law, in this year Curll was found guilty of an obscene libel for publication of a scandalous book, *Venus in the Cloister.* This is the first recorded instance of a conviction on grounds of obscenity in the English-speaking world. A similar case in 1708 had led to the dismissal of an indictment against a printer for publishing a bawdy book, because, as the Justice said, "there is no law against it." The irrepressible Curll was noted, in part, for his enemies: Daniel Defoe attacked his less respectable publications and Alexander Pope mocked him in *The Dunciad.*

Swedenborg, Emanuel (1688–1772)

Principia; or the First Principles of Natural Things, 1721
Amor Conjugalis, 1768

1738 Italy–Rome: *Principia* placed on the *Index* where it remained in the 1948 edition.

1909 United States–Philadelphia, Pa.: *Amor Conjugalis* was seized by the Post Office authorities on grounds of obscenity.

1930 Soviet Union: All works banned.

Montesquieu, Baron Charles Louis (1689–1755)

Lettres Persanes, 1721
L'Esprit des Lois, 1748

1721 France: *Lettres Persanes,* a satire on the social, political, ecclesiastical, and literary follies of the day, was published anonymously. It so shocked Fleury that Montesquieu was not admitted to the Academy until seven years after publication.
Italy–Rome: *Lettres Persanes* listed on the *Index,* where it remained in 1948.

1751 France: The Sorbonne planned but did not carry out a regular censure of the author for denouncing the abuse of the French monarchical system in *L'Esprit des Lois.*
Italy–Rome: Prohibited by the church authorities, although not with the entire approval of the Pope.

Richardson, Samuel (1689–1761)

Pamela; or Virtue Rewarded, 1740

1755 Italy–Rome: The French translation by Abbé Prévost was listed on the *Index*; still cited in 1948.
England: This volume was abridged, not for moral reasons, but for length, and given as a reward of virtue to children who excelled in their lessons. Sir Walter Scott feared *Pamela* would rather "encourage a spirit of rash enterprise than vigorous resistance." Charles Lamb pictured a young lad retreating from the book "hastily with a deep blush."

Voltaire (François Marie Arouet) (1694–1778)

Puero Regnante, 1717
J'ai Vue, 1717
Temple du Goût, 1733
Lettres Philosophiques sur les Anglais, 1734
Diatribe du Docteur Akakia, 1752
Histoire des Croisades, 1754
Cantiques des Cantiques, 1759
Candide, 1759
Dictionnaire Philosophique, 1764

1716 France: The author was exiled to Tulle, and later to Sully, for composing lampoons against the Regent, the Duke of Orléans.
1717 The author thrown into the Bastille for writing *Puero Regnante*, and *J'ai Vue*, on grounds that they libeled Louis XIV.
1734 *Lettres Philosophiques sur les Anglais* condemned and burned by the high executioner on the grounds that it was "scandeleux, et contraire à la réligion."
Temple du Goût, a satire on contemporary French literature, was condemned. Copies were seized and burned, and a warrant was issued against the author, who was not to be found.
1752 Prussia: *Diatribe du Docteur Akakia*, a lampoon against Frederick the Great, caused the author to be arrested, and copies of the book to be burnt. In consequence, Voltaire ended his connection with the Court of Frederick.
Italy–Rome: *Lettres Philosophiques* placed on the *Index*, followed by *Histoire des Croisades* and *Cantiques des Cantiques*.
1764 France and Switzerland–Geneva: *Dictionnaire Philosophique* banned.
1929 United States–Boston, Mass.: *Candide* was seized by U.S. Customs

way to a class in French literature at Harvard, but was
 d later in a new edition.

Customs, after 170 years, discovered Voltaire and banned
Candide as obscene, although it was being studied in college classrooms the world over as a literary masterpiece. The defense was prepared by two Harvard professors.

No one writer of the eighteenth century contributed so many
books to the flames as Voltaire.

Erroneously attributed to Voltaire was one of the best known
quotations on the freedom of speech: "I disapprove of what you say,
but I shall defend to the death your right to say it." The phrase was
coined by S. G. Tallentyre (Miss E. Beatrice Hall) in her book *The
Friends of Voltaire*, London, 1906, and was not originated by
Voltaire.

1935 Soviet Union: All philosophical works suppressed.

1944 United States–New York City: Concord Books, Inc., issued a sale
catalogue of 100 books for $.49 each, including *Candide*. They were
notified by the Post Office Department that the catalogue violated
the section relating to the mailing of obscene literature, and that the
title must be blocked out before it could be mailed. This was done.

1956 United States–New York City: *Candide* made into a successful
Broadway musical, with text by Lillian Hellman, score by Leonard
Bernstein, and directed by Tyrone Guthrie; restaged with enormous
success in 1976.

Arabian Nights' Entertainments or *The Thousand and One Nights*

Origin unknown, first translation from the Arabic by A. Galland,
Paris, 1704–1712

1927 United States–New York City: The Customs held up 500 sets of the
translation by the French scholar, Mardrus, which were imported
from England.

1931 Ban lifted on the unexpurgated translation (1885–1888), by Richard
Francis Burton, but the prohibition was maintained on the Mardrus
edition. (*See also* Sir Richard Francis Burton [1821–1890].)

Fielding, Henry (1707–1754)

Pasquin, a Dramatick Satire, 1736

Tom Jones, 1749

Inquiry into the Causes of the Late Increase in Robberies, 1750

1730 England–London: Some of Fielding's early plays contained criticism
of the political corruption of Sir Robert Walpole. The Prime
Minister was so enraged that he forced a bill through Parliament

which brought on the Licensing Act of 1737, enabling the Lord Chamberlain to license or suppress plays at will. Fielding turned to writing novels.

1749 France–Paris: *Tom Jones* banned on publication.

1750 *Inquiry into the Causes of the Late Increase in Robberies*, led to a parliamentary act governing the licensing of music halls in and near London.

1963 A somewhat frank film of *Tom Jones* was highly successful although widely criticized in some sedate circles.

Cleland, John (1709–1789)

Memoirs of a Woman of Pleasure, also known as *Fanny Hill*, 1749

1749 England: Arraigned before the Privy Council for writing a literary obscenity, Cleland pleaded poverty. He was reprimanded and given a pension of £100 annually on condition that he not repeat the offense. The book went underground and remained the chief erotic classic for more than 200 years.

1821 United States: Banned in Massachusetts in the first known obscenity case in the United States.

1963 United States: Published openly by Grove Press, the book was attacked by "decency" groups. The highest state court in New York cleared it; the highest courts of New Jersey and Massachusetts declared it obscene; and on March 21, 1966, the U.S. Supreme Court reversed the unfavorable judgments, clearing *Fanny* for publication.

1965 Illinois: Prosecution of the book in Illinois was a major factor in the closing of a bookstore, Paul Romaine, Books, in Chicago, according to Mr. Romaine.

During the period when the book was emerging into the open market, it was seized in Berlin, burned in Manchester, England, and burned in Japan.

Rousseau, Jean-Jacques (1712–1778)

Julie, ou la Nouvelle Héloïse, 1761

Émile, ou de l'Éducation, 1762

Du Contrat Social, 1762

Lettres de la Montagne, 1763

Lettre à Christophe de Beaumont, Archevêque de Paris, 1763

Confessions, 1770

1762 France: *Émile* condemned by the Parliament of Paris to be torn and burned at the foot of the great staircase; the Archbishop published a pastoral against the author, who went in exile to Geneva, his birth-place.

1763 Switzerland: Condemned by the Council of Geneva, whereupon Rousseau renounced his citizenship, attacked the Council, and the Geneva constitution, in *Lettres de la Montagne*, and fled to Neuchâtel, where he had the protection of Frederick the Great, who was the elected prince of this Swiss canton as well as King of Prussia. Italy–Rome: Both books placed on the *Index*.

1766 Italy–Rome: *Du Contrat Social*, and *Lettre à Christophe de Beaumont, Archevêque de Paris* were placed on the *Index*.

1806 *Julie, ou la Nouvelle Héloise* placed on the *Index*.

1929 United States: *Confessions* was banned by the Customs Department as being injurious to public morals.

1935 Soviet Union: All philosophical works forbidden.

1936 Works permitted in Soviet Union.

Diderot, Denis (1713–1784)

L'Encyclopédie, 1751–1780

1752 France: The first two volumes were suppressed by the King's Council for political and religious outspokenness.

1754 Louis XV issued a privilege for the continuation of the work.

1759 Although innocent of treason, this work was looked upon with suspicion and alarm in official circles. Consequently, the royal privilege was withdrawn. The work, however, was continued surreptitiously by the publisher, Le Breton, who had been censoring Diderot's work without his knowledge. For a century and a half, scholars despaired of recovering Diderot's original text, for the manuscript had been destroyed as the matter was set in type, but about 200 years later a volume containing Le Breton's corrections of the proof turned up and was acquired by an American collector. Italy–Rome: The first seven volumes were condemned by the *Index*.

1804 The complete work was placed on the *Index*.

Sterne, Laurence (1713–1768)

A Sentimental Journey through France and Italie by Mr. Yorick, 1768

1819 Italy–Rome: The translation by Ugo Foscolo was listed on the *Index*.

Hely-Hutchinson, John (1724–1794)

The Commercial Restraints of Ireland Considered, 1779

1779 England–London: Hely-Hutchinson, borrowing from Adam Smith, wrote what Lecky called "one of the best specimens of political literature in Ireland," which accused England of maintaining policies damaging to Irish trade. His work was condemned and is reported to be the last work burned by the common hangman.

Kant, Immanuel (1724–1804)

Critique of Pure Reason, 1781
Die Religion Innerhalb der Grenzen der Blossen Vernunft, 1793

1793 Prussia: *Die Religion Innerhalb der Grenzen der Blossen Vernunft*, second part, was suppressed by the strongly Lutheran Prussian State because it was opposed to the literal doctrines of the Lutheran Church.
      Königsberg: Both parts were published, and Frederick William II promptly forbade the author to lecture or write on religion, not so much because of his religious unorthodoxy, as for his supposed sympathy with French revolutionary ideas.

1827 Italy–Rome: *Critique of Pure Reason*, in the Italian, was placed on the *Index*.

1928 Soviet Union: All works banned.

1939 Spain: Franco purged the libraries of "such disgraceful writers" as Kant.

Casanova de Seingalt, Giovanni Jacopo (1725–1798)

Mémoires: Écrites par lui-même, 1826–1838

1820 Germany–Leipzig: The original manuscript was confined to the safe of the publisher, Brockhaus, and never published in unexpurgated form until the twentieth century, although it was an invaluable record of morals, manners and etiquette of the eighteenth century.

1834 Italy–Rome: Placed on the *Index*.

1863 France: Condemned by "le grand procès de Lille."

1929 United States: An unexpurgated edition translated by Arthur Machen, with an appreciation by Havelock Ellis, was sold freely.

1931 Customs ban on imported copies was lifted, except for editions containing risqué illustrations.

1933 Ireland: Banned.

1934 United States–Detroit, Mich.: Seized by the police.

1935 Italy: Banned by Mussolini.

1967–1971 Complete works, 12 volumes, published under the title *History of My Life*, by Harcourt, Brace (Helen & Kurt Wolff Books).

Goldsmith, Oliver (1728–1774)

History of England, 1764

1823 Italy–Rome: The Italian translation was listed on the *Index*, *donec corrigetur*—until it is corrected.

1948 *An abridged History of England from the Invasion of Julius Caesar to the Death of George II*, remained on the *Index*.

Beaumarchais, Pierre Augustin Caron de (1732–1799)

Le Barbier de Séville, 1773

Mémoires, 1774

Le Mariage de Figaro, 1778

c.1770–c.1780 During his service as a secret agent of Louis XV and Louis XVI, Beaumarchais traveled abroad to seize writings condemning Mme. Du Barry and Marie Antoinette.

1773 For two years *Le Barbier de Séville* was forbidden to be performed on the stage. A revised version was successful in 1775.

1774 France: *Mémoires* was condemned to flames by Parliament for criticizing the state powers.

1778 *Le Mariage de Figaro* was suppressed for six years by Louis XVI at court and in public performances on the ground of profound immorality. The author was imprisoned in St. Lazare.

1792 Beaumarchais was charged with treason against the Republic and his works were suppressed. Released, he became an émigré for four years.

Lord Chamberlain

1737 England: By the Licensing Act of this year the Lord Chamberlain was empowered to license plays, giving rise to the popular phrase "legitimate theater." The history of theatre censorship is itself long and complicated, and extends at least from medieval Europe down to the present. But the particular function of the Lord Chamberlain led to many clashes over works that have since become classics—even so seemingly harmless a piece as Gilbert and Sullivan's *Mikado*.

1968 The power of the Lord Chamberlain to license plays was revoked by Parliament.

Forskål, Peter (1736–1763)

1759 Sweden: After being rebuffed by the faculty of the University at Uppsala, and by the Chancery Council of Sweden, which possessed the final authority to license printing, Forskål privately printed his *Thoughts on Civil Liberty*. He was reprimanded by the King, and the case was investigated by a committee of the Swedish Parliament.

1766 As a result of the Forskål episode, censorship was abolished in Sweden.

Gibbon, Edward (1737–1794)

The History of the Decline and Fall of the Roman Empire, 1776–1788

1783 Italy–Rome: The first volume, in Italian (1779), was placed on the *Index* because it contradicted much official church history. In his vindication, which refers to attacks, more by Protestants than by Catholics, Gibbon says: "I stand accused . . . for profanely depreciating the promised land. . . . They seem to consider in the light of a reproach, the idea which I had given of Palestine, as a territory scarcely superior to Wales in extent and fertility; and they strangely convert a geographical observation into a theological error. When I recollect that the imputation of a similar error was employed by the implacable Calvin, to precipitate and to justify the execution of Servetus, I must applaud the felicity of the country, and of this age, which has disarmed, if it could not mollify, the fierceness of ecclesiastical criticism."

1826 England: An expurgated edition was published by Thomas Bowdler.

Paine, Thomas (1737–1809)

The Rights of Man, 1791–1792

The Age of Reason, 1793

1792 England: Paine's writings were the subject of bitter controversy in America, where he supported the cause of the colonies, and in England, where his attack on English institutions in his *Rights of Man* led to his indictment for treason and his flight to France.
France: Paine was imprisoned because of his hostility to the Jacobins.
England: Pitt commented: "Tom Paine is quite in the right . . . but if I were to encourage his opinion we should have a bloody revolution."

1797 England: T. Williams was prosecuted for publishing *The Age of Reason*, a defense of Deism against Christianity and Atheism, and was found guilty.

1819 Richard Carlile prosecuted for publishing the works of Paine, was heavily fined and imprisoned. (*See also* Elihu Palmer [1764–1806] entry.)

Sade, D. A. F., Marquis de (1740–1814)

Justine, or the Misfortunes of Virtue, 1791
Juliette, 1798

1791 France: The authorities doggedly suppressed *Justine* and *Juliette*, and the Marquis spent much of his life in prison. Grandmothers, misled by the title, are said to have given *Justine* to their frivolous granddaughters to read as an object lesson.

1929 United States: *L'Oeuvre du Marquis de Sade*, from which the term "sadism" was derived, remained on the list of prohibited Customs importations, although pirated editions circulated surreptitiously within the barrier.

1948 Italy–Rome: Books still listed on the *Index*.

1955 France–Paris: A complete edition of the works of Sade in 26 volumes, begun in 1947, finally in 1954 came to the attention of the Commission Consultative, which, under a decree of 1940, was empowered to advise the Minister of Justice to initiate prosecutions. Despite such notable witnesses for the defense as Jean Cocteau, the publishers were fined and the books ordered destroyed, although most of them had long since been sold.

1962 England–London: *Justine* seized by British Customs.

1965 United States: Many of the suppressed works published openly.

Cagliostro, Alessandro (Giuseppe Balsamo) (1743–1795)

Mémoires Authentiques de Cagliostro, 1786
Maçonnerie Égyptienne, 1789

1789 Italy–Rome: Cagliostro, alchemist and impostor, was imprisoned by the Inquisition for pamphlets advocating necromancy and astrology.
Spain: The *Mémoires* and *Maçonnerie Égyptienne* were placed on the Spanish *Index* for encouraging superstition.

1795 Italy–Rome: The author died in prison. He was arrested as a heretic on the denunciation of his wife and sentenced to death, but the punishment was commuted to imprisonment for life. His collection of books and instruments was publicly burned, including a manuscript which denounced the Inquisition as a godless institution, degrading to the Christian religion.

Jefferson, Thomas (1743–1826)

A Summary View of the Rights of British America Set Forth in Some Resolutions Intended for the Inspection of the Present Delegates of the People of Virginia, now in Convention. By a Native, and Member of the House of Burgesses, 1774

Mélanges Politiques et Philosophiques. Extraits des Mémoires et de la Correspondence de T. Jefferson.

1774 England: The pamphlet on the *Rights of British America* by the author of the Declaration of Independence was printed by sympathetic friends, without Jefferson's knowledge, and says "Our emigration to this country gave England no more rights over us than the emigration of the Danes and the Saxons gave to the present authorities of their mother country over England." It contained material rejected by the Virginia Constitutional Convention. The Declaration of Independence uses much of the language of this book. Popular in America, the British edition caused the proscription of Jefferson's name by the English House of Parliament.

1833 Russia: *Mélanges Politiques et Philosophiques* was banned for political reasons under Nicholas I.

Goethe, Johann Wolfgang von (1749–1832)

The Sorrows of Werther, 1774
Faust, 1790

1776 Denmark: *The Sorrows of Werther* was prohibited under a strict censorship exercised by the Lutheran authorities.

1808 Germany–Berlin: The State authorities suppressed the production of *Faust,* until certain "dangerous passages" concerning freedom were deleted.

1939 Spain: Franco purged the libraries of the works of "such disgraceful writers" as Goethe.

Radishchev, Alexander (1749–1802)

Putishestvie (Journey from Petersburg to Moscow), 1790

1790 Russia: *Putishestvie,* a book of travel with emphasis on the evils of serfdom and Tsarist absolutism, was one of the most famous books suppressed by the Tsars. Catherine II declared that the book was an attempt to propagate the ideas of the French revolution, and ordered the edition burned by the public executioner. The author was sentenced to death, but the sentence was commuted to ten years in Siberia.

1801 Author granted amnesty by Alexander I, but, unwilling to "reform," he took poison the following year.

1935 Moscow: A facsimile copy of the first edition was published.

Barlow, Joel (1754–1812)

Advice to the Privileged Orders, 1791–1795

1792 England–London: Eulogized by Fox on the floor of the House of Commons, whereupon the Pitt Ministry suppressed the work and proscribed the author.

Schiller, Johan Christoph Friedrich von (1759–1805)

Die Räuber: ein Schauspiel, 1781

1782 Germany: The Duke of Württemberg, annoyed with Schiller for running away from his medical post at Stuttgart to see his drama performed at Mannheim, put him under a fortnight's arrest and forbade him to write any more "comedies" or to hold intercourse with anyone outside Württemberg. The Duke was also irritated by a complaint from Switzerland of an uncomplimentary reference to Graubünden in *Die Räuber*. All the author's poetic dramas and philosophical works were written after this affair.

Babeuf, François Noel (Gracchus Babeuf) (1760–1797)

Le Tribun du Peuple, 1794

1794 France–Paris: Father of revolutionary socialism, Babeuf attacked, in his *Journal de la Liberté de la Presse*, later called, *Le Tribun du Peuple*, not only the fallen terrorists after the execution of Robespierre, but also the economic theories of the Directoire.

1795 Number 33 of the *Tribun* was burned in the Théâtre des Bergères, by the foes of Jacobinism.

1796 Number 40 of the *Tribun* rallied thousands of workmen under Babeuf's slogan, "Nature has given to every man the right to the enjoyment of an equal share in all property."

1797 The author was arrested, tried, and convicted, in spite of the efforts of his Jacobin friends to save him. He stabbed himself before being summoned to the guillotine.

Chénier, André Marie de (1762–1794)

Avis au Peuple Français, 1790

Ode à Charlotte Corday, 1792

Iambes, 1795

Jeune Captive, 1795

1792 France: His political writings, including *Avis au Peuple Français* and *Ode à Charlotte Corday*, were privately printed and publicly banned.

1794 France–Paris: While imprisoned in the Saint Lazare by the Committee of Public Safety for protesting too violently against the Reign of Terror, Chénier wrote *Iambes*, attacking the Convention (the revolutionary legislature), and *Jeune Captive*, a poem of despair. He was guillotined, on a false charge of conspiracy, three days before Robespierre. The two books were published the year after his death.

Palmer, Elihu (1764–1806)

Principles of Nature, 1801

1819–1824 England–London: This rather simplified expression of ideas like those of Thomas Paine was first issued in America. In London, 1819, it was published by the boldly defiant bookseller Richard Carlile (the work was done by his wife Jane, while Richard was in jail on an 18-month 1817 sentence for other publications). He was further sentenced for Palmer's book. In 1820, Jane was prosecuted for other radical items, but the conviction was quashed. In 1821, Richard's sister Mary Anne Carlile was convicted for publishing Paine material. In 1824, Campion, Perry, and other booksellers were jailed, each for three years, for publishing Paine and Palmer.

Staël-Holstein, Anne Louise Germaine de (1766–1817)

Corinne, ou l'Italie, 1807

De l'Allemagne, 1810

1807 Italy–Rome: *Corinne* was listed on the *Index* for immorality.

1810 France–Paris: *De l'Allemagne*, extolling the merits of German culture, was condemned by Napoleon as "not French" in its political philosophy. The author was exiled from the country and her book was destroyed. She took refuge on her father's estate on Lake Geneva until the fall of the Emperor. The condemnation was no doubt due to Napoleon's personal animosity for Mme. de Staël, and his fear of her ambitions, as her salon was largely devoted to organizing political intrigues against him. Her political views were alleged to be so contaminating that Mme. Rècamier was exiled for frequenting her salon, since she was undoubtedly implicated as well.

Stendhal (Marie Henri Beyle) (1783–1842)

Le Rouge et le Noir, 1831

1850 Russia: *Rouge et Noir*, and all other works, banned by Nicholas I.

1939 Spain: Works purged by Franco.

1948 Italy–Rome: Still listed on the *Index*.

Shelley, Percy Bysshe (1792–1822)

The Necessity of Atheism, 1811

Queen Mab, a Philosophical Poem, 1813

Alastor, 1816

The Revolt of Islam, 1817

Prometheus Unbound, 1818

The Cenci, 1819

1811 England: Shelley and his friend Hogg were dismissed from Oxford as mutineers against academic authority, for publishing *The Necessity of Atheism.*

1816 *Alastor* was rejected by a library on grounds of immorality.

1822 In 1813, at 21, Shelley had published *Queen Mab* in a very small private edition. In 1817, it was cited in his custody trial to show the author was an atheist and free-love advocate; hence it could not be copyrighted, and, up to 1845, was pirated in 14 or more editions. In 1821 William Clarke issued one of those, and in 1822 he was prosecuted by the Society for the Suppression of Vice (formed in 1802) and jailed four months. Also in the 1820s, Richard Carlile was jailed for publishing the poem, among others.

1840–1842 Edward Moxon, a leading publisher, began issuing Shelley's works (including those listed above). He and three other publisher-booksellers were prosecuted, partly to test if there was one law for "the low booksellers of the Strand" and another for the more aristocratic ones, who were freely publishing books at least as outspoken as *Queen Mab*. Moxon was released, but had to give up all copies of his edition.

One reason for official hostility to *Queen Mab* in this entire period was that it became a basic text for lower- and middle-class radicals and for the Chartist and Owenite reform movements. The period of Shelley's life was an especially repressive one, politically, in Britain, a nation badly frightened by the French Revolution.

Goodrich, Rev. Samuel G. (1793–1860)

Peter Parley's Annual. A Christmas and New Year's Present for Young People, 1832

1843 Russia: Prohibited unconditionally by Nicholas I.

More than 170 books were published under the pseudonym, Peter Parley, used by Goodrich, Boston publisher and writer, beginning with *The Tales of Peter Parley about America*, 1827. These were moral and historical tales, distinguished by their breakaway from religiosity. Some seven million copies reportedly were sold, and they were popular all over the world; pirated editions in England were illustrated by Cruikshank, Leech, and Phiz. Hawthorne was among writers Goodrich employed to write under the Peter Parley pseudonym.

Heine, Heinrich (1797-1856)

Reisebilder, 1826-1831
Die Lorelei, 1827
De la France, 1835
De l'Allemagne, 1836
Neue Gedichte, 1844

1833 Germany: The Federal Diet issued a decree banning all works by members of a radical literary group called "Young Germany." Anticipating such suppression, and attracted by the revolution of 1830, Heine had taken up residence in Paris in 1831, where he wrote freely and received an annual stipend from a fund for political refugees. A Jew, he embraced Christianity in 1825.

1836 Italy-Rome: *De la France, Reisebilder*, and *De l'Allemagne*, were placed on the *Index*, where they remained in 1948.

1844 *Neue Gedichte* was listed on the *Index*, where it remained in the edition of 1948.

1933 Germany: Works burned in the Nazi bonfires.

1939 *Die Lorelei* listed as the work of Anonymous instead of Heine, for although his works were banned, the poem was too well loved to suppress.

1954 German Democratic Republic-East Berlin: Works banned by the Soviet occupation authorities. Later republished.

Balzac, Honoré de (1799-1850)

Novels: *La Commédie Humaine*, 1831-1847
Les Contes Drôlatiques (*Droll Stories*), 1832-1837

1841 Italy-Rome: All works listed on the *Index*.

1850 Russia: All works banned.

1914 Canada: *Droll Stories* banned by the Customs.

1930 United States: Customs ban lifted.

1944 New York City: Concord Books, Inc. issued a sale catalogue of 100 books for $.49 each, including *Droll Stories*. They were notified by the Post Office Department that the catalogue violated the section relating to the mailing of obscene literature, and that the title must be blocked out. This was done.

1953 Spain: Franco purged the libraries of "such disgraceful writers" as Balzac.
Soviet Union: Works published in large editions.

Circulating Libraries

19th century England: The high price of books led to the growth of circulating libraries which, for a modest subscription price, supplied to readers a continuous flow of popular novels. The most famous of these organizations, Mudie's, while never a monopoly, came very close to being one, with the result that the decision by Mudie's to buy or reject a novel often determined the fate of a book. The pressure thereby placed upon publishers to conform to the standards imposed by Mudie's made virtually impossible the honest treatment of thematic material by authors. The clashes of authors with their publishers are too numerous to mention, but the famous works that were excluded from the circulating libraries comprise a list of classic English fiction. George Gissing's *New Grub Street* is a vivid fictional account of an author unable to find a market for his works because of the tyranny of the system. George Moore's *Esther Waters*, Thomas Hardy's *Jude the Obscure*, H. G. Wells' *Ann Veronica* and Compton MacKenzie's *Sinister Street* were only four of the titles around the turn of the twentieth century which were excluded from circulating libraries.

The effect of this kind of "respectable" censorship on British literature is impossible to calculate, but it is against this background that some of the rebellious English authors of the period after World War I can be seen in a new dimension, e.g., Lawrence, Huxley, Graves.

Owen, Robert Dale (1801–1877)

Moral Physiology, 1836

1877 England–London: Edward Truelove, a 70-year-old bookseller and disciple of Owen, who had achieved great fame in the United States, was imprisoned for four months for selling *Moral Physiology*, which was considered designed to deprave public morals.

Hugo, Victor Marie (1802–1885)

Hernani, 1830

Marion Delorme, 1831

Notre Dame de Paris, 1831

Le Roi s'Amuse, 1832

Napoléon le Petit, 1851

Les Misérables, 1862

1829 France: Performance of the play, *Marion Delorme*, was prohibited by the official censors because it showed Louis XIII as a "weak, superstitious and cruel prince," and this depiction might provoke public malevolence and lead to disparagement of Charles X. Hugo appealed to the king. A royal veto sustained the prohibition; but Charles offered to raise the poet's pension from 2,000 to 6,000 francs. After Charles was removed by the Revolution of 1830, the play was produced at the Théâtre Français and published for the first time, in 1831.

1830 France–Paris: The Inspector General of Theatres ordered the correction of such passages in *Hernani* as, "Thinkest thou that kings to me have aught of sacredness?" A literary war ensued: classicists and romanticists fought nightly in the theater and out. The classicists hired professional claques. Theophile Gautier organized a troop of volunteers "resolved to take their stand upon the rugged mount of Romanticism, and to valiantly defend its passes against the assault of the Classics." In the end Romanticism triumphed; but not without a martyr, for a young man died fighting a duel over the play.

1832 *Le Roi s'Amuse* was prohibited after the first performance, by order of the Prime Minister, Guizot, for derogatory allusions to Louis-Phillipe. It was produced 50 years later under the supervision of the author.

1834 Italy–Rome: *Notre Dame* placed on the *Index*.

1850 Russia: All works banned by Nicholas I.

1853 France: Copies of *Napoléon le Petit* were seized by the police. This satire was written one year after the author had been banished by Napoleon III and began his 20-year exile for criticizing the government.

1864 Italy–Rome: *Les Misérables*, published two years earlier, was listed on the *Index*. Removed from the *Index* in 1959.

Hawthorne, Nathaniel (1804–1864)

The Scarlet Letter, a Romance, 1850

1852 Russia: Banned by Nicholas I in the "censorship terror."
United States: Rev. A. C. Coxe argued "against any toleration to a popular and gifted writer when he perpetrates bad morals—let this brokerage of lust be put down at the very beginning."

1856 Russia: Ban lifted by Alexander II.

1925 United States: The screen version was made to comply with the demand by the board of censorship for the marriage of Hester.

Andersen, Hans Christian (1805–1875)

Wonder Stories, 1835

1835 Russia: Banned by Nicholas I during the "censorship terror." Ban removed in 1849.

1954 United States–Illinois: Stamped "For Adult Readers" to make it "impossible for children to obtain smut."

Browning, Elizabeth Barrett (1806–1861)

Aurora Leigh, 1857

Lord Walter's Wife, 1857

1857 United States–Boston, Mass.: *Aurora Leigh* was condemned as "the hysterical indecencies of an erotic mind."
England: Thackeray declined to publish *Lord Walter's Wife* because of its "immoral situation"; and it was excluded from the monopolistic circulating libraries. (See page 40.)

Mill, John Stuart (1806–1873)

System of Logic, 1843

Principles of Political Economy with some of their Applications to Social Philosophy, 1848

1856 Italy–Rome: The *Index* listed these works, which epitomized the social and philosophical theories of the more educated English radicals of the day.

Daumier, Honoré (1808–1879)

La Caricature, 1832

1832 France: As a staff artist for the journal, *La Caricature*, Daumier did a satirical drawing of the King as Gargantua, for which he served six months in prison at Ste. Pélagie, and the journal was suppressed.

Darwin, Charles Robert (1809–1882)

On the Origin of Species, 1859

1859 England–Cambridge: The entire edition of 1,250 copies was sold on publication date. The Master of Trinity College refused to allow a copy of the book to be placed in the library, although Darwin was a graduate of Cambridge.

1925 United States–Dayton, Tenn.: John T. Scopes was found guilty of having taught evolution based on *The Origin of Species*, in a high school, and was fined $100 and costs. Chief counsel for the prosecution was William Jennings Bryan, and chief defense counsel was Clarence Darrow. As a result of the decision a law was passed forbidding any teacher in the state "to teach any theory that denies the story of the Divine creation of man as taught in the Bible, and to teach instead that man has descended from a lower order of animals." This law remained on the statute books until 1967.

successor to those given by traveling companies for a century—was protested by blacks as a caricature of reality. At this period, also, "Uncle Tom" was becoming a derogatory phrase implying submissiveness.

Froude, James Anthony (1818–1894)

The Nemesis of Faith, 1849

1849 England–Oxford: Froude, primarily a historian, wrote this novel when he had broken from the Oxford Movement (Anglo-Catholic). It described an Anglican's loss of faith. At Exeter College where Froude was a Fellow, the outraged Senior Tutor burned the novel publicly in the Great Hall of the college and demanded the author's resignation. Froude did resign, and decided to become a professional man of letters.

Marx, Karl (1818–1883)

Rheinische Zeitung, 1842

Manifesto of the Communist Party, 1847

Das Kapital, 1867–1895

1843 Germany–Cologne: *Rheinische Zeitung*, a journal of advanced political and social ideas, was suppressed one year after Marx became editor. He was exiled in Paris and Brussels, but returned at the outbreak of revolution in 1848.

c.1845 France: Marx was expelled at the instance of the Prussian Foreign Office for contributing to the radical magazine *Vorwärts*, which was then liquidated.

1849 Prussia: *Neue Rheinische Zeitung* published, "an organ of democracy," which advocated nonpayment of taxes, and armed resistance against Emperor Frederick William. Publication of the *Zeitung* was suspended, and the editor, Marx, was tried for treason. Although unanimously acquitted by a middle-class jury, he was expelled from the country. Being unwelcome in Paris, he made London his home for the rest of his life.

1878 Germany: Following two attempts on the life of William I, Bismarck persuaded the Reichstag to enact stringent measures against the Social Democrats, and prohibited their literature, including the *Manifesto*.

1929 China: The Nationalist Government sent armies against the sporadic Communist outbreaks in the provinces, and stopped, where possible, the reading of the *Manifesto* and *Kapital*.

1950–1953 United States: Marx's works, along with Communist writings generally, were heavily criticized in the United States. The Boston

Public Library, under attack by the Boston *Post* for including
Communist works in its collections, put the issue to a vote of its
trustees, who upheld the inclusion of such works by a 3–2 vote.

Eliot, George (Mary Ann Evans) (1819–1880)

Adam Bede, 1859

1859 England: *Adam Bede*, although a popular success, was attacked as
"the vile outpourings of a lewd woman's mind," and was soon withdrawn from the circulating libraries of the period.

Whitman, Walt (1819–1892)

Leaves of Grass, 1855

1855 United States: The poems shocked American puritanism and
English victorianism, although Ralph Waldo Emerson wrote to the
New York Times, calling the book "the most extraordinary piece of
wit and wisdom that America has yet contributed."

The Library Company of Philadelphia was the only American
library known to have bought a copy on publication.

1868 England–London: After reading *Leaves of Grass*, Mrs. Anne
Gilcrist defended his use of banned words in *A Woman's Estimate
of Walt Whitman* and said: "A quarrel with words is more or less a
quarrel with meanings . . . If the thing a word stands for exists (and
what does not so exist?), the word need never be ashamed of itself;
the shorter and more direct the better. It is a gain to make friends
with it, and see it in good company."

1881 United States–Boston, Mass.: The District Attorney, at the urging
of agents of the Society for the Suppression of Vice, threatened
criminal prosecution unless the volume was expurgated. The book
was withdrawn in Boston but published in 1882 in Philadelphia.

Whittier, in a rage of indignation, threw his first edition into the
fire, although he himself had suffered persecution for his abolitionist
poems.

Wendell Phillips' comment was: "Here be all sorts of leaves except
fig leaves."

Vizetelly, Henry (1820–1894)

*Extracts Principally from English Classics: Showing that the Legal
Suppression of M. Zola's Novels Would Logically Involve the
Bowdlerizing of Some of the Greatest Works in English Litera-
ture*, 1888

1888 England–London: A work compiled by and privately printed for
Vizetelly, publisher of Flaubert, Goncourt, Gautier, Maupassant,

Daudet, Bourget, Zola, and others in translation, and many out-standing writers in English. At the instigation of a powerful "purity" group, the National Vigilance Association, founded in 1884, Vizetelly was prosecuted, on the basis of selected passages, for publishing five works of Zola, two of Maupassant, one of Bourget. Aged 70, and ill, he was convicted and jailed for three months, and died shortly after release. It was apparently his espousal of books about the depressed classes in society, as much as the "coarse" scenes in some books, that caused outrage and led the respectable to rationalize that he was a mere exploiter of vulgarity.

Baudelaire, Charles Pierre (1821–1867)

Les Fleurs du Mal, 1857
Les Épaves, 1866

1857 France–Paris: The author, publisher, and printer were prosecuted under the Second Empire, for an "outrage aux bonnes moeurs." Baudelaire was arrested and fined 300 francs.

1866 Belgium–Brussels: Six poems suppressed from *Les Fleurs du Mal* were published under the title of *Les Épaves*, and were widely circulated in France.

1949 France: Ban lifted.

Burton, Sir Richard Francis (1821–1890)

First Footsteps in East Africa, 1856
Journals, Notes, Papers
Translations

1856 England–*First Footsteps in East Africa*: the publisher tore out an appendix, written in Latin, which dealt with sexual customs of certain tribes. Partly from this experience, Burton learned the techniques of publishing to avoid Victorian censorship.

1883–1890 Burton was the principal translator of several works which, in order to sidestep obscenity laws, he issued "privately" and, ostensibly, abroad. Among these were: *The Kama Sutra of Vatsayana*, 1883 (the classic Hindu sex manual); *The Book of the Thousand Nights and a Night*, 1883–1888 (see also *The Arabian Nights' Entertainments*, p. 28); *The Perfumed Garden . . . A Manual of Arabian Erotology*, 1886; and other works, all of which bore imprints such as: "Printed for the Kama Shastra Society for Private Subscribers Only, Benares."

1890 Upon the death of the explorer, anthropologist, writer and translator, his widow, Lady Isabel Burton, destroyed all his remaining private diaries and most of his everyday journals, many private letters and papers, and the notes for a revised edition of *The Perfumed Garden*, which he referred to as *The Scented Garden*. Many of the writing and reading public condemned her.

1896 Lady Burton died, and the annual report of the National Vigilance Association boasted that she had entrusted with it, for burning, books and papers "which in her opinion, could not be read by an indiscriminate public," and they burned, "on one occasion, books to the value of £1,000." In the same year, her surviving sister burned still more of the remaining Burton papers.

Eddy, Mary Baker (1821–1910)

1909 Boston: The Christian Science Church acquired and destroyed the plates and copies of Georgine Milmine's biography of Mrs. Eddy.

1927 The Church successfully suppressed Adam Dickey's *Memories of Mary Baker Eddy*.

1930 Christian Science Church officials called on Scribner's to object to Edwin F. Dakin's *Mrs. Eddy: The Biography of a Virginal Mind* (1929). Scribner rejected the complaints, whereupon members and committees of the church called on booksellers throughout the country demanding withdrawal of the book or removal from display and advertising; many complied.

1931 The American Council of Learned Societies resisted Church pressure to withdraw the biography of Mrs. Eddy in the *Dictionary of American Biography*.

Flaubert, Gustave (1821–1880)

Madame Bovary, Moeurs de Province, 1856
Salammbô, 1862
The Temptation of St. Anthony, 1874
November (written 1842)

1857 France–Paris: The author was taken to court for "outrage aux bonnes moeurs," as depicted in *Madame Bovary*. He was acquitted on the ground that the passages cited by the prosecution, though reprehensible, were few in number compared with the extent of the whole work. His counsel pleaded that in depicting vice, the author was only endeavoring to promote virtue.

1864 Italy–Rome: *Madame Bovary* and *Salammbô* were placed on the *Index*.

1927 United States: *The Temptation of St. Anthony* was unsuccessfully attacked by the New York Society for the Suppression of Vice.

ᴇw York City: *November* was seized at customs as obscene but ᴇleased by literary experts of the Customs Bureau.

New York City: The Society for the Suppression of Vice attacked *November*, but Magistrate Jonah J. Goldstein discharged the complaint, saying: "The criterion of decency is fixed by time, place and geography and all the elements of a changing world. A practice regarded as decent in one period may be indecent in another." Three years earlier this book had been on the Book-of-the-Month Club's selected list.

1954 United States: *Madame Bovary* was on the blacklist of the National Organization of Decent Literature.

Dumas, Alexandre, fils (1824–1895)

La Dame aux Camélias, 1848

1850 England–London: The authorities permitted the play's performance as an opera, *La Traviata*; but the translation of the text, as a libretto, was forbidden.

1852 France: After being forbidden on the Paris stage for three years, the play was produced through the efforts of Morny, the influential minister of Napoleon III.

1863 Italy–Rome: All love stories listed on the *Index*.

1958 Soviet Union: Works formerly banned reported to be extremely popular.

Ibsen, Hendrik (1828–1906)

Ghosts, 1881

1881 Norway: The play, being a diagnosis of the diseases of modern society, and intended as a reform, was received with ill will.

1892 England: Application for license was refused by the Lord Chamberlain. Long after Ibsen's position had been recognized in modern letters, the censor still interposed his shocked and obstinate personality between the British public and the great Norwegian author.

c.1915 Ban removed by the Lord Chamberlain.

1939 Spain: Works purged by the Franco government.

1958 Soviet Union: Works formerly banned reported to be extremely popular.

Rossetti, Dante Gabriel (1828–1882)

Verses, 1847

1833–1846 Italy–Rome: Some of the author's poems, translated into Italian, were placed on the *Index*.

1871 England: Robert Buchanan, under the pseudonym c
Maitland," in an article in the *Contemporary Revie*
Rossetti and the "fleshly school of poetry" as immoral, aิน์น ง...
sonnets as "one profuse sweat of animalism." Rossetti, deeply hurt,
replied in an article called "The Stealthy School of Criticism."

Tolstoy, Leo (1828–1910)

The Kreutzer Sonata, 1889

1880 Russia: Various works forbidden publication were printed in
Switzerland, England, and Germany. In his early days, the writings
of Tolstoy were greatly influenced by the philosophy of Rousseau,
especially as expressed in *Émile*.

1890 United States: The Post Office Department barred from the mails
copies of a newspaper serializing *The Kreutzer Sonata*; the U.S.
Attorney General ruled the department could do this with respect to
any installments containing material postal officials considered
obscene. Theodore Roosevelt, then a state politician, denounced the
author as a "sexual and moral pervert."

1926 Soviet Union: Many ethical works were banned or confined to the
large libraries.
Hungary: All works banned.

1929 Italy: All works banned except in expensive editions.

1936 Soviet Union: Works topped the sales of books.

Dodgson, Charles L. (Lewis Carroll) (1832–1898)

Alice's Adventures in Wonderland, 1865

1931 China: Banned by the Governor of Hunan Province on the ground
that "Animals should not use human language, and that it was
disastrous to put animals and human beings on the same level."

Clemens, Samuel Langhorne (Mark Twain) (1835–1910)

The Adventures of Tom Sawyer, 1876
The Adventures of Huckleberry Finn, 1885

1876 United States–Brooklyn, N.Y.: *The Adventures of Tom Sawyer*
was excluded from the children's room in the Public Library.
Denver: Excluded from the Public Library.

1885 Concord, Mass.: In the home town of Henry David Thoreau, *The
Adventures of Huckleberry Finn* was banned by the Public Library
as "trash and suitable only for the slums." The Concord Free Trade
Club retaliated by electing the author to honorary membership.

1905 Brooklyn, N.Y.: The books were excluded from the children's room of the Public Library as bad examples for ingenuous youth. Asa Don Dickinson, Librarian of Brooklyn College, appealed to the author to defend the slander. His reply, which was not published until 1924, said: "I am greatly troubled by what you say. I wrote *Tom Sawyer* and *Huck Finn* for adults exclusively, and it always distressed me when I find that boys and girls have been allowed access to them. The mind that becomes soiled in youth can never again be washed clean."

Note: Mrs. Clemens censored *Huckleberry Finn* and deleted the profanity and other strong passages, but left some which have at times been criticized, such as: "All kings is mostly rapscallions" (Ch. 23) and "so the king he blatted along" (Ch. 25). The London Athenaeum has called it one of the six greatest books ever written in America.

1930 Soviet Union: Books confiscated at the border.

1946 Books had become best sellers in the Soviet Union.

1957 United States–New York City: Dropped from list of approved books for senior and junior high schools, partly because of objections to frequent use of the term "nigger" and the famed character, "Nigger Jim."

Gilbert, W. S. (1836–1911) and Sullivan, Arthur (1842–1900)

H.M.S. Pinafore, 1878

The Mikado, or the Town of Titipu, 1885

c.1905 England: The British Foreign Office was much distressed for, although *The Mikado* had been first performed in 1885, and had been a great popular success, the Lord Chamberlain suddenly awoke to the unsuspected dangers in the piece, and forbade its further production on the ground that it might "give offense to our Japanese allies." As a matter of fact, the music was being played by Japanese bands on Japanese ships on the Medway River during the ban.

Lewis Carroll (C. L. Dodgson) earlier attended a performance of *Pinafore* given by children and of the famous "Damme, it's too bad," of the Captain and the chorus he wrote: "I cannot find words to convey to the reader the pain I felt in seeing those dear children taught to utter such words to amuse ears grown callous."

Woodhull, Victoria (1836–1927)

Woodhull and Claflin's Weekly, 1872

1872 United States: The November 2 issue, containing an exposé of the private life of Henry Ward Beecher, minister of Plymouth Congregational Church in Brooklyn, N.Y., was suppressed at the instance of Anthony Comstock (who organized the New York Society for the Suppression of Vice the following year) for obscenity and libel. The feminist editors were jailed.

Swinburne, Algernon Charles (1837–1909)

The Queen Mother, Rosamond—Two Plays, 1860
Poems and Ballads, 1866
The Devil's Due, 1875

1860 England: *The Queen Mother* and *Rosamond* were withdrawn from circulation because of strenuous objections to their alleged licentiousness.

1866 *Poems and Ballads* evoked a storm of excitement over the author, whom Robert Buchanan classed with Rossetti and his circle as "the fleshly school." Swinburne's "hound of a publisher" became frightened and withdrew the book, which was later issued by John Hotten.

1875 *The Devil's Due*, an open letter to Buchanan, was immediately suppressed as libelous.

Hardy, Thomas (1840–1928)

Tess of the D'Urbervilles: A Pure Woman Faithfully Portrayed, 1891
Jude the Obscure, 1895

c.1891 England: *Tess* was banned by the circulating libraries which held a virtual censorship over popular reading.
United States–Boston, Mass.: Highly disapproved by the Watch and Ward Society.

1896 England: *Jude the Obscure* banned by the circulating libraries.

Zola, Émile (1840–1902)

Nana, 1880
La Terre, 1887
J'accuse, 1898

1888 England: Vizetelly, the publisher, was imprisoned for publishing *La Terre*; even in their expurgated editions, Zola's novels outraged the Victorian era.

1894 Italy–Rome: All Zola's works were placed on the *Index*.

1898 France: In 1894 Capt. Alfred Dreyfus was degraded and sentenced to Devil's Island for life for allegedly selling military secrets. Firm exonerating evidence was found in 1896, but Army circles suppressed it, denying a new trial, and causing intense protests. Zola denounced the military authorities in an open letter, *J'accuse*. He was convicted of libeling the Army, fled to England, and was amnestied in a few months. Dreyfus was pardoned in 1899 and exonerated formally in 1906. The cases convulsed French political life and society.

1929 Yugoslavia: All works banned.

1953 Ireland: All works banned.

1954 United States: *Nana* disapproved by the National Organization of Decent Literature.

France, Anatole (Jacques Anatole Thibault) (1844–1924)

A Mummer's Tale, 1921

1921 Sweden: Author awarded the Nobel prize for literature.

1922 Italy–Rome: The *Index* placed its most stringent prohibition on the reading of the works of France by listing simply and conclusively *Opera Omnia*—all the works.

1953 Ireland: *A Mummer's Tale* banned.

Maupassant, Henri René Albert Guy de (1850–1893)

Des Vers, 1880

Mademoiselle Fifi, 1882

Une Vie: L'Humble Vérité, 1883

1880 France: Legal proceedings against *Des Vers* were withdrawn through the influence of Senator Cordier. Flaubert, the teacher of Maupassant, who had been prosecuted for *Madame Bovary*, congratulated his pupil on the similarity of their literary experiences.

1883 The sale of *Une Vie* was forbidden at railway bookstalls. The prohibition drew much attention to the master of the short story.

1930 Canada: Many of this author's works were on the blacklist of the Customs Office.

1956 United States: A paperback edition of *Mademoiselle Fifi* was banned from the mails for line illustrations showing female nudity.

Warren, Mortimer A. (c.1850?–?)

Almost Fourteen, 1892

1897 United States–Massachusetts: This sensitive little book of sex information "for parents and for young people," approved by leading clergymen, had circulated without objection, and was used in some Sunday school libraries, until an aggressive reformer started to give it general circulation, and the Watch and Ward Society got wind of it. On their complaint a seller was convicted, Warren was driven from his job as a school principal, and the publisher, Dodd, Mead, felt it could no longer sell the book.

Chopin, Kate O'Flaherty (1851–1904)

The Awakening, 1899

1899 United States–Missouri: The novel dealt realistically and artistically with one woman's intellectual, spiritual, and sexual "awakening," and Stone & Kimball sold it fairly well. However, reviewers immediately condemned it for bringing up an indelicate subject and criticized its morality. St. Louis libraries accordingly banned it from their shelves. Some readers apparently confused it with Tolstoy's supposedly scandalous *Awakening*, which was being condemned at the same time.

1964 The book was republished by Putnam in a Capricorn reprint, later by other publishers, as interest in the author revived.

Moore, George (1852–1933)

Flowers of Passion, 1878

A Modern Lover, 1883

A Mummer's Wife, 1885

Esther Waters, 1894

A Story Teller's Holiday, 1918

c.1878 Ireland: Edmund Yates called the author of *Flowers of Passion* a "bestial bard," and advised whipping him and burning the book.

1883 England: Moore was told by a spokesman for W. H. Smith, one of the circulating library and bookstore chains, that it was withdrawing *A Modern Lover* from stock because of objections by "two ladies from the country." Mudie's Circulating Library also barred the book. In effect, the circulating (rental) libraries were exercising censorship, because patrons borrowed and few bought the expensive three-volume novels of the day. Moore vowed revenge and published his next novel, *A Mummer's Wife*, in an inexpensive single volume, thereby starting a vogue to break the monopoly of circulating libraries.

1894 Circulating libraries refused to stock *Esther Waters*.

1929 United States: The Customs refused admittance to *A Story Teller's Holiday*. The officer who seized the copy, which contained the author's autograph, vandalized it by marking out offending passages.

This incident, together with the banning of *Lady Chatterley's Lover*, touched off a lengthy and often acrimonious debate in the U.S. Senate which led finally to some easing of the regulations of the U.S. Customs. This reform in turn precipitated the famous decision to allow Joyce's *Ulysses* into the United States.

1932 The Customs Court judged *A Story Teller's Holiday* obscene.

1933 The Treasury Department admitted it as a modern classic.

George Moore once remarked that if all the books objected to by censors as sexually stimulating were swept from the face of the earth, the spring breeze would still remain to awaken desires in man and woman.

Harris, Frank (1855–1931)

My Life and Loves, 4 vols., 1922–1927

1922 England: Banned. Not published in that country until 1938.

1922–1956 United States: Imports banned, and frequently destroyed, by Customs.

1925 United States–New York City: The Society for the Suppression of Vice, under John S. Sumner, seized about 300 copies of the second volume and prosecuted Harris' New York agent, who eventually was sentenced to 90 days in the workhouse.

Shaw, George Bernard (1856–1950)

Mrs. Warren's Profession, 1898

Man and Superman, 1903

The Shewing-up of Blanco Posnet, 1909

The Adventures of the Black Girl in Her Search for God, 1932

1905 United States–New York City: The New York Public Library withdrew *Man and Superman* from the public shelves to reserve judgment, and Anthony Comstock complained to Arnold Daly, producer of *Mrs. Warren's Profession*, which had been suppressed in London and called it "reekings." Shaw, infuriated, coined the word "Comstockery." Comstock retaliated and took arms against "this Irish smutdealer's books." *Mrs. Warren's Profession* was taken to court, where it was held not actionable. The Comstock publicity greatly increased the attendance at the stage production; police reserves were called out on opening night to dispel the crowds. One newspaper critic referred to the play as "tainted drama" and another, fearful of the word "prostitution," accused it of having "an unspeakable theme." The play soon closed.

1909 England–London: The Lord Chamberlain refused a license for performance of *The Shewing-up of Blanco Posnet*. Shaw thereupon wrote a statement, privately printed, for submission to a parliamentary committee of inquiry. In its published report, the committee deliberately omitted Shaw's remarks, whereupon Shaw made them the preface to the published version of the play.

1925 Sweden–Stockholm: Shaw was awarded the Nobel prize for literature.

1929 Yugoslavia: All works banned from the public libraries.

1933 England: *The Adventures of the Black Girl in Her Search for God*
was banned from the Cambridge Public Library.

1939 Italy: Shaw, informed that his works and those of Shakespeare were
the only English books exempted by the Propaganda Ministry from
the sanctions reprisals, replied that he was greatly flattered to be in
such good company.

Wilde, Oscar Fingal O'Flahertie Wills (1856–1900)

Salomé, 1893

1892 England: The play was being rehearsed in London by Sarah
Bernhardt when the Lord Chamberlain withheld its license on the
ground that it introduced biblical characters. The London *Times*
called it "an arrangement in blood and ferocity; morbid, bizarre,
repulsive and very often offensive in its adaptation of scriptural
phraseology to situations and the reverse of sacred."

1895 France: Played by Sarah Bernhardt.
United States–Boston, Mass.: Banned in book form.

1907 Boston, Mass.: The New England Watch and Ward Society
prevented Mary Garden from appearing in Richard Strauss' celebrated opera *Salomé* and banned the performance.

Obscene Publications Act (1857–1930) and Comstock Act (1873)

1857 England: This law, enacted at the urging of Lord Chief Justice
Campbell, who was incensed by Dumas' *The Lady of the Camellias*,
established the ground upon which obscenity convictions were
obtained in England in the following century and in the United
States nearly as long. It was a particularly troublesome law because
it provided for the seizure of materials under a general search
warrant, and put the burden of proof upon the accused. While it did
not alter the existing common law on the definition of obscene libel,
it provided the means of forestalling sales through early seizure and
destruction.

1868 The significant change in legal emphasis came in this year when Lord
Chief Justice Cockburn enunciated the so-called Hicklin doctrine:
"The test of obscenity is this, whether the tendency of the matter
charged as obscenity is to deprave and corrupt those whose minds
are open to such immoral influences and into whose hands a publication of this sort may fall."

1873 United States: The Comstock Act was enacted by the U.S. Congress
with similar acts in the states, all producing effects similar to those

of the English law. While the Comstock Act has never been repealed, its effect has been largely nullified by successive court decisions.

1959 England: A new act replaced the 102-year-old law of 1857. Its liberal provisions include the now generally accepted doctrine that a work must be considered in its entirety, and that if a work can be proved to have merit, any incidental obscenities become irrelevant. The law also provides for the taking of expert testimony.

Doyle, Sir Arthur Conan (1859–1930)

The Adventures of Sherlock Holmes, 1892

1929 Soviet Union: Banned because of its references to occultism and spiritualism.

Ellis, Havelock (1859–1939)

Studies in the Psychology of Sex, 1897–1910

1887 England–London: As editor of the Mermaid series of British dramatists, Ellis issued the first volume, on Christopher Marlowe, which reproduced a document that had been used against the Elizabethan playwright. Because of protests the publisher, Vizetelly, suppressed some of the offending language in subsequent reprints. After Vizetelly was prosecuted for publishing Zola's works, Fisher Unwin took over the Mermaid series, dismissed Ellis, and further bowdlerized the texts that Ellis had prepared.

1898 England–London: *Studies in the Psychology of Sex* was condemned as "lewd, wicked, bawdy, scandalous and obscene," and the prosecution raised a storm of protest. Ellis was not allowed to defend the scientific nature of his work in court, so he formed a Defense Committee including George Bernard Shaw, George Moore, and others. The first publisher willing to sponsor the book proved to be dishonest, was arrested, took poison said to be hidden in his ring, and died. A copy of the first volume under a Leipzig imprint was bought by the police from G. Bedborough, who was arrested but later released on turning State's evidence. The second volume was seized and burned. It was barred from the library of the British Museum. Ellis resolved to publish the subsequent volumes outside England.

1901 United States–Philadelphia, Pa.: F. A. Davis Company, medical publishers, issued the seven volumes for sale to physicians only.

It was not until after Joyce's *Ulysses* had been cleared in court that the *Studies* were offered to the general public and also became available in England, where the Royal Society of Physicians made Ellis a Fellow.

1941 United States: Various writings banned from the mail by the Post

Office Department unless they were addressed to doctors. The same materials meanwhile were freely sold in bookstores.

1953 Ireland: Banned.

Maeterlinck, Maurice (1862–1949)

Monna Vanna, 1902

1909 England: *Monna Vanna* was censored by the Lord Chamberlain as improper for the stage, asserting, "Our decision was almost universally upheld."

1914 Italy–Rome: All works listed on the *Index*.

1926 Soviet Union: Works restricted to the large libraries.

Schnitzler, Arthur (1862–1931)

Reigen, 1900

Casanova's Homecoming, 1918

1924 United States: The English translation of *Casanova's Homecoming* was indicted as obscene. The indictment was attacked, whereupon Judge Wagner maintained that the book was sufficiently corrupting for the indictment to stand, his point being: "We may assert with pride, though not boastfully, that we are essentially an idealistic and spiritual nation, and exact a higher standard than some others." The publisher withheld publication and the case was not tried. Meanwhile the book circulated freely in the original German.

1929 New York: A bookseller was convicted by the Court of Special Sessions for selling a copy of *Reigen*. The Appellate Division upheld the conviction, basing their decision more on the "exquisite handling of the licentious" described in the introduction rather than the text. Since the book had been pirated and privately printed, the author was in complete ignorance of the introduction. The conviction was sustained by the highest state court. Shortly afterwards *Reigen*, which had been studied widely in college and university courses in German literature, was published by the Modern Library, and no further attempt was made to suppress it. *Reigen* had been played abroad since 1903.

1930 John S. Sumner, secretary of the New York Society for the Suppression of Vice, brought Simon and Schuster to court for publishing *Casanova's Homecoming*. The case was dismissed.

1939 Italy: *Casanova's Homecoming* was banned by Mussolini.

D'Annunzio, Gabriele (1863–1938)

Writings, 1880–c.1900

1898 United States–Boston, Mass.: *The Triumph of Death*, 1894, was brought to court by the Watch and Ward Society, but not convicted.

1911 Italy–Rome: All love stories and plays placed on the *Index*.

1926 Rome: In spite of the fact that many of D'Annunzio's works were on the *Index*, the Italian Government voted to publish them in a deluxe edition. D'Annunzio's admirers subscribed 6,000,000 lire for the purpose.

1928 While the author lived at Lake Garda, enshrined as Italy's beloved patriot and poet, the *Index* further prohibited his mystic poetry and mystery plays.

1935 Autobiography banned by Mussolini.

1936 Rome: The Government Tourist Bureau postponed indefinitely the presentation of D'Annunzio's play *The Martyrdom of Saint Sebastion*. The Bishop of Pompeii highly disapproved of it and forbade all Catholics to attend.

1937 Appointed president of the Royal Italian Academy by Mussolini.

1938 After the death of the great patriot, the catafalque was covered with the trophies of his campaigns and included a semiofficial statement from the Vatican denying the widespread impression that he had been excommunicated. Mussolini and members of his Cabinet joined the thousands of mourners at the bier.

Glyn, Elinor (1865?–1943)

Three Weeks, 1907

1907 England–London: The book was banned as immoral.
Canada: Sale forbidden on government trains.

1908 United States–Boston, Mass.: A representative of the publisher was arrested for selling a copy of the novel, and was held on bail. The action was instituted by the Watch and Ward Society, which submitted copies of the book to the District Attorney and the judges of the lower court. Referred to the Grand Jury, whose indictment said that "the language on certain pages of the book is improper to be placed upon the court records and offensive to the court."
(*See also* Disney, Walt [1901–1966].)

Kipling, Rudyard (1865–1936)

A Fleet in Being: Notes of Two Trips with the Channel Squadron, 1898

1898 England: Suppressed on grounds that the book betrayed naval secrets, although the author was well known as an intense patriot.

Wells, H. G. (1866–1946)

The World of William Clissold, 1926

1929 United States–Boston, Mass: Banned.

Phillips, David Graham (1867–1911)

Susan Lenox, 1917

1917 New York City: Attacked by John S. Sumner, the publisher, D. Appleton, was prepared to defend in court this novel about a prostitute who rises to respectability. However, the author's sister and literary executor persuaded the publisher to remove the offending passages.

Przybszkewski, Stanislaw (1868–1927)

Homo Sapiens, 1915

1915 United States–New York City: Brought before magistrate's court by John S. Sumner, Alfred Knopf was charged with publishing an obscene book. Knopf, who had started his firm that year, yielded to pressure, withdrew the book, and melted down the plates.

Dimnet, Abbé Ernest (1869–1954)

La Pensée Catholique dans l'Angleterre Contemporaine, 1905

1907 Italy–Rome: Listed on the *Index*.

Gide, André Paul Guillaume (1869–1951)

If It Die, 1926

1935 United States–New York City: The owner of the Gotham Book Mart was arrested by a patrolman who had bought *If It Die* and taken it to John S. Sumner, who considered some of the passages obscene. At the time the book was taken to court 100,000 copies had been sold in France and Germany, and the limited edition of 1,500 copies published in America had been sold out.

1936 Magistrate Nathan D. Perlman said in his decision that the author had "unveiled the darker corners of his life," but he held that "the book as a complete entity was not obscene" and dismissed the case.

1938 Soviet Union: Gide incurred a Soviet ban on his works following his split with Communism.

1952 Italy–Rome: Although a Nobel prize winner, all the author's works were placed on the *Index*.

1953 Ireland: *If It Die* banned.

1954 Germany–East Berlin: Writings forbidden by the Soviet occupation authorities.

Lenin, Vladimir Ilyich (Ulyanov) (1870–1924)

The State and Revolution, 1917
Proletarian Revolution in Russia, 1918

1927 United States–Boston, Mass.: *The State and Revolution* was seized as obscene.

Hungary: Seized as subversive.

1928 Canada: *Proletarian Revolution in Russia* burned by the authorities.

1940 United States–Oklahoma City, Okla.: A vigilante organization made an unofficial raid on the bookshop of Robert Wood, state secretary of the Communist Party, and seized many books, including *The State and Revolution*, Communist literature, works of fiction and economics, *The Declaration of Independence* and the *Constitution of the United States*. These books were publicly burned at the City Stadium. Mr. and Mrs. Wood, customers in the shop and a carpenter repairing shelves were arrested on charges of criminal syndicalism and held incommunicado. Of the 18 arrested, six were held as witnesses. Mr. Wood was charged with distributing literature advocating violence, and Mrs. Wood and two others with belonging to the Communist Party. All six were sentenced to ten years in prison and fined $5,000, the only evidence being books and pamphlets relating to the party. There was no attempt to show that the defendants had committed an overt act against the government, or were guilty of anything except selling books. No witnesses for the defense were permitted. The convictions were protested by many organizations, publishers, and writers.

1943 The Court of Appeals reversed the convictions.

1954 Providence, R.I.: The local post office attempted to withhold from delivery to Brown University 75 copies of *The State and Revolution* as "subversive."

Louÿs, Pierre (1870–1925)

The Songs of Bilitis, 1894

Aphrodite, 1896

The Twilight of the Nymphs, 1903

1929 United States: *Aphrodite* banned by the Customs Department as lascivious, corrupting, and obscene, as well as *The Songs of Bilitis* and *The Twilight of the Nymphs*.

1930 New York City: E. B. Marks, book dealer, was fined $250 for possessing a copy of *Aphrodite*, in violation of the state laws against objectionable literature.

1935 The importation of copies of *Aphrodite* was forbidden in a deluxe edition, although a $.49 copy was freely advertised in the *New York Times Book Review*, and delivered for $.10 extra through the U.S. mails.

1954 *Aphrodite* condemned by the National Organization of Decent

Literature and other local censorship groups throughout the country.

Dreiser, Theodore (1871–1945)

Sister Carrie, 1900
The Genius, 1915
An American Tragedy, 1925
Dawn, 1931

1900 United States–New York City: *Sister Carrie* printed by Doubleday. An undetermined number of advance copies were released before the publisher's wife objected. The remainder of the edition was suppressed. Although an English edition appeared in 1901, the American public did not have ready access to this modern classic until the second edition in 1907.

1916 New York City: *The Genius* was suppressed.

1923 *The Genius* was republished; the jacket blurb flaunted the fact that the volume had been suppressed by the New York Society for the Suppression of Vice.

1930 Boston, Mass.: The Superior Court condemned *An American Tragedy* and fined the publisher $300, but across the Charles River it was required reading for a Harvard English course.

1932 Ireland: *Dawn* was banned.

1933 Germany: *The Genius* and *An American Tragedy* were burned by the Nazis because "they deal with low love affairs."

1935 United States–Boston, Mass.: *An American Tragedy* still banned, though obtainable by mail.

1958 United States–Vermont: *Sister Carrie* still banned.

Rasputin, Grigori Yefimovich (1871–1916)

My Thoughts and Meditations, 1915

1915 Russia: In the preface the editors commented on the author's meteoric rise from lowly peasant origin. He resented this and forced it to be deleted from the book.

Dennett, Mary Ware (1872–1947)

The Sex Side of Life, an Explanation for Young People, 1918

1922 United States–New York City: Originally written for the instruction of Mrs. Dennett's sons, the material was published by the *Medical Review of Reviews*, reprinted as a pamphlet in 1919, and used by the Y.M.C.A., Union Theological Seminary, government hospitals and others. But in 1922 it was declared unmailable by the Post Office Department.

1928   Mrs. Dennett received a request for the pamphlet from a "Mrs. Miles" in Virginia. The lady turned out to be a postal inspector who had been instructed to trap the author.

1929   Author tried and sentenced by jury to a $300 fine for sending obscene matter through the mails.

1930   Conviction reversed on appeal.

Russell, Bertrand (1872–1970)

What I Believe, 1925

1929   United States–Boston, Mass.: Banned.

1940   New York City: Russell was appointed Professor of Philosophy at the College of the City of New York. Bishop William T. Manning of the Episcopal Church denounced the appointment because Russell was a "recognized propagandist against religion and morality." A Brooklyn housewife instituted suit against the Board of Higher Education on the ground that her daughter might be injured if she enrolled in one of Russell's classes. The Court supported the woman's suit, and Russell's appointment was voided. Despite a national outcry of protest, New York authorities refused to appeal the decision.

La Motte, Ellen N. (1873–1961)

The Backwash of War, 1916

1919   England: Suppressed for its pacifistic thesis.

Anderson, Sherwood (1874–1959)

Many Marriages, 1922
Horses and Men, 1923
Dark Laughter, 1925

1923   England: *Many Marriages* aroused legal action.

1930   United States–Boston, Mass.: *Dark Laughter* was blacklisted.

1931   Ireland: *Horses and Men* banned.

Simkhovitch, Vladimir G. (1874–1959)

Marxism Versus Socialism, 1913

1917   Russia: The Russian translation was burned at the outbreak of the Revolution. It is now unprocurable; but the volume is available in French, German, Italian, English, and Japanese.

American Library Association (organized 1876)

1918 The American Library Association (ALA), which had undertaken to administer the book program for soldiers, was chastised by the War Department for permitting the inclusion in servicemen's libraries of Ambrose Bierce's *In the Midst of Life* and Henri Barbusse's *Under Fire*, a prize-winning, realistic French novel about the war. The ALA thereupon withdrew these books from its program.

London, Jack (1876–1916)

The Call of the Wild, 1903

1929 Italy: All cheap editions were banned.
Yugoslavia: All works banned as too radical.

1932 Germany: Various works were cast into the Nazi bonfires.

Sinclair, Upton (1878–1968)

The Jungle, 1906
Oil!, 1927
No Pasarán, 1937
Wide Is the Gate, 1943

1910 United States: A campaign was started to ban *The Jungle*, but it was unsuccessful.

1927 Boston, Mass.: *Oil!* was forbidden because of its comments on the Harding administration. The author defended the case himself and addressed a crowd of 2,000 on Boston Common on the character and aim of his book. The nine pages objected to, including the two pages quoted from the *Song of Solomon*, were covered by a large black fig leaf. The bookseller was fined $100, and the trial cost the author $2,000.

1929 Yugoslavia: All works banned by the public libraries.

1933 Germany: Works burned in the Nazi bonfires because of Sinclair's socialist views.

1938 South Africa–Johannesburg: *No Pasarán*, a book against fascism in Spain, banned.

1953 Ireland: *Wide Is the Gate* banned.

1956 East Germany–Berlin: Sinclair's works banned as inimical to Communism.

Cabell, James Branch (1879–1958)

Jurgen, A Comedy of Justice, 1919
The Devil's Own Dear Son, 1949

1920   United States: *Jurgen* was prosecuted by the New York Society for the Suppression of Vice. Several hundred people prominent in public and literary life presented petitions protesting against the action. This publicity established a hitherto obscure novel as a best-seller.

1922   Although indicted as obscene two years before, the book was now deemed a "work of art," and the indictment was dismissed.

1935   Volume unobtainable in many large public libraries.

1953   Ireland: *Jurgen* and *The Devil's Own Dear Son* banned.

Lindsay, Norman (1879–1969)

The Cautious Amorist, 1932

1941   United States: Barred from the U.S. mails.

Trotsky, Leon (Bronstein, Lev Davidovich) (1879–1940)

Second Congress of the Russian Socialist Democratic Workers' Party: Report of the Siberian Delegation, 1903

1903   Russia: *Report* banned by the Imperial Government.

1927   Soviet Union: Banned by the Government. Therefore the same writings were banned by two opposing ideologies for the same reason—that they opposed the existing philosophies of government.

1930   United States–Boston, Mass.: Works banned.

1933   Germany: All works banned.
Soviet Union: All works banned.

1934   Italy: All works banned except in deluxe editions.

Asch, Sholem (1880–1857)

The God of Vengeance, 1923

1923   United States–New York, N.Y.: Asch's play was closed by police and the leading performer was fined.

Noyes, Alfred (1880–1958)

Voltaire, 1936

1938   England: Noyes, a Roman Catholic, was denounced to the Holy Office for his biography of Voltaire. The volume was withdrawn by the publishers and revised to meet the demands of the censors.

Stopes, Marie Carmichael (1880–1958)

Wise Parenthood, 1918
Married Love, 1918

Contraception: Its Theory, History and Practice, 1923

Vestia, 1926

1918 England: On publication, *Wise Parenthood* was made a notorious test case.

Canada: Prohibited.

England: 700,000 copies of *Married Love* were sold.

1921 United States–New York State: A physician was convicted for selling a copy of *Married Love*.

1930 *Contraception* was refused entry by the U.S. Customs, but after vindication the case cleared the way for future importation of birth control literature.

1931 New York City: Ban on *Married Love* raised by Judge John M. Woolsey. His decision was: "I cannot imagine a normal mind to which this book would seem to be obscene or immoral within the proper definition of these words, or whose sex impulses would be stirred by reading it. . . . Instead of being inhospitably received it should, I think, be welcomed within our borders."

Customs ban raised on *Married Love*.

Ireland: All works banned.

England: The Lord Chamberlain refused to license *Vestia* for the stage, although it was legally circulated in book form.

1939 United States: After the sale of one million copies of *Married Love*, it was published in a $.49 reprint.

Ireland: *Married Love* banned in English.

1953 Ireland: All works banned.

Joyce, James (1882–1941)

Dubliners, 1914

Ulysses, 1922

1912 Ireland–Dublin: After years of delay and wrangling, *Dubliners* was printed in an edition of 1,000 copies. All but one copy was destroyed by the printer, John Falconer, because he found passages objectionable.

1914 *Dubliners* finally published.

1918 United States: Early installments of *Ulysses*, appearing in *The Little Review*, were burned by the Post Office Department.

1922 Imported copies of *Ulysses* burned.

Ireland: Burned.

Canada: Burned.

1923 England: 499 copies burned by the Customs authorities at Folkstone.

United States: 500 copies burned by the Post Office Department. The court ruled against its publication. Consequently, there being no copyright, Joyce, who was becoming blind, did not benefit by the royalties of the thousands of pirated and bowdlerized editions.

1929 England: Banned.

1930 United States–New York City: A copy of *Ulysses* sent to Random House was seized by the Collector of Customs as obscene, although this book had for more than a decade won enthusiastic critical acclaim and had profoundly influenced literature.

1933 New York City: A copy addressed to Alexander Lindey, mailed from Paris, was detained by Customs. Lindey petitioned the Treasury Department to admit *Ulysses* as a classic, which they did, under a Tariff Act provision which permits entry of so-called classics for noncommercial purposes at the discretion of the Secretary of Treasury.

The book was taken to court and defended by Morris L. Ernst. The ban was raised by Judge John M. Woolsey in a notable decision: "A rather strong draught . . . emetic, rather than aphrodisiac . . . a sincere and honest book . . . I do not detect anywhere the leer of a sensualist."

On appeal, U.S. Attorney Martin Conboy tried to convict the book on irreligious instead of obscene grounds, contending that "whatever constituted a reflection on the Church was indecent." Judge Woolsey's decision was upheld by a vote of two to one in an opinion written by Judge Augustus N. Hand.

Henry Seidel Canby said: "Its indecency would have appalled Rabelais and frightened Chaucer; but such a book is valuable in a world trying to be sane, trying to save itself by humor or insight from the perversion of honest instincts and from mental confusion only because of its new and brilliant technique, and the passages of undoubted genius."

This book has been translated into many languages and is on the reading lists of the English courses of many universities. It is considered one of the masterworks of the twentieth century.

1960 A Caedmon recording of the soliloquies of Leopold and Molly Bloom was bowdlerized.

MacKenzie, Compton (1882–   )

Sinister Street, 1913–1914

1913 England: Banned by circulating libraries.

Magruder, Frank Abbott (1882–1949)

American Government, 1942 ed.

1947-1955 United States: The text, the leading schoolbook in its field for 38 years, was the victim of unfounded attacks in the postwar period. Much of the distorted information came from pamphlets, articles, and pretended reviews by Allen A. Zoll and Lucille C. Crain, who called Magruder's book procommunist by using falsified, invented and distorted "quotations." Some school systems were thus misled to the extent that Georgia dropped the book and attempted to dump 30,000 copies in other areas, and the Houston, Tex., and Little Rock, Ark., school boards banned it.

Leading educators, magazines and dailies counterattacked, exposed Zoll and Crain and ended the mischief. The 1955 edition was approved in all states, but the pressure had caused some revisions.

Goodman, Daniel Carson (1883-1957)

Hagar Revelly, 1913

1914 United States–New York City: Although *Hagar Revelly* was written by a social hygienist hoping to instruct the young in the dangers of vice, it was attacked by Anthony Comstock. The publisher was acquitted after a brief trial in Federal Court. The importance of this case lay in the opinion of Judge Learned Hand, which contained the first serious legal challenge to the Hicklin Rule.

Sanger, Margaret (1883-1966)

Family Limitation, 1915

Happiness in Marriage, 1926

My Fight for Birth Control, 1931

1915 United States–New York City: *Family Limitation* was brought to court by the New York Society for the Suppression of Vice and found to be "contrary not only to the law of the state, but to the law of God," and Mrs. Sanger was jailed. William Sanger was jailed for 30 days for distributing his wife's pamphlets on birth control.

1923 England–London: The book was suppressed.

1929 United States–New York City: On complaint of a chapter of the Daughters of the American Revolution to the Police Commissioner, Mrs. Sanger's clinic was raided. Three nurses and two doctors were arrested and carried off in a patrol wagon, along with thousands of case histories. They were defended by five eminent physicians in a crowded courtroom, and the case was dismissed. Representatives of the Academy of Medicine declared that there had been unwarranted interference with the freedom of physicians engaged in their lawful practice and warned against further interference.

1931 Ireland: Pamphlets banned.
Italy: Pamphlets banned.
Yugoslavia: Pamphlets banned.
United States–Boston, Mass.: *My Fight for Birth Control* was
omitted from the collection of the public library.

1950 Japan–Tokyo: Mrs. Sanger was refused permission by General
MacArthur to enter the country for a lecture tour. The General was
quoted as saying that birth control was a matter for the Japanese
people and the Occupation had a policy of hands off.

1953 Ireland: *Happiness in Marriage* and *My Fight for Birth Control*
banned.

1954 Japan–Tokyo: Mrs. Sanger, speaking on birth control, became the
first woman from the United States to testify before the Japanese
Diet.

Feuchtwanger, Lion (1884–1958)

Power, 1926

1914–1919 Germany: Works constantly suppressed during the war.

1930 United States–Boston, Mass.: *Power* was banned for immorality.

1933 Germany: All works were burned in the Nazi bonfires. The author
was exiled and his property confiscated.

Durant, Will (1885–   )

The Case for India, 1930

1931 India: Banned, with many other pro-Gandhi books, by the British
Viceroy of India.

Kazantzakis, Nikos (1885–1957)

The Last Temptation of Christ, trans. 1960

1962–1965 United States–California: The novel was a central point in
a three-year attack by right-wing groups in Long Beach against the
city public library and its librarian for stocking this title, along with
Jessica Mitford's *The American Way of Death* and the works of the
poet Langston Hughes. The attack was ultimately unsuccessful.

Lawrence, David Herbert (1885–1930)

Sons and Lovers, 1913
The Rainbow, 1915
Women in Love, 1920
Lady Chatterley's Lover, 1928
The Paintings of D. H. Lawrence, 1929

Love among the Haystacks, 1930
The First Lady Chatterley, 1944

1915 England–London: Under Lord Campbell's Act of 1857 over 1,000 copies of the first edition of *The Rainbow* were ordered destroyed by the magistrate's court. As a result, the book was not republished in England until 1926, in expurgated form. The full text did not appear again until 1949.

1922 United States: *Women in Love* seized by John S. Sumner of the New York Society for the Suppression of Vice. The case was dismissed in court, but the countersuit for libel was sustained.

1929 *Lady Chatterley's Lover, Women in Love*, and *Paintings* were barred by Customs. For 20 years, Lawrence's books were confiscated at Customs whenever detected.
England: *The Rainbow*, freely circulated in America, was banned, while *Women in Love* was not objected to.

1930 United States–Washington, D.C.: *Lady Chatterley's Lover* had prominence in the famed "decency debates" in the Senate between Senator Bronson Cutting of New Mexico, who was in favor of modifying the censorship laws, and Senator Reed Smoot of Utah, who was against it. Cutting enraged Smoot by witty insinuations that *Lady Chatterley* was a favorite with the Mormon Senator.

1932 Ireland: *Lady Chatterley's Lover* banned.
Poland: *Lady Chatterley's Lover* banned.

1944 United States–New York City: John S. Sumner appeared at the offices of the Dial Press with a search warrant and seized 400 copies of *The First Lady Chatterley*. It is the first version of *Lady Chatterley's Lover*, published in the 1920s in Italy, but not issued in its entirety in America before. Magistrate Charles G. Keutgen declared the book obscene and committed the case for trial in the Court of Special Sessions, where it was exonerated by two of the three judges and the case dismissed.

1953 England: *Lady Chatterley's Lover* was removed from the shelves of two retail establishments as being obscene. The magistrate hearing the case declared it "absolute rubbish" and said had he read the unexpurgated edition he would have chucked it on the fire.
United States: *Lady Chatterley* and *Love among the Haystacks* were on the blacklist of the National Organization of Decent Literature.

1959 United States–New York City: Grove Press published the unexpurgated edition of *Lady Chatterley's Lover*, copies of which were seized by the Post Office and impounded. Challenged in court, the Post Office seizure was overturned.
During the succeeding years the novel was banned in several

nations, including Australia, Japan, and India. A film based on the novel was also widely attacked.

1960 England–London: Penguin Books published the unexpurgated edition, which was challenged by the Director of Public Prosecutions under the Obscene Publications Act of the previous year. A lengthy trial ensued, which itself became the subject of a book. The jury returned a "not guilty" verdict, thus freeing Lawrence's novel after more than 30 years of litigation, piracy, smuggling, and suppression.
Canada–Montreal: Banned by court order. Ban lifted by the Supreme Court in 1962.

1961 Canada: Customs held up the import of *The Trial of Lady Chatterley*, which was itself not obscene, but was merely a detailed report of the court case involving Lawrence's novel.

Lewis, Sinclair (1885–1951)

Elmer Gantry, 1927

Ann Vickers, 1933

It Can't Happen Here, 1935

Cass Timberlane, 1945

Kingsblood Royal, 1947

1927 United States–Boston, Mass.: *Elmer Gantry* was banned because a religious hero was depicted as obscene. The publishers defended the suit and expressed their amazement at the discretionary powers invested in local officials.
Washington, D.C.: The Post Office Department upheld postmasters as censors.
Banned by the libraries of Camden, New Jersey; Glasgow, Scotland; and others.

1930 Sweden–Stockholm: Lewis was the first American to be awarded the Nobel prize for literature.

1931 Ireland: *Elmer Gentry* was banned as offensive to public morals.
United States–New York City: The Post Office Department banned any catalogue listing the book.

1936 Hollywood, Calif.: A storm was aroused by the refusal of a moving picture company to film the antifascist novel *It Can't Happen Here*. Lewis accused Will Hays, head of the motion picture industry, of forbidding the production. Hays replied that the decision had been made by the producing company. In the meantime there was a storm of protest from the press and the controversy doubled the sale of the book.

1938 Cohasset, Mass.: Lewis appeared in a revised version of the play *It Can't Happen Here*, playing the part of Doremus Jessup.

1953 Illinois: *Kingsblood Royal* was one of the 6,000 books "relating to sex" which were removed from state libraries on a mother's complaint that her daughter had borrowed a book that was offensive. Ireland: *Ann Vickers, Cass Timberlane*, and *Elmer Gantry* banned.

1954 Germany–East Berlin: Works banned.

Hall, Radclyffe (1886–1943)

The Well of Loneliness, 1928

1928 England–London: Withdrawn from sale by the publisher at the request of the Home Office, followed by contradictory decisions of several courts and much controversy. Among those who protested the suppression of the novel were George Bernard Shaw, Laurence Housman, Rose Macaulay, John Buchan, Lytton Strachey, Laurence Binyon, and others.

1929 United States–New York City: John S. Sumner, Secretary of the New York Society for the Suppression of Vice, acting under a warrant issued by Chief Magistrate McAdoo, raided the office of the publisher and removed 865 copies remaining from the sixth edition, then raided Macy's book department.

1939 New York City: The book, defended by Morris L. Ernst, was finally cleared. The case was significant because the judge sought to inject a new element into the obscenity law in declaring the subject matter, rather than words or phrases, "offensive to decency."

1944 Miss Hall received the Femina Vie Heureuse Prize and the James Tait Black Prize for her novel, *Adam's Breed*.

The New York *Herald-Tribune* wrote: "*The Well of Loneliness* is much more of a sermon than a story, a passionate plea for the world's understanding and sympathy, as much a novel of problem and purpose as *Uncle Tom's Cabin*, as sentimental and moralistic as the deepest-dyed of the Victorians."

Rugg, Harold O. (1886–1960)

An Introduction to Problems of American Culture and later revisions retitled *Our Country and Our People*, 1929–1940

1939–1941 United States: Editions of this widely used Ginn & Co. text, one of many by Dr. Rugg, were targets of a campaign by the Advertising Council of America against its continued use, since it was thought to be critical of advertising practices. It was attacked also by the American Legion, in its magazine and in local posts, for supposedly undermining American institutions. The author fought back energetically, backed by educators and civic leaders nationally, but in some schools his books were withdrawn.

Clarke, Donald Henderson (1887–1958)

Female, 1933

1933 United States–New York City: Criminal proceedings for obscenity were brought in Manhattan against the publisher of *Female*. However, the judge dismissed the complaint.

Five months later, a clerk in an Astoria, Long Island, lending library rented a copy of the novel to a police officer and was subsequently served with a summons and held for trial. The defendant was found guilty of renting an obscene book and sentenced to a fine of $100 or 20 days in jail.

O'Neill, Eugene (1888–1953)

Desire under the Elms, 1924

Strange Interlude, 1928

1925 United States–New York City: *Desire under the Elms* was closed by New York police.

1928 New York City: *Strange Interlude* opened and brought the playwright his third Pulitzer Prize.

1929 Massachusetts: *Strange Interlude* was banned in Boston but performed in Quincy. The censorship was supported by the influential Catholic paper, *The Pilot*, but attacked by the secular press.

1936 Sweden–Stockholm: O'Neill awarded the Nobel prize for literature.

Hitler, Adolf (1889–1945)

Mein Kampf, 1925–1927

1932 Germany: The authorized translation was considerably abridged for foreign consumption.

Czechoslovakia: Banned for its fierce militaristic doctrines.

1936 United States–New York City: A first edition containing many passages suppressed later was sold at the American Art Association Anderson Galleries for $250. It was the first time the book had been sold at auction on either side of the Atlantic and the first time that police protection had been needed at an American book auction. Threats of a demonstration during the sale caused Mr. Parke to send for the police.

1937 Palestine: Once banned, the testament became a best seller among the Arabs.

Connelly, Marc (1890–)

The Green Pastures, 1929

1929   England: The play was forbidden on the ground that the Deity ought not to be represented on the stage.
United States: Awarded the Pulitzer Prize.

1933   Norway: Forbidden to be played in the National Theatre.

Pasternak, Boris Leonidovich (1890–1960)

My Sister Life, 1922

Themes and Variations, 1923

Doctor Zhivago, 1958

1923   Soviet Union–Moscow: The two early books of poems, highly considered abroad, caused the author to be denounced in the Soviet Union as a "decadent formalist." Consequently he turned to translating Shakespeare and other poets to earn a living.

1958   Soviet Union–Moscow: Pasternak submitted his novel, *Doctor Zhivago*, to the State Publishing House and sent a copy to a publisher in Italy. Moscow condemned the book and did not publish it. The author was compelled to ask the Italians to return the manuscript for "revisions," which they refused to do. The novel became a best seller in Europe and the United States and resulted in the author being awarded the Nobel prize for literature. The Soviet Union denounced the award with a scathing attack on the Swedish judges for a "hostile political act for recognizing a work withheld from Russian readers which was counterrevolutionary and slanderous." Pasternak was formally read out of the Soviet Union of Authors, deprived of his title of "Soviet writer," and forced to refuse the award, saying "in view of the meaning given to this honor in the community in which I belong, I should abstain from the undeserved prize that has been awarded to me."
United States–New Haven, Conn.: Yale University students and faculty signed a petition written by President A. Whitney Griswold protesting the vilification of Pasternak and urging that he go to Stockholm to receive the Nobel Prize and to welcome him back to continue his distinguished writing.

1961   A year after the death of Pasternak his friend and collaborator Olga Ivinskaya was arrested for allegedly receiving foreign royalties for Pasternak's works. She was sentenced to eight years imprisonment and hard labor in Siberia, and her daughter received three years for alleged complicity.

Marks, Percy (1891–1956)

The Plastic Age, 1924

1927 United States–Boston, Mass.: Banned for revealing casual standards of college life.

Miller, Henry (1891–   )

Tropic of Cancer, 1934
Tropic of Capricorn, 1938
Sexus, 1949

1934 United States: *Tropic of Cancer* banned by U.S. Customs.

1946 France–Paris: A prosecution of Henry Miller was undertaken, but owing to almost unanimous support for Miller from literary figures, the case was dropped.

1950 France: *Sexus* banned.

1953 United States–San Francisco, Calif.: U.S. Court of Appeals upholds ban on the two *Tropics.*

1956 Norway: *Sexus* banned after trial and appeal.

1961 United States: Grove Press published *Tropic of Cancer,* touching off a national controversy which led to many court decisions against the book, notably in New York, Florida, California, Massachusetts, and Illinois.

1964 United States: The U.S. Supreme Court found *Tropic of Cancer* not obscene.

1974 Following U.S. Supreme Court decisions of June 21, 1973, Greenleaf Classics, California, reportedly shredded thousands of Miller books, since paperback wholesalers were returning them in quantities too great for storage.

Towsley, Lena (1891–   )

Peggy and Peter, What They Did Today, 1931

1931 United States–New York City: The first edition of this photostory book was printed without a picture of the children saying their prayers at bedtime, as a quasi-intellectual parent did not want the trouble of explaining the picture to her children, who had never heard of God or religion. In later editions the questionable picture was tipped in.

(The Soviet Government, feeling somewhat the same way about religion, had acted similarly in a case in 1930. Before the opening of the school season one million copies of a new primary textbook were ready for release. Suddenly a horrified official discovered that in a poem by Nekrasov the word God [Bog] was spelled with a capital letter. To reduce Bog to bog involved changing 16 pages in each of the million copies; but the change was made, regardless of expense, and the books reached the Soviet children uncontaminated.)

Aldington, Richard (1892–1962)

Death of a Hero, 1929

1929 England: In his preface, Aldington complained that he had reluctantly deleted certain words and passages because his publisher feared prosecution.

Posselt, Eric, compiler (1892–?)

Give Out: Songs Of, For and By the Men in the Service, 1943

1943 United States: Although sold at armed forces installations, and described by *Time* magazine as presenting "well-scrubbed lyrics," this book of well-known songs was banned from the U.S. mails.

Huxley, Aldous   (1894–1963)

Antic Hay, 1923
Point Counter Point, 1928
Brave New World, 1932
Eyeless in Gaza, 1936

1930 United States–Boston, Mass.: *Antic Hay* banned on grounds of obscenity.
Ireland: *Point Counter Point* banned on the ground of "offending public morals."

1932 Ireland: *Brave New World* banned.

1936 Ireland: *Eyeless in Gaza* banned.

1953 United States: *Antic Hay* was placed on the list of publications disapproved by the National Organization of Decent Literature.
Ireland: *Eyeless in Gaza* unbanned by Appeal Board. *Point Counter Point* and other books still banned.

Kinsey, Alfred (1894–1956)

Sexual Behavior in the Human Male, 1948
Sexual Behavior in the Human Female, 1953

1953 West Germany: Both books banned in U.S. Army post exchanges in Europe as having "no worthwhile interest for soldiers." Not stocked in Army libraries.
South Africa: Banned upon publication by the Interior Minister.
Ireland: Banned.

1954 Soviet Union–Moscow: *Sexual Behavior in the Human Female* reviewed eight months after publication and called "the cheapest pornographic hash clumsily masked as science."

1956 United States: Kinsey's collection of books, pictures, etc., imported from Europe and the Orient for the Institute for Sex Research Inc., brought to trial in Federal Court in New York after being held for six years by the U.S. Customs. The *New York Times* reported Dr. Kinsey as saying: "This is a real test of the right of scholars to have access to their material. . . . They have taken the position that the same prohibitions apply to us as would to a commercial enterprise. . . ."

1957 The right to import for scientific purposes was upheld and Customs agreed to base its future policy on the decision. Kinsey's collection formed a nucleus of suppressed works at the University of Indiana, many of which were later issued along with scholarly analyses of them, e.g., *My Secret Life*, one of the most revealing examples of Victorian English pornography.

Graves, Robert (1895–   )

I, Claudius, 1934

1955 South Africa: Banned under the Customs Act of 1955. The Board of Censors still maintains a list of over 4,000 prohibited titles, including Tennessee Williams' *Streetcar Named Desire* and D. H. Lawrence's *Aaron's Rod*.

1976–1977 Great Britain and United States: The public television film based on the book had tens of millions of viewers.

Wilson, Edmund (1895–1972)

Memoirs of Hecate County, 1946

1946 United States–New York City: 130 copies were confiscated by the police from four Doubleday bookshops after the New York Society for the Suppression of Vice charged that it was salacious and lascivious. Fifty thousand copies had been sold in the four months since publication. The Court of Special Sessions adjudged the book obscene in a 2–1 decision and the publisher, Doubleday, was fined $1,000. The District Attorney warned that anyone who sold a copy could be sentenced to a year's imprisonment.
Los Angeles, Calif.: Booksellers were fined for sale of the book. The conviction was later upset upon appeal.
San Francisco, Calif.: A bookseller was acquitted on a second trial, after the first trial resulted in a hung jury.
Philadelphia, Pa.: Copies confiscated by police.
Massachusetts: Publishers ceased shipment to the state because of its censorship law.

Nationwide, the Hearst newspapers used *Hecate County* as a principal focus in their ongoing campaign against "indecent" books.

1947 New York State: Decision affirmed in the State Supreme Court's Appellate Division and later upheld by the State Court of Appeals.

1948 United States: The first U.S. Supreme Court test of a state "obscene literature" statute, as applied to a book, resulted in a 4–4 split decision, allowing the conviction to stand.

1956 United States: Banned from the U.S. mails.

1959 Farrar, Straus & Giroux published an edition newly revised (though not expurgated) by Wilson.

1961 United States–New York City: New American Library published a paperback edition of the 1959 edition, but carried on the cover the legend, "Not for Sale in New York State."

1966 United States–New York City: Ballantine Books issued a paperback of the 1959 edition, described on the cover as "authentic and unexpurgated," and "still banned in the State of New York."

Faulkner, William (1897–1962)

Soldier's Pay, 1926

Mosquitoes, 1927

Sanctuary, 1931

Pylon, 1935

The Wild Palms, 1939

The Hamlet, 1940

1948 United States–Philadelphia, Pa.: After a complaint from a fundamentalist minister that obscene books were being sold, the Chief Inspector of the Vice Squad assigned a patrolman to investigate. He bought about 25 books and marked the so-called improper words and passages—thus becoming the judge of what the people of Philadelphia should read. A raid without warrant followed on 54 bookshops and approximately 2,000 allegedly obscene books were seized, including *Mosquitoes, Sanctuary* and *The Wild Palms*. While action was pending, the police obtained warrants for the arrest of five booksellers and indictments against nine books. Also included in this case were such books as James T. Farrell's *Studs Lonigan* and *A World I Never Made*. The defense of these books was vigorously undertaken by their publishers.

1949 Judge Curtis Bok dismissed the indictments against the booksellers and said that the books "were an obvious effort to show life as it was."

1950 Sweden–Stockholm: Faulkner was awarded the Nobel prize for literature.

Pennsylvania: The Superior Court of Pennsylvania upon appeal by the Commonwealth upheld the judgment of Judge Bok.

1954 *Sanctuary, Pylon* and *Soldier's Pay* were on the disapproved list of the National Organization of Decent Literature, and were also condemned by many local censorship groups throughout the country.

Ireland: Most of the author's writings were banned.

Reich, Wilhelm (1897–1957)

The Sexual Revolution, trans. 1945

Character Analysis, trans. 1945

The Mass Psychology of Fascism, trans. 1946

Function of the Orgasm, trans. 1949

1956 United States: Charging that the refugee psychoanalyst's "orgone energy" theory for sex therapy involved fraudulent practices, the Food and Drug Administration obtained a court order forbidding him to publish information on his therapy devices. Refusing, he was sent to prison in 1956 for two years and died there. FDA agents burned copies of his books, translated from the German by Theodore P. Wolfe and published by Reich's Orgone Institute. Farrar, Straus & Giroux has since published his books.

Smith, Lillian (1897–1966)

Strange Fruit, 1944

1944 United States–Boston, Mass.: *Strange Fruit* was forbidden to be sold in bookshops by the Board of Retail Book Merchants and the Commissioner of Police. Boston's behind-the-counter censorship of books was defied for the first time in 66 years by the Civil Liberties Union of Massachusetts. The case was forced into the courts through the purchase of the novel from a Cambridge bookseller by Bernard De Voto. In court the book was ruled obscene, indecent, and impure because of its language. The bookseller was fined $200, but this was later reduced to $25.

New York: The publisher was informed that the U.S. Post Office Department had seized six copies of *Strange Fruit* and would not receive any more copies for mailing, although 200,000 copies had been sold.

Detroit, Mich.: As in Boston, the majority of bookstores entered into a "gentlemen's agreement" with the Police Department and removed the book from sale. However, the United Automobile Workers' Book Shop refused to withdraw the title as long as it could be obtained from the Public Library, and appealed to its parent union, which prepared to defend them legally if necessary. The Public Library insisted upon keeping the book in circulation and the police ended the controversy by lifting the ban.

1945 Boston, Mass.: The Superior Court of Massachusetts on an appeal from the Supreme Court upheld the 1944 conviction and declared the novel a menace to the morals of youth.

1953 Ireland: Banned.

Guttmacher, Dr. Alan F. (1898–1974)

The Complete Book of Birth Control, 1961

1961 United States–Illinois: The Chicago Post Office returned to the sender, W. F. Hall Printing Co., 7,000 copies of this Ballantine paperback, written by a leading family planning authority, with coauthors Winfield Best and Frederick S. Jaffe. For almost two months, Ballantine was not officially informed. When it protested, the Post Office Department ruled that the ban was in error and that prior rulings allowed birth control information and materials to be mailed in commercial channels from producer to distributor or retailer.

Hemingway, Ernest (1898–1961)

The Sun Also Rises, 1926

A Farewell to Arms, 1929

To Have and Have Not, 1937

For Whom the Bell Tolls, 1940

Across the River and into the Trees, 1950

The Old Man and the Sea, 1952

1929 Italy: *A Farewell to Arms* was banned because of its painfully accurate account of the Italian retreat from Caporetto.
United States: The screen version was privately censored through Italian influence.
Boston, Mass.: Five issues of *Scribner's Magazine* were prohibited because they contained the story.
Robert Herrick attacked *A Farewell to Arms* in an article entitled "What Is Dirt?" in the November issue of *Bookman*.

1930 Boston, Mass.: *The Sun Also Rises* was banned.

1933 Germany: Works burned in the Nazi bonfires.

1938 United States–Detroit, Mich.: *To Have and Have Not* was removed from public sale and from circulation in the public library, but preserved among works by "writers of standing." It was also barred from sale by the Prosecutor of Wayne County on complaint of Catholic organizations. The novel was reported by the American Civil Liberties Union as the only book suppressed during the year. New York: Distribution forbidden in the Borough of Queens.

1939 Ireland: *A Farewell to Arms* banned.

1941 United States–New York, N.Y.: When the Pulitzer Prize Advisory Board recommended *For Whom the Bell Tolls* for the 1940 prize, Columbia University President Nicholas Murray Butler said, "I hope that you will reconsider before you ask the University to be associated with an award for a work of this nature." There was no Pulitzer Prize for fiction for 1940. The Post Office in the same year declared the book nonmailable.

1953 *The Sun Also Rises* and *Across the River and into the Trees* were banned in Ireland.

1954 Sweden–Stockholm: Awarded Nobel prize for literature for *The Old Man and the Sea.*

1956 South Africa–Johannesburg: *Across the River and into the Trees* was banned as "objectionable and obscene."

1960 United States–California: *The Sun Also Rises* banned from San Jose schools. All of Hemingway's books withdrawn from Riverside school libraries.

1962 "Texans for America" opposed textbooks which referred students to books by Hemingway.

Remarque, Erich Maria (1898–1970)

All Quiet on the Western Front, 1929
The Road Back, 1931
Three Comrades, 1937
Flotsam, 1941

1929 United States–Boston, Mass.: *All Quiet on the Western Front* was banned on grounds of obscenity, although it had already been expurgated at the suggestion of the Book-of-the-Month Club, whose selection it was.
Chicago, Ill.: Copies of the English translation were seized by U.S. Customs.
Austria: Soldiers were forbidden to read the book.
Czechoslovakia: Barred from the military libraries by the war department.

1930 Germany–Thuringia: Banned.

1933 Italy: The Italian translation was banned because of the book's anti-war propaganda.
Germany: All works consigned to the Nazi bonfires.

1953 Ireland: *The Road Back, Flotsam*, and *Three Comrades* were still banned.

Waugh, Alec (1898-   )

The Loom of Youth, 1917

1917 England: Waugh, in his autobiography, says "In many schools the book was banned and boys were caned for reading it." Despite this attack—or, in part, assisted by it—the book has never been out of print.

Nabokov, Vladimir (1899–1977)

Lolita, 1955

1955 Nabokov completed *Lolita* in 1954, but could not find a publisher. Olympia Press issued it in Paris and it was held admissible by U.S. Customs, but not by the British. Graham Greene's praise of it set off a long controversy.

1956 France–Paris: Banned as obscene. U.S. Customs pronounced the book unobjectionable. *Lolita* thus could not be legally exported from France, but smuggled copies could be legally imported into the United States.
United States: Publishers thought the book unworthy of publication, but it came out abridged in a magazine, *Anchor Review 2*.

1958 The book was finally published by Putnam.

1959 England: Freely published.
France: Ban lifted.
Argentina–Buenos Aires: The court said *Lolita* was not banned because of crude passages, but because the whole work reflected moral disintegration and reviled humanity. The ban was again upheld in 1962.

1960 New Zealand: Banned by the Supreme Court.

Disney, Walt (1901–1966)

Mickey Mouse (internationally syndicated comic strip)

1932 United States: A *Mickey Mouse* cartoon was suppressed because it showed a cow resting in a pasture reading Elinor Glyn's *Three Weeks*.

1937 Yugoslavia–Belgrade: The *Mickey Mouse* comic strip was banned because of a supposedly anti-monarchical story picturing a plot against a young king and a conspiracy to place an impostor on the throne. Concurrently a regency headed by Prince Paul was ruling the country during the minority of King Peter.

1938 Italy–Rome: The National Conference of Juvenile Literature decided that *Mickey Mouse* was unsuitable for the minds of children, and editors were instructed to eliminate it as contrary to "Italian inspiration as to racism, and exaltation of the imperial, Fascist and Mussolinian tone in which we live." Children, they said, should be trained in the principles of "sleeping with the head on a knapsack." However, a distinction was made between guns handled by organized youth and gunplay as depicted in the comics.

1954 Germany–East Berlin: Communists raided the schools in search of Western books. They found *Mickey Mouse* comics and banned them because *Mickey* was classed as an anti-Red rebel.

Guthrie, Alfred Bertram, Jr. (1901–   )

The Big Sky, 1947
The Way West, 1949

1962 United States–Texas: Banned in Amarillo, along with many other novels.

Hanley, James (1901–   )

Boy, 1931

1931 England: The second and third editions were progressively bowdlerized by the publisher. A reprint of the third edition was seized at a circulating library in Manchester. The book was later defended eloquently by E. M. Forster at a meeting of the International Congress of Authors in Paris.

Steinbeck, John (1902–1968)

The Grapes of Wrath, 1939
The Wayward Bus, 1947

1939 United States–St. Louis, Mo.: Seven months after publication of *The Grapes of Wrath*, three copies were ordered burned by the public library because of the vulgar words employed by the characters. After a protest by the National Council on Freedom from Censorship, the book was placed on a shelf for "adults only."
Kansas City, Mo.: Banned here and in towns in Oklahoma.
New York City: The book was assigned reading in sociology classes at the College of the City of New York. At this time, there were 360,000 copies in print.
California: The Associated Farmers of Kern County, whose policies had been attacked, mapped a statewide ban in schools and libraries against the book as being derogatory to the state.

1942–1943 Germany: By order of the Propaganda Administration, *The Grapes of Wrath* was issued in a German translation.

1953 United States: *The Wayward Bus*, although a Pulitzer Prize winner, was placed on the list of books disapproved by the Gathings Committee (a House of Representatives select committee on indecent literature) and by censorship groups in many cities.
Ireland: Works banned.

Caldwell, Erskine (1903–   )

Tobacco Road, 1932
God's Little Acre, 1933

1933 United States–New York: *God's Little Acre*, taken to court on charges of obscenity by the New York Society for the Prevention of Vice, was exonerated. The decision handed down by City Magistrate Benjamin Greenspan marked a milepost in the fight against censorship. It rested on the fact that the book must be considered in its entirety, not in isolated passages; that a cross-section of representative opinion was relevant to the case; that the book was honest and sincere in its intent, and obviously "not a work of pornography"; that it "has no tendency to incite its readers to behave like its characters"; and that its use of coarse and vulgar language was not censurable, since "the court may not require the author to put refined language in the mouths of primitive people."

1935 Chicago, Ill.: The play *Tobacco Road* was banned as indecent and forbidden in many other cities as well, including Detroit, Mich.; St. Paul, Minn.; Minneapolis, Minn.; Utica, N.Y.; and Tulsa, Okla. In Washington, D.C., Representative Deen of Georgia made an impassioned appeal to Congress to stop the showing of "the infamous, wicked, untruth (sic) portrait" of his district as portrayed in *Tobacco Road*. However, a posse of six assistant district attorneys was dispatched to the theater to see for themselves and they returned a verdict favorable to the play.

1941 United States: *Tobacco Road* barred from the mails, as was *God's Little Acre* in the same era, although both admittedly were selling heavily in bookstores.

1946 St. Paul, Minn.: *God's Little Acre* was banned but was readily available across the Mississippi in Minneapolis.

1947 Denver, Colo.: The novel was banned in the $.25 edition to keep the book out of the hands of teenage children.

1948 Philadelphia, Pa.: Seized in the mass bookstore raid by the police, and later exonerated.
Ireland: Banned.

1950 Boston, Mass.: Banned from the state as indecent, obscene, and impure by the full bench of the Massachusetts Supreme Court. The world's best-selling modern novel, more than 6,500,000 copies of the paperback edition alone were sold.

1953   Chicago, Ill.: *God's Little Acre* was listed as disapproved by the National Organization of Decent Literature.

England: The novel was included in the *National Newsagent Bookseller Stationer* list of nearly 700 books named for destruction by local magistrates. Also included was *Studs Lonigan* by James T. Farrell. (See below.)

United States: Blacklisted by the Gathings Committee.

Ireland: *God's Little Acre* and *Tobacco Road* banned.

1960   Australia: *God's Little Acre* found obscene and banned by the Supreme Court.

Connell, Vivian (1903–   )

The Chinese Room, 1942

September in Quinze, 1952

1953   United States–New Jersey: Matthew F. Melko, prosecuting attorney of Middlesex County, sent to wholesalers a list of objectionable titles compiled by a citizens' committee, suggesting that such books be withdrawn. The publishers of *The Chinese Room*, Bantam Books, represented by Horace S. Manges, brought suit. Judge Sidney Goldman of the Superior Court ruled that the prosecutor violated the constitutional guarantee of freedom of the press and held that the book in question was unobjectionable.

1954   The New Jersey Supreme Court sustained this ruling, but deleted certain broader principles of the judgment which had denied the prosecutor's right to promulgate lists, enlist aid from unofficial committees, and threaten sellers. A rehearing was denied.

Great Britain–London: By jury trial, *September in Quinze* was judged an obscene libel, and its publishers were fined $4,200. This verdict followed the so-called Secker case in which Justice Stable acquitted the publishers of *The Philanderer* by Stanley Kauffmann with his widely praised reversal of the traditional Cockburn (Hicklin) decision. These cases were among several that led to the writing of more liberal legislation in Britain, the Obscene Publications Act of 1959.

Farrell, James T. (1904–   )

Studs Lonigan: A Trilogy, 1932–1935

A World I Never Made, 1936

1936   United States–New York: Advertising for *A World I Never Made* was refused by the *New York Times* on publication.

1937 New York: The novel was the only book prosecuted by the New York Society for the Suppression of Vice during the year, although it was written on a Guggenheim Fellowship. In court, where many prominent writers testified favorably, Magistrate Henry H. Curran exonerated *A World I Never Made* and ruled that "a whole novel should not be condemned because of objection to parts as obscene, lewd and lascivious."

Milwaukee: The novel was seized by the Chief of Police as vulgar, obscene and unfit for children. The author appealed to the Socialist Mayor and to the Socialist Chief of Police "as a Socialist comrade to do all in your power to halt this illegal action on the part of the police."

New York: Farrell was awarded a $2,500 Book-of-the-Month-Club Fellowship. The award was made "to the man rather than to a particular book."

1942 England–London: The trilogy *Studs Lonigan* was dropped from the American Library Association list of books interpreting the United States. Consequently Constable & Co., publishers, were refused a permit to import American sheets. This amounted to a virtual ban in England as they had insufficient paper to publish it there. However when paper was secured 5,000 copies were printed.

Germany: The sending of *Studs Lonigan* to prisoners of war was banned.

Canada: *Studs Lonigan* was refused entry as being of an indecent and immoral character.

1948 United States–Pennsylvania: Both works were seized among 2,000 others in police raids on Philadelphia bookshops. Indictments were dismissed in 1949 by Judge Curtis Bok.

1953 United States: *Studs Lonigan* and *A World I Never Made* were on the blacklists of the Gathings Committee and the National Organization of Decent Literature.

St. Cloud, Minn.: Works banned.

Ireland: Works banned.

1957 Works were banned in overseas libraries controlled by the U.S. Information Agency.

Kantor, MacKinlay (1904–1975)

Andersonville, 1955

1956 United States–New York City: Awarded Pulitzer Prize.

1962 Texas: Widely attacked in the United States, it was successfully banned in Amarillo.

McHugh, Vincent (1904–   )

The Blue Hen's Chickens, 1947

1947 United States–New York City: An agent of the New York Society for the Suppression of Vice bought a copy from the Random House receptionist; the society's director John S. Sumner showed up the next day with a summons and seized several copies of the book, apparently objecting to a segment, *Suite from Catullus*, which was based on classic erotic poems. A N.Y. County grand jury found no obscenity and declined to indict. The head of Random House, Bennett Cerf, welcomed the seizure as a boost to sales of poetry, which ordinarily were very small.

Stevens, Sylvester (1904–   )

Pennsylvania—Birthplace of a Nation, 1966

1967 United States–Pennsylvania: Helen Clay Frick, daughter of the nineteenth-century industrialist Henry Clay Frick tried to halt distribution of this state history (issued by Random House), objecting to statements in it about her father. Historians feared that, if successful, her suit would allow any books involving historical figures to be threatened by their descendants. A federal court declined to rule on the author's claim that such a suit in itself violated his freedom to write; but a Pennsylvania court, vindicating the book, dismissed Miss Frick's complaint.

Delmar, Viña (1905–   )

Bad Girl, 1928

1928 United States–Boston, Mass.: Banned by the Watch and Ward Society, although it was a selection of the Literary Guild of America.

1933 Ireland: Prohibited for describing an illegal abortion too graphically.

O'Hara, John (1905–1970)

Appointment in Samarra, 1934

Ten North Frederick, 1955

1941 United States: *Appointment in Samarra* declared nonmailable by the Post Office Department, although it was freely sold.

1957 A series of local bans and seizures spread over a two-year period during the height of *Ten North Frederick*'s popularity. Cleveland, Ohio; Albany, N.Y.; and Omaha, Nebr. were involved.

Detroit, Mich.: This book, which won the 1956 National Book Award for fiction, was banned in the paper edition by Police Commissioner Piggins, acting under the Michigan obscenity statute. Although in hardcover it had been sold in Detroit bookstores for a year and was available in the Public Library it also fell under the ban. A Federal District Court ruled against the Detroit Police Commissioner.

1958 New York: The Albany County Supreme Court indicted Bantam Books, John O'Hara, and the distributors of *Ten North Frederick* for conspiring to publish and distribute an obscene book. The defendants examined the testimony and found that only certain passages had been read. This appears to be the first time following the Roth decision that the validity of an indictment involving a charge of obscenity has been challenged in any jurisdiction on the ground that the entire publication had not been read to or by the grand jury. The ban was lifted.

United States–Michigan: Detroit police banned sale of both the Random House hardcover and Bantam Books paperback edition, and the publishers obtained a permanent injunction against the ban. Detroit authorities later dropped the case.

Sartre, Jean-Paul (1905–   )

1948 Italy–Rome: Works listed in the *Index*.

1954 Works removed from U.S. Information Agency libraries throughout the world.

Steig, William (1907–   )

Sylvester and the Magic Pebble, 1969

1977 United States–Illinois: Illinois Police Association writes to librarians asking them to remove the book because its characters, all shown as animals, present police as pigs—though in favorable portrayals. American Library Association reports "problems" of similar nature in 11 states.

Baker, Samm Sinclair (1909–   )

The Permissible Lie, 1968

1966 The book, subtitled "The Inside Truth about Advertising," was printed for publication by Funk & Wagnalls, but before publication date, Reader's Digest Association bought the firm, and when shipment to the trade was to begin, withdrew publication. World Publishing Co. then took over F&W, and, while releasing the book, barred ads that called it "the book that Reader's Digest suppressed."

Genet, Jean (1910–   )

Our Lady of the Flowers, 1942

1957 England: A two-volume edition of Genet's novels, in French, ordered by the Birmingham Public Library, was seized.

1964 According to a letter by Genet's publisher, Maurice Girodias, to *Newsweek*, the English translation was banned in France "five or six years ago" but the original French text was available.

Durrell, Lawrence (1912–   )

The Black Book, 1938

1961 United States: Seized by the Customs Bureau. Subsequently successfully published in the United States.

Robbins, Harold (1912–   )

The Carpetbaggers, 1961

1961 United States–Connecticut: Police in Waterbury and Bridgeport requested local wholesalers and retailers to withdraw the novel on grounds of obscenity. Pocket Books, the paperback reprinter of the book, sued for damages and a permanent injunction. This was denied, but in 1967 the U.S. Supreme Court dismissed the local indictments and reaffirmed the rule that a book must be considered in its entirety.

   Sale of *The Carpetbaggers* was also restricted in Warwick, Rhode Island; Rochester, New York; and Mesquite, Texas. Sales by mid-1962 were about three million copies.

Williams, Garth (1912–   )

The Rabbits' Wedding, 1958

1959 United States–Alabama: After attacks by White Citizens Council and state senators, this Harper juvenile was moved out of open circulation shelves and into reserves by order of the state Public Library Service Division; critics thought the story encouraged racial integration.

Bissell, Richard (1913–1977)

A Stretch on the River, 1950

1951 United States–Iowa: A county attorney ordered police raids on bookstores, three department stores and the public library to pick up copies of the book. Library patrons who borrowed it were to be subpoenaed to testify about it.

Shulman, Irving (1913–   )

The Amboy Dukes, 1947

1949 Canada–Brantford, Ontario: Cleared of obscenity charges by Judge D. J. Cowan.

1949–1950 United States: Book under fire by local authorities in Milwaukee, Wis.; Detroit, Mich.; Newark, N.J.; and elsewhere.

1954 On disapproved list of National Organization of Decent Literature.

Burroughs, William (1914–   )

The Naked Lunch, 1959

1965 United States–Boston, Mass.: Found obscene in Superior Court. The finding was reversed by the State Supreme Court the following year. Burroughs' book was one of many that came under widespread attack in the 1960s.

Fast, Howard (1914–   )

Citizen Tom Paine, 1943

1947 United States–New York: Banned from the high school libraries in a vote of 6–1 by the Board of Education because it was allegedly written by a spokesman of a totalitarian movement and because it contained incidents and expressions not desirable for children, and was improper and indecent.

Almost a million copies of the book had been sold. It had been distributed to the armed forces abroad and to citizens of liberated countries.

The ban was strongly opposed at a public meeting by Marc Connelly, head of the Censorship Committee of the Authors League of America, and by other organizations. Connelly demanded that "the bigotry behind its condemnation be investigated in the interest of public welfare." The ban was supported by Rupert Hughes, president of the American Writers Association, who said the Board must not "yield to a propaganda drive."

1953 Soviet Union–Moscow: The Stalin Peace Prize was awarded to Howard Fast for "strengthening peace between peoples." The prize was established in 1950 in honor of Stalin's seventieth birthday and is said to be worth $25,000.

United States: The book was withdrawn from U.S. Information Agency libraries overseas.

1957 United States: Following the Soviet invasion of Hungary, Fast renounced his loyalty to Communism, despite the enormous popularity of his works in the Soviet Union and the honors bestowed upon him by the Soviet government.

Williams, Tennessee (1914–   )

1965 Portugal: All writings banned.

Davie, Emily (1915–   )

Profile of America, 1954

1954 The U.S. Information Agency sent 30,000 copies overseas.

1955 A House of Representatives Subcommittee on Appropriations specified that no U.S. Information Agency funds were to be used for any reorders of *Profile of America*. Subcommittee Chairman Rooney called it a "fine book for American consumption. But when it comes to showing foreigners what foul balls we are, that is something different." Objections were based on a photograph of an eighteenth-century school, a quotation from Thoreau, and an excerpt from *Ah, Wilderness!* alleged to be obscene. Despite Senate approval, the funds were not granted for reorder.

Miller, Arthur (1915–   )

A View from the Bridge, 1955

1956 England–London: The Lord Chamberlain refused a license for performance of the play, which had won both the New York Drama Critics Circle Award and the Pulitzer Prize.

Kauffmann, Stanley (1916–   )

The Philanderer, 1953

1954 England–London: The novel, originally published in America under the title of *The Tightrope* (1952), was involved in the British courts in a nominal damage verdict brought against a lending library on the Isle of Man. In London the Director of Public Prosecutions charged that the book was "obscene in the sense that it tends to corrupt and deprave the minds of those into whose hands it might fall, not only in certain passages but in the whole tendency of the book." This charge was worded to comply with the traditional test of obscenity under British law, Justice Cockburn's decision in 1868 in *Regina* v. *Hicklin*.

Justice Stable, in his charge to the jury, emphasized that the 1868 test had to be applied in the light of modern standards. He pointed out that while there were two schools of thought on the subject of sex which were "poles apart," the stand taken by average, decent people was somewhere in between.

The jury was given three days in which to read the book and charged that their verdict would have great bearing on where the line was to be drawn between liberty and license. The publishers

Secker & Warburg were found not guilty and Justice Stable's charge was heralded as a fresh reappraisal of the 1868 decision.

Merriam, Eve (1916–   )

The Inner City Mother Goose, 1969

1972 United States–New York: An Erie County judge called for a grand jury investigation of this satirical book of adult nursery rhymes, alleging it taught crime; complaint came from Buffalo city council members. Similar controversies were reported in Baltimore, Md.; Minneapolis, Minn.; San Francisco, Calif.

1976 Police criticism of the book in West Orange, N.J., and Baltimore, Md.

Solzhenitsyn, Aleksandr Isayevich (1916–   )

One Day in the Life of Ivan Denisovich, 1962
The First Circle, 1964
Cancer Ward, 1966
Stories and Prose Poems, trans. 1971
August 1914, 1972
The Love Girl and the Innocent, trans. 1972
Candle in the Wind, trans. 1973
The Gulag Archipelago, 1974

1964 Soviet Union–Moscow: A decorated officer in World War II, Solzhenitsyn was imprisoned for criticizing Stalinist methods, but was released under Khrushchev, and publication of his labor camp novel (*One Day*) was authorized. After Khrushchev lost power in 1964, Solzhenitsyn's works were barred from publication in the Soviet Union, though published in part in *samizdat* (private, underground, often typewritten copies), or abroad.

1970 The author was forbidden to go to Stockholm to receive the Nobel Prize on pain of being refused reentry to his homeland.

1974 He still published books abroad, and he was stripped of Soviet citizenship and deported.

Wallace, Irving (1916–   )

The Fan Club, 1974

1974 United States–California: The 26 branch librarians of Riverside County were advised that the book was not selected for circulation, and patrons should be told the county selection committee could not in good conscience spend tax money on it; further, that it was not their policy to purchase "formula-written commercial fiction."

Burgess, Anthony (1917–   )

A Clockwork Orange, 1962

1973 United States–Utah: Under the 1973 Supreme Court "local standards" decision, the town of Orem passed a highly specific obscenity
ordinance and charged a bookseller, Carole Grant, citing *A Clockwork Orange*, also *Last Tango in Paris* by Robert Ailey, 1973, and
The Idolators, by William Hegner. Charges were dropped, but Mrs.
Grant had to close her store; she opened a new one, however, in
Provo, where moves for a similar ordinance began.

The Little Review

1917 United States–New York City: An issue of this famous periodical
was confiscated by postal authorities, whose action was later upheld
by a Federal Court. The occasion was the publication of a story by
Wyndham Lewis which reflected adversely on war.

1921 New York: Margaret Anderson, the editor of *The Little Review*,
having been arrested the previous summer for printing "obscene"
excerpts from Joyce's *Ulysses*, was found guilty and fined $50. The
New York Times, commenting on the case, observed that *Ulysses*
was a trivial work, not worth the trouble of prosecuting.

Salinger, J. D. (1919–   )

The Catcher in the Rye, 1951

1955 United States: Beginning this year and extending to the present, this
book has been a favorite target of censors. Literally hundreds of
attempts have been made to ban the book in schools throughout
the United States, many of them successful. As recently as 1968, a
group in Minnesota attacked a high school administration for permitting it in the library.

1957 Australia: Despite a presentation gift by the U.S. Ambassador,
Australian Customs seized a shipment of this book.

1960 United States–Oklahoma: Tulsa teacher fired for assigning book
to 11th grade high school students; case "settled" by reinstating
the teacher, and removing the book from teaching programs.

1961 In a locally organized censorship campaign, wholesalers were assailed in a legislative hearing in Oklahoma City, Okla. for carrying
the paperback edition. Outside the capital building the groups
parked a "Smutmobile" displaying ("Free—Adults Only") many
books including *Lust for Life* by Irving Stone, Pocket Books; *Sons
and Lovers* by D. H. Lawrence, New American Library; *Tobacco
Road* and *God's Little Acre* by Erskine Caldwell, NAL; *Male and
Female* by Margaret Mead, NAL; and 43 magazines. Mid-Continent

News Co., the Oklahoma City paperback wholesaler, dropped a dozen of the criticized titles as a result of the campaign.

Winsor, Kathleen (1919–)

Forever Amber, 1944

1946 United States–Springfield, Mass.: A temporary injunction was issued against sale of the book, the first to come under the new Massachusetts censorship law of 1945, which although it did not change the definition of obscenity, set up a new procedure in the case of books sold to persons 18 years of age or older, whereby the action was to be against the book, not the distributor, and must be instigated by the district attorney or attorney general.
England: Copies burned at British ports and by the public library in Birmingham.

1947 Boston, Mass.: The book was acquitted in Suffolk County Superior Court. On appeal, the decision was upheld in 1948 by the Massachusetts Supreme Court. Judge Frank J. Donahue found the novel to be "obscene, indecent or impure," but he added that it was "a soporific rather than an aphrodisiac . . . that while the novel was conducive to sleep, it was not conducive to a desire to sleep with a member of the opposite sex."
   This was the first instance of a book being cleared by the high court of Massachusetts, four others having been condemned since the turn of the century. These were Elinor Glyn's *Three Weeks*, Dreiser's *An American Tragedy*, Lawrence's *Lady Chatterley's Lover*, and Lillian Smith's *Strange Fruit*.

1953 Ireland: Banned.

Comfort, Alex (1920–)

The Joy of Sex, 1972
More Joy of Sex, 1975

1978 United States–Kentucky: These and other contemporary sex instruction books were confiscated from three bookstores by police in Lexington under a new county ordinance prohibiting the display of sexually-oriented materials in places frequented by minors. Lexington's mayor, who had backed the ordinance, said, "These are not the type of thing I had in mind." Other bans were reported in scattered localities, 1972–1978.

Griffin, John Howard (1920–)

The Devil Rides Outside, 1952
Black Like Me, 1961

1954 United States–Detroit, Mich.: *The Devil Rides Outside* was one of 192 books classified as "objectionable" by the city prosecutor's office, 46 others having been previously classified as "partly objectionable" under the Detroit system of police censorship established in 1951.

The district sales manager of Pocket Books, publisher of the paperbound reprint edition, was charged with the sale of an obscene book, found guilty and fined.

1957 In a notable decision, *Butler* v. *Michigan*, the Supreme Court reversed the conviction. Justice Frankfurter said that the statute under which the conviction was obtained would "reduce the adult population of Michigan to reading what was fit for children." The decision was a breakthrough in eliminating American application of the Hicklin rule.

1966 The paperback edition of *Black Like Me* was widely attacked as unfit for children. In Wisconsin, a man sued his local school board for damage to his child; the case was dismissed.

Keats, John (1920–   )

Howard Hughes: A Biography, 1967

1966 United States: Agents for the multimillionaire Howard Hughes sought to prevent publication of this Random House book about him, but a final appeal for an injunction was denied in the U.S. Supreme Court.

Gilot, Françoise (1921–   )

Life with Picasso, trans. 1964

1964 France: Pablo Picasso, supported by many fellow-artists in France, sought unsuccessfully to suppress these memoirs by his former companion on grounds that they constituted "an infringement on my personal privacy."

Jones, James (1921–1977)

From Here to Eternity, 1951

1951 United States: This book was unofficially censored in Holyoke and Springfield, Massachusetts and in Denver, Colorado.

1953 New Jersey, Jersey City: Police "suggested" to dealers that they remove the title from newsstands and book outlets. Most dealers complied, but after it had been pointed out by a representative of the American Book Publishers Council that this was contrary to a New Jersey court decision, the book was again placed on sale.

1954 United States: On disapproved list of the National Organization of Decent Literature.

1955 Declared nonmailable by the Post Office, although it was a best-seller for four years.

Bishop, Leonard (1922–   )

Down All Your Streets, 1952

1953 United States–Youngstown, Ohio: The Chief of Police of this city had ordered some 335 paperbound books removed from newsstands as allegedly obscene. Suit was brought by the New American Library, publisher of *Down All Your Streets* and some of the other books so banned, with Roosevelt, Freidin, and Littauer serving as attorneys. Federal Judge Charles J. McNamee, of the U.S. District Court in Cleveland, enjoined the police officer from such action, pointing out that he "was without authority to censor books."

1954 The city of Youngstown, Ohio brought suit against a local distributor of paperbound books on the charge of distributing for sale a book of "obscene and immoral nature." Municipal Judge Forrest J. Cavalier dismissed the charges, agreeing with the defense that the word "immoral" in the original affidavit was too vague.

Manchester, William (1922–   )

The Death of a President, 1967

1966 Jacqueline Kennedy, who had authorized the writing of this work, demanded deletions in the manuscript, items said to be of personal material. Legal actions and settlements followed, involving Mrs. Kennedy, Robert Kennedy, the author, *Look* magazine (which was serializing the book), and Harper & Row, the publisher. The changes sought by the President's widow were made. This was the most widely reported of several disputes at this period over deletions demanded in books or manuscripts. (*See also* John Keats [p. 94], Milton J. Shapiro [p. 98], and Sylvester Stevens [p. 86].)

Vonnegut, Kurt, Jr. (1922–   )

Slaughterhouse-Five, 1969

Cat's Cradle, 1971

God Bless You, Mr. Rosewater, 1971

1972 Ohio: The Strongsville school board voted to require withdrawal from the school libraries of *Cat's Cradle* and *God Bless You, Mr. Rosewater*. The action was overturned in 1976 by a U.S. District Court, thus upholding the faculty's professional decisions.

1973 United States–Iowa: *Slaughterhouse-Five* banned and 32 paperback copies burned by order of this town's school board, reportedly because the book contained some four-letter words. Job of teacher who assigned it to a high school English class was threatened; he later moved elsewhere.

McBee, S.C.: High school teacher using *Slaughterhouse-Five* in English classes was arrested and charged with use of obscene materials.

1975 Island Trees, Long Island, N.Y.: School district censors personally removed ("stole," their opponents said) *Slaughterhouse-Five* and books of several other authors from the high school library.

Willingham, Calder (1922–   )

End as a Man, 1947

1947 United States–New York City: John S. Sumner of the New York Society for the Suppression of Vice sought a ban on this frank portrayal of life in a South Carolina military college. However, charges were dismissed by Magistrate Frederick L. Strong in New York's Municipal Term Court a few weeks later.

1948 Philadelphia, Pa.: *End as a Man* was among 2,000 titles seized in the Philadelphia raids. Judge Curtis Bok in the Court of Quarter Sessions dismissed the indictments. (*See also* William Faulkner [1897–1962].)

1950 Pennsylvania: Judge Bok's decision was appealed to the Pennsylvania Superior Court, but it was upheld.

Heller, Joseph (1923–   )

Catch 22, 1961

1972 United States–Ohio: The Strongsville school board voted to require withdrawal from school libraries of *Catch 22* and books by Kurt Vonnegut. The board's action was overturned in 1976 by a U.S. District Court, thus upholding the faculty's professional decisions.

Mailer, Norman (1923–   )

The Naked and the Dead, 1948

1949 England: This book created quite a stir when publication was first announced. But on May 23, according to the *New York Times*, Attorney General Sir Hartley Shawcross told the House of Commons that no action would be taken against the distribution of the book.

Canada: Rinehart, the U.S. publisher, was informed by Canadian Customs that the book "cannot be permitted entry into Canada."

Australia: Banned.

1954 United States–Georgia: The State Literature Commission investigated this novel, together with several joke books and magazines.

Baldwin, James (1924–   )

Another Country, 1962

1963 United States–New Orleans, La.: Considered obscene, the book was banned from the public library. After a year of litigation, it was restored.

1964 New Zealand: The Indecent Publications Tribunal found *Another Country* not obscene.

1965 United States–Illinois: After a parent's complaint, the Chicago City Council ordered removal of *Another Country* from a course list at Wright Junior College, but the college dean refused to comply.

Metalious, Grace (1924?–1964)

Peyton Place, 1956

1958 Canada: Temporary ban lifted.

1960 United States–New York: Accepted by New York public libraries.

Donleavy, James Patrick (1926–   )

The Ginger Man, 1955

1955 England: Originally published by Girodias in Paris, Donleavy expurgated the text himself to permit publication in England.

Ginsberg, Allen (1926–   )

Howl and Other Poems, 1956

1957 United States–California: U.S. Customs at San Francisco seized 520 copies printed abroad for the publisher, City Lights Bookstore. These were later released; meanwhile, the publisher had an edition printed in the United States. San Francisco police seized copies at the bookstore, claiming they were not suitable for children, although the shop was not a children's store. A municipal court ruled the book not obscene.

Selby, Hubert, Jr. (1928–   )

Last Exit to Brooklyn, 1964

1965 Massachusetts: A local city attorney sought an injunction against the book, but State Attorney (later U.S. Senator) Brooke directed dismissal of the complaint.

1966 United States–Connecticut: A circuit court issued a temporary injunction against the book, as "obscene and pornographic." (Grove and Dell both published editions.)

1967 England: The British publishers, Calder and Boyars, were prosecuted and the book was found obscene by a jury, under the Obscene Publications Act of 1959, which provided that a book could not be condemned unless it would deprave and corrupt by inciting its readers to act as the characters in the novel did, and that even then it must not be condemned if its publication would be of benefit to literature, science, or learning. In 1968, the Court of Appeal quashed the conviction because the judge had not made these points clear to the jury.

Shapiro, Milton J. (dates unreported)

The Warren Spahn Story, 1958

1967 United States–New York: The baseball star was upheld in New York State courts in his suit to suppress this fictionalized biography (written for young people) because, he said, it contained misstatements and fictitious episodes and invaded his right of privacy. The U.S. Supreme Court reversed the New York decision, upholding the author and Julian Messner, the publisher.

Thomas, Piri (1928–　)

Down These Mean Streets, 1971

1972 United States–New York City: Removed from a Queens school district junior high school library; right to remove upheld in State court; U.S. Supreme Court let this decision stand.

Ireland

1929 A Censorship of Publications Board was established and empowered to report to the Minister of Justice on books to be registered and banned for obscenity or for dealing with contraception or abortion, the Minister then to issue prohibition orders, without right of appeal. Modifications in 1956 and later provided that books must be considered in their entirety rather than on selected passages; more members would be added to the board; and an appeals procedure was established. The result was a heavy reduction in books banned and named in the *Register of Prohibited Publications*. By 1970 that list contained about 4,000 titles.

Maas, Peter (1929–　)

The Valachi Papers, 1968

1966 United States: The Department of Justice, which had engaged Maas as a freelance to edit the papers of the Mafia leader Joseph Valachi, sued to restrain his publishing a book of the memoirs. Grounds were that it would hamper law enforcement and be inconsistent with the Bureau of Prisons rule against publishing prisoners' manuscripts that dealt with their lives in crime.

1968 Suit settled, book published by Putnam.

Wilson, Colin (1931–)

The Sex Diary of Gerard Orme, 1963

1964 United States–Connecticut: A bookseller in New Britain was arrested for selling the Dial Press and Pocket Books novel. The state's Appellate Division ruled it not obscene, pending establishment of contrary constitutional standards.

Roth, Philip (1933–)

Portnoy's Complaint, 1969

1969 United States: Throughout the year, many libraries were attacked for carrying this Random House novel, and some librarians' jobs were threatened.

Royko, Mike (1933–)

Boss: Richard J. Daley of Chicago, 1971

1972 United States–Connecticut: The Ridgefield school board barred the title from the high school reading list, alleging that it "downgrades police departments."

Agee, Philip (1935?–)

Inside the Company: CIA Diary, 1974

1974–1977 United States: To avoid the problems faced by Marchetti (p. 100), Agee arranged for publication of his book by Penguin in England; he had already left the United States in 1971. Penguin could not place the book with U.S. publishers because Penguin would not honor their warranty clauses. Imported copies were sold out in two Washington, D.C. bookstores in 1974, but U.S. Customs stopped delivery of any more. When the American Civil Liberties Union promised to defend the book, Stonehill Publishing Co., New York, issued it in 1976 and Bantam published a reprint. Meanwhile, Britain ordered Agee's deportation; the U.S. Department of State in 1977 said he could return without prosecution, since no cause for action had so far been found.

Cleaver, Eldridge (1935–   )

Soul on Ice, 1968

1969 United States–California: California Superintendent of Instruction Max Rafferty barred Cleaver's book and *Dutchman* by LeRoi Jones from elective courses in black studies.

Marchetti, Victor (dates unreported) and Marks, John D. (1942?–   )

The CIA and the Cult of Intelligence, 1974

1972 Announcement of this book by Knopf led the Central Intelligence Agency (CIA) to obtain a U.S. court injunction against its publication on grounds that the author, as a CIA employee, had signed a contract not to write about the CIA without its approval of the manuscript. This action was opposed by Knopf, the Association of American Publishers, the Authors League and the author, raising the question of whether a citizen can sign away his First Amendment rights.

1974 The book was published with 168 passages deleted out of 339 deletions originally demanded by the CIA.

1977 In March 1977 Marchetti asked the Department of Justice to get the injunction lifted, and asked the CIA to permit the restoration of most deletions because they were capricious, arbitrary, or confined to information since published elsewhere.

Snepp, Frank (1943–   )

A Decent Interval, 1978

1978 United States: The Justice Department filed a civil complaint against the author for failing, as required by his contract when employed by the Central Intelligence Agency (CIA), to submit to the agency the manuscript of this Random House book on the chaotic American withdrawal from Vietnam. The suit demanded a lifetime ban on his writing or speaking about the CIA; and asked damages equal to any profits from the book, in part for allegedly undermining trust in the agency (which was already undermined). The case was, in part, a test of a contract restraining speech and press where no use of classified information was charged. It introduced also a claim that even without a restrictive contract, a past or present government official has a "fiduciary duty" to submit writings before publication.

Zilg, Gerard Colby (1945–   )

Du Pont: Beyond the Nylon Curtain, 1974

1975 United States–New York City: This Prentice-Hall book was withdrawn by the Book-of-the-Month Club (BOMC) as a choice of its

Fortune Book Club, after a telephoned complaint by a du Pont corporation spokesman to the operating head of BOMC, according to a *New York Times* report.

Alabama

1953 Alabama enacted a law requiring that every publisher doing business with the state would have to swear whether or not each author of a book being submitted for state textbook adoption was a Communist; this would apply also to writers mentioned in supplementary reading lists.

Indiana

1953 United States–Indiana: A State Textbook Commission member demanded the story of *Robin Hood* (thirteenth century, ff.) be removed from textbooks for promoting "Communist doctrines"— taking from the rich to give to the poor. The same commissioner demanded removal of all mention of Quaker religion from textbooks, claiming pacifism tended to support Communism. Modern Sheriff of Nottingham told the United Press, "Robin Hood was no Communist!" Moscow *Pravda* blamed "Wall Street." Indiana governor defended the Quakers, but was silent on Robin Hood. No actual banning reported.

Rhode Island

1962 U.S. Supreme Court ruled unconstitutional the extrajudicial censorship action of the state's Youth Commission to Encourage Morality, which had sent lists to wholesalers, citing books and magazines deemed objectionable for sale to persons under 18 years of age. The Court noted this meant banning in effect, and said: "Adult readers are equally deprived of the opportunity to purchase the publications in the State."

Russian Books

1963 United States–Ohio: A Columbus city ordinance against the selling of "Communist-made goods" forced Long's College Bookstore to remove several Russian books, and also caused the arrest of a rare books dealer. A local court judge found this law unconstitutional because only Congress has the right to regulate foreign trade.

China: Cultural Revolution

1965–1974 Inspired by Mao Tse-Tung and beginning as a reaction against elitism in education, the Great Proletarian Cultural Revolution convulsed China, struck down vestiges of class structure, and violently disrupted universities, which were closed until reorganized. An American scientist, visiting in 1971 and 1972, found science emphasized, art and literature minimized. He wrote: "It seems that not only is literary creativity stifled, but cultural insularity is imposed."

Kendel, Lenore (dates unreported)

The Love Book, 1966

1966 United States–California: San Francisco police arrested three booksellers (in the City Lights Bookstore and the Psychedelic Shop) for selling this book of poems, alleging it violated an obscenity ordinance.

1967 Banned after a month-long jury trial. Meanwhile, the publisher, Jeff Berner (Stolen Paper Editions) promised one percent of the profits to the city Patrolmen's Benevolent Association for helping the sales. Grove Press then published the poem in a collection of the author's work, *Word Alchemy*.

American Heritage Dictionary, 1969

1978 United States–Missouri: Banned in Eldon library because of 39 "objectionable" words.

Zap Comics #4, 1969

1969 Managers of two outlets were convicted on the presumption that they were aware that contents of this publication were obscene; conviction upheld, 1973, by New York State Court of Appeals. (In 1959, however, the U.S. Supreme Court had ruled [*Smith* v. *California*] that such awareness must be proved.)

Report of the Commission on Obscenity and Pornography, 1970

1970 United States: Calling the traffic in obscenity and pornography "a matter of national concern," the Congress in Public Law 90–100, 1967, set up the commission to examine legal aspects of the question, distribution of materials, and effects of obscenity and pornography, and to make recommendations for legislative, administrative, or other action "to regulate the flow of such traffic without in any way interfering with constitutional rights." The report, with its recommendations, and with majority and several minority statements, were published by Random House and Bantam Books with an introduction by Clive Barnes. The findings were denounced by President Nixon without reading the full report. However, it remains the most extensive study made of the subject.

Valliéres, Pierre (dates unreported)

White Niggers of America, 1968

1970 Canada: Subtitled "The Precocious Autobiography of a Quebec 'Terrorist,'" this book, part personal history, part Quebec history and revolutionary doctrine, was written in jail in French and was confiscated when the author was charged with sedition. A French import was/banned in Canada under the War Measures Act. Published in the United States in 1971 in English by Monthly Review Press.

Hansen, Søren (dates unreported) and Jensen, Jesper (dates unreported)

The Little Red Schoolbook, trans. 1971

1971 United States: Published by Pocket Books in a U.S. version by Wallace Roberts, this Danish book made a stir with its radical challenge to traditional education and lifestyles, its section on sex and sex knowledge, and suggestions to teenagers on organizing for reform.
England: A translation was banned in 1971 under the Obscene Publications Act.
France: A French version was banned.

1972 Italy: Mario Guaraldi, publisher, believed he had expurgated material not proper under Italian law, but his edition was confiscated anyway; the book would still incite youth to corruption, authorities claimed.

The Pentagon Papers, 1971

1971 United States: In mid-1967, Secretary of Defense Robert S. McNamara commissioned a massive top-secret history of the United States role in Indo-China. It was completed about the end of 1968, in 3,000 pages of narrative and more than 4,000 pages of documents, covering the history from the 1940s to May 1968. The *New York Times* obtained most of the material, and began June 13, 1971 to publish a series of articles based on them with selected, key documents. On June 15 the Justice Department obtained from a U.S. District Court in New York a temporary restraining order against further publication. The *New York Times* and the Washington *Post*, which had also begun publishing articles on the history, appealed, and on June 30, 1971 the U.S. Supreme Court ruled 6–3 that the right to a free press overrode any subsidiary legal considerations, and permitted publication. In July, 1971, Bantam Books issued a paperback edition of the *New York Times* articles and documents.

1972 A copy of the Pentagon report obtained by Sen. Gravel (D., Alaska) was published by Beacon Press (Unitarian-Universalist Association) in four volumes. (Justice Department and a federal grand jury in Boston, Mass., had meanwhile been investigating both the Press and the church.) The U.S. Supreme Court ruled 5–4 that publication of the *Papers* was not protected under the First Amendment; and that Sen. Gravel's congressional immunity regarding them did not extend to publication. Sale of the volumes continued, however.

Ashman, Charles R. (dates unreported)

Connally: The Adventures of Big Bad John, 1974

1974 United States–Texas: Several major retail outlets and broadcasting stations cancelled appearances by the writer of this Morrow book about the Texas politician; shortly, however, other stores and media in the same cities (Dallas, Austin, San Antonio) invited the author to appear.

Male and Female under 18, 1973

1977 United States–Massachusetts: This Avon Books anthology, edited by Nancy Larrick and Eve Merriam, was banned by the Chelsea school board from the high school library because of objections to one poem by a teenage girl. A local defense group and state library association sued to prevent the board's interference with the librarian.

APPENDIX 1

Trends in Censorship

Control of Books and Reading
by Religious and Political Powers

In the history of censorship, the oldest and most frequently recurring controls have been those designed to prevent the expression of unorthodox religious or political ideas. A notable example of the former, until very recently, was the Roman Catholic *Index Librorum Prohibitorum (Index of Prohibited Books)*, which was intended to regulate the reading of the world's Catholic population.

The Church's regulation of books can be traced back to Apostolic times, when the Ephesian converts of St. Paul made a bonfire of hundreds of volumes which they viewed as catering to superstition.

Most of the early lists and decrees, however, were concerned with establishing which books were to be accepted as part of the Bible, which were recommended reading and which were heretical. In 1515 the Lateran Council established the principle of ecclesiastical licensing, a procedure which was formalized and given potency by the Council of Trent in 1546, with the forbidding of the sale or possession of anonymous religious books. It was Pope Paul IV who authorized the first list of banned books in 1557. For nearly 400 years, the list was issued in numerous editions, with occasional additions and deletions. The last edition was published in 1948, with a list of more than 4,000 titles, mostly obscure titles disapproved for doctrinal reasons, but including also some of the masterworks of the Western world. Publication of the *Index* ceased in 1966.

At about the time that the Vatican's *Index* was formalized, the Spanish Church established an *Index* of its own, as seen in several examples cited in this book. In modern times, the Republic of Ireland set up in 1929 a registry of books banned, mainly for moral reasons, and did not soften its application until 1967.

In this century, political censorship has consistently taken more dramatic forms and received far greater notoriety than religious bannings. However, recent episodes of suppression, although numerous, are quite limited in scope when compared to those of the Stalin period in the Soviet

Union and its satellites, and the National Socialist (Nazi) era in Germany and its conquered territories.

The first large-scale demonstration in Germany occurred on May 10, 1933, when students gathered 25,000 volumes by Jewish authors and burned them in the square in front of the University of Berlin. The bonfire was watched by 40,000 unenthusiastic people in a drizzling rain. Joseph Goebbels, the Minister of Public Enlightenment, delivered an address on "the symbolic significance of the gesture." Similar demonstrations were held at many other German universities. In Munich 5,000 school children, who had formerly seen Marxist literature publicly burned, were enjoined: "as you watch the fire burn these un-German books, let it also burn into your hearts love of the Fatherland." Students entered the bookstores and took without remuneration the books they considered eligible for the bonfire, and had to be prevented from confiscating books from the University Library.

The following list names some of the most important authors whose works were sacrificed at the fires:

Sholem Asch, Lion Feuchtwanger, Maxim Gorky, Stefan Zweig, Karl Marx, Sigmund Freud, Helen Keller, Jack London, Ernest Hemingway, John Dos Passos, Jakob Wasserman, Emil Ludwig, Arthur Schnitzler, Leon Trotsky, V. I. Lenin, Josef Stalin, Grigori S. Zinoviev, Alfred Adler, Gotthold Lessing, Franz Werfel, Hugo Munsterberg, Thomas Mann, Heinrich Mann, Erich Maria Remarque, Albert Einstein, Heinrich Heine, Felix Mendelssohn, Maximilian Harden, Kurt Eisner, Henri Barbusse, Rosa Luxemburg, Upton Sinclair, Judge Ben Lindsay, Arnold Zweig.

This great destruction of books by the Nazis continued until World War II. In 1938 they made a cultural purge of Austria. Booksellers were forced to clear their shelves of proscribed works, and either to conceal or destroy them. When word of the purge reached the United States, many offers to buy the books were sent to Vienna by universities and individuals. Some eventually did reach this country.

In Salzburg 15,000 people watched a "purification bonfire" of one copy each of 2,000 volumes, including Jewish and Catholic books. The ceremony was started by a schoolboy who threw a copy of Chancellor Schuschnigg's *Three Times Austria* on the gasoline-soaked pyre. Meanwhile the crowd sang "Deutschland Über Alles" in the gaily lighted square. The proceedings were under the auspices of the National Socialist (Nazi) Teachers' Association, which had appealed to the public to give up all "objectionable literature," and it was said that the destruction of 30,000 more volumes would follow.

In Leipzig many of the same titles that had been burned in the Nazi bonfire of 1933 were suppressed, and in Czechoslovakia the Education Ministry ordered all public libraries to remove and destroy all "unpatriotic" books, particularly by patriots including ex-President Beneš.

In 1944 the great "book city" of Leipzig suffered the loss of many valuable books by the Allied bombings, and in 1946 the Coordinating Council of the American Military Government in Germany ordered Nazi memorials to be destroyed. The object was to eliminate the "spirit of German militarism and Nazism as far as possible." This order to cleanse the German mentality was issued just as the eleventh anniversary of the Nazi "Burning of the Books" was being observed by the free world, and it caused much sharp comment. Included were the works of Hitler, Goebbels, Mussolini, and Karl Marx. The books were placed on the restricted lists in libraries, or in some instances pulped, but no burnings were known to have taken place. At the same time the Communists in East Germany were doing the same thing from their own point of view.

In 1953, in East Germany, the Communist cultural advisers removed from the libraries, schools, and bookshops at least five million volumes by German, Nazi, and foreign authors. Even Marx and Engels did not escape and were expurgated or rewritten "with historically important additions." It is said that books written before the war about the "good old days" were especially feared.

In 1953–1954 it was reported by refugees from East Berlin that all printed matter including picture papers and crossword puzzles sent to East Germany was confiscated at the border. As recently as 1969, East German guards at Rudolphstein refused passage to West Berlin of copies of Konrad Adenauer's memoirs and of road maps showing Germany's boundaries before World War II.

There is no room here to cite all the known specific instances of censorship in Communist nations. The right of the state to determine what shall or shall not be read is firmly established in Communist countries, and the catalog of banned or emasculated works is long. Soviet censorship is particularly fascinating because it appears to rise and fall in intensity in accordance with the currents of policy. Notable literary figures in the Soviet Union have experienced periods of freedom and repression. Some have been isolated from the Union of Soviet Writers, cut off from contact with peers, incarcerated in psychiatric institutions or labor camps. Others have conformed, at least outwardly.

The story of Soviet censorship has become known, though incompletely, since the time of Stalin's consolidation of power. The purge trials of the 1930s established political and cultural controls that have chilled independent literary and artistic production ever since. Similar controls have been reported generally from other "socialist" countries. Even in spite of a "thaw" after Stalin's death, and Khrushchev's denunciation of Stalinism, the spirit of repression still was reaffirmed in the crushing of the Hungarian uprising in 1956 and of the attempt to estabish "communism with a human face" in Czechoslovakia in 1968. Nevertheless, in the Soviet Union and neighboring lands, original literary production, unsanctioned by authority, has persisted in the form of underground writings—*samizdat*—circulated in typewritten or hectographed form.

The more spectacular censorship moves in the Soviet Union include the unsuccessful effort to prevent publication abroad of *Doctor Zhivago* by Boris Pasternak. The degree of effort that the Soviet Union is willing to expend to suppress information is astonishing to Westerners. Following the death of Stalin, Lavrenti Beria, the head of the Soviet Secret Police, was discredited and later executed. *The Great Soviet Encyclopedia*, which had already been published and distributed abroad, contained a lengthy article on Beria. This article was ordered to be excised from all existing copies and sheets containing an article on the Bering Sea were substituted.

In 1961 the Soviet Union permitted publication of Aleksandr Solzhenitsyn's book about Stalin's labor camps, *One Day in the Life of Ivan Denisovich* (Praeger). But after the author extended his criticisms, he was forced to publish abroad or not at all, and at last, having gained world attention, he was expelled from his native land (1974). At the same period, the activities of the distinguished physicist and dissident Andrei Sakharov were sharply restricted. In 1975 the Soviet Union was one of the signers of the international Helsinki Agreement, which included provisions to safeguard free and critical expression. Monitoring groups sprang up in Soviet cities to report on violations of this agreement, but authorities gradually broke them up.

Meanwhile, however, the worldwide civil liberties organization, Amnesty International (winner of the Nobel Peace Prize in 1977), was focusing attention on specific violations of human rights in many countries. International P.E.N., the writers' organization, was also intervening to defend persecuted writers. It is believed that the lives of many writers and other dissidents or independents may have been saved by the publicity which these activities produced, and by floods of letters from many countries, appealing to leaders of authoritarian régimes.

Countries where freedom of thought and expression has been thus defended include the Soviet Union, Poland, South Korea; South Africa and other African régimes; Iran, Greece, Philippines, Chile, Argentina, Brazil, and many more.

Unfortunately there was no effective world pressure group to protect books and writers in Spain and Portugal during the years of military dictatorship from the 1930s to the 1970s. There was no influence strong enough to dissuade Yugoslavia's Marshall Tito from jailing his one-time associate Milovan Djilas in 1956 after Djilas wrote a critique of Communism, *The New Class* (Praeger, 1957), and supported the Hungarian freedom fighters. Human rights efforts were not organized in time to stop the suppression of classics in Greece under the military régime of 1966–1974. They did not prevent soldiers in Chile in the 1973 rightist coup from burning books seized in citizens' homes (as was shown on American television, with an English-speaking officer explaining that it was necessary to destroy "harmful" books).

In the late 1970s, however, it appears that open protests against suppression can have positive results and can, at the very least, let independent spirits know that they are not alone. Undoubtedly these efforts on behalf of civil liberty are reinforced by the adoption of the human rights principle as a major, ongoing element of American foreign policy under President Jimmy Carter.

It is difficult to learn what specific books may have figured in the persecution of writers in any of the countries just mentioned. More important, it is impossible even to speculate what books were never written because the climate of a society was stifling to its potential writers.

Book Banning in Overseas Libraries

In 1953 a great outcry went up over book banning and alleged book burning in the approximately 200 U.S. Information Agency (USIA) libraries overseas. More than two million books stood on their shelves and they were visited by 36 million people a year. The purpose of these centers has been to provide a "balanced presentation" of American life and ideas through books and periodicals. Early in 1953 a Senate subcommittee, headed by Senator Joseph R. McCarthy, had been investigating the activities of the International Information Administration of the State Department. A series of confusing directives, which came from the State Department during that spring, led to different interpretations in libraries in the various capitals, the resulting book bannings causing serious damage to U.S. prestige abroad. During this time Senator McCarthy's staff men, Roy Cohn and David Schine, were making a hasty survey of USIA overseas libraries. They visited seven European countries in 18 days and turned in the spectacular report that there were 30,000 books by "pro-Communist" authors in the libraries. Upon examination this report turned out to be a gross exaggeration.

It was said that more than 40 authors were involved in the books withdrawn during this period. The debate over the selection of books for the overseas libraries culminated in July of that year with a directive from the State Department reaffirming the fundamental policy of selecting books which would reflect a representative picture of the United States. The books of eight known or avowed Communists were permanently banned. The books of some 20 other writers who had refused to testify as to their Communist affiliations before Senate investigating committees were banned "pending further examination."

Secretary of State John Foster Dulles testified that to his knowledge only 11 books had actually been burned by overzealous librarians, and that the other books in question had been withdrawn from circulation for further consideration—a very small percentage of the two million books which have proved invaluable in the many countries where the libraries of the USIA have operated so efficiently and so successfully.

On June 14, 1953, President Eisenhower made his famous speech at Dartmouth College, "Don't join the book burners." He argued that Communism would be defeated only by our understanding of what it is and what it teaches. In order "to fight it with something better," we also should not attempt "to conceal the thinking of our own people . . . even if they think ideas that are contrary to ours." Excitement blazed anew and the press questioned the connection between the speech and the overseas library furor. The President, at a press conference, claimed that there was no connection between the two, that he was not familiar with the State Department directives to the libraries, but said he was against book burning and the suppression of ideas. However, to quote from the press conference record, the President also said that, "it is perfectly proper to bar certain books from the mails, as is done, and he would do it now"; that "he did not believe the standards of essential human dignity and decency ought to be violated," and that "Overseas, he saw no reason for bringing these (questionable) books out unless there was some area where we believed we had to show a particular group what Communism was, out of the mouths of the Communist leaders themselves. He added that he was not an apostle of the doctrine that all generalizations are always true."

Although the McCarthy episode had long passed, new accounts of library censorship overseas arose later on. The USIA banning of *The Ugly American* (Norton) by William J. Lederer from its overseas libraries generated a great deal of unfavorable publicity in 1958. A year later the ban was lifted. In December 1969, *Newsweek* magazine reported that the USIA had barred the distribution of some two dozen books to one of its European libraries. The magazine went on to explain that six full-time reviewers screen books for the USIA into three categories: (1) recommended, to be "pushed hard" for overseas use (about 70 titles a month make the grade); (2) noncontroversial books that any USIA library can get by specifically requesting them from Washington; (3) books that raise questions about American policy and that the USIA believes might be "misunderstood" or "offensive" overseas.

Some of the banned books and the official USIA reasons for refusing them follow:

Henry Steele Commager's *Freedom and Order* (Braziller; NAL): "The value of the rest of the book does not begin to overcome the liability of the 30-plus pages condemning American policies in Vietnam."

George R. Stewart's *Not So Rich as You Think* (Houghton Mifflin): "The book just wouldn't help to 'glamorize our program,' nor will it help other nations prevent or solve similar problems."

James Baldwin's *Tell Me How Long the Train's Been Gone* (Dial; Dell):

"A quote from Mr. Baldwin to the effect that 'My countrymen impressed me simply as being, on the whole, the emptiest and most unattractive people in the world.'"

Government Papers, the CIA, Official Materials

Court decisions affecting the Pentagon Papers; legislation providing means for the release of government reports and for the disclosure of "security" files about oneself; and congressional investigations of the Central Intelligence Agency (CIA)—all these have combined to bring new concepts into the whole complex field of government secrecy. The issues are often confused; policies and practices are still in flux.

The *New York Times* in 1971 printed extensive excerpts from the Department of Defense report on the history of America's embroilment in Vietnam, the report that quickly became known as the Pentagon Papers. The right of the *Times* to print the material was upheld by the U.S. Supreme Court. The court did not, however, find that the reading into the *Congressional Record* of the complete papers by a U.S. Senator was sufficient to permit their publication by the Beacon Press in four volumes, but Beacon was not prevented from issuing its edition.

Controls Applied by Government Bureaus

Censorship carried out as a function of government bureaus, particularly the Post Office and the Bureau of Customs, is a study in itself. Numerous instances of book banning by these agencies are cited in the main body of this book, under the names of the authors. For a proper understanding of this subject, the reader is referred to the profoundly researched, highly readable study, *Federal Censorship: Obscenity in the Mail* by James C. N. Paul and Murray L. Schwartz (The Free Press of Glencoe, 1961). These two legal scholars describe the roots of postal and customs (import) censorship in America; its growing application, at first to pictures, later to books; nineteenth-century laws culminating in the widely restrictive Comstock Act of 1873; changes under the Tariff Act of 1930, still restrictive; disputes in the courts; administrative changes after the obscenity decisions of 1957; and recommendations for reform.

A quite different kind of action against books, one involving allegations of fraud, is described in this book under the name of the author in question, the psychiatrist Wilhelm Reich. In that case the book banning agency was the Food and Drug Administration.

Censorship of Library Books, Attacks on Librarians

Libraries in the United States felt the pressure of censorship long before the overseas libraries were subjected to such investigation. As early as 1941 Governor Eugene Talmadge of Georgia ordered removed from college and school libraries in his state books unfavorable to the South, the Bible, or the state of Georgia. He announced that he would ask the 1943 legislature to order the burning of library books advocating interracial cooperation. Although this particular censorship move did not materialize, others occurred. In 1959 the Georgia Board of Education voted to require a stamp of approval from its literary committee on all library books after a board member warned that pro-integration literature was worming its way into the libraries. Two years later, the Georgia Library Association was forced to appeal to Chatham County grand jurors and to the president of the county board of education to protect their libraries from what it called "witch hunts." The action stemmed from the removal by the grand jury of four titles from Savannah high school libraries because they allegedly contained immoral material.

In Iowa, early in 1951, city and county officers suddenly raided the Dubuque public library, under a warrant, and seized an assortment of books charged with being obscene. Among them were the works of Rabelais, Boccaccio's *The Decameron*, and Henry Fielding's *Tom Jones*.

The librarian of Bartlesville, Oklahoma, was dismissed in 1950 after 31 years of service because she had participated in local group discussions on race relations and had certain magazines on the library shelves which a Citizens' Committee considered undesirable. Although the library had been administered by an autonomous board, which supported the librarian's position in all but one respect, the City Commission passed a new ordinance gaining control of the library and dismissing the old library board. The librarian and a member of the old board carried the case to the Oklahoma Supreme Court where, in 1952, the court ruled against them.

In the fall of 1952 the Boston Public Library was attacked by the Boston *Post* for having Communist material, not on its open shelves, but in its reference collection. The director of the library argued that all aspects of political, international, and other questions must be available for the information of the citizens of the city. This established policy of the library was upheld by its board by a 3–2 vote.

Several other cities, notably San Antonio, Texas, and Dubuque, Iowa, faced similar censorship attacks on their public libraries in recent years. In Illinois some 400 titles, involving between 6,000 and 8,000 volumes, were removed from circulation in the state libraries in December 1953, after the mother of a 13-year-old girl complained that she obtained a book which was "offensive." However, these were all reclassified "for adult consumption" early in 1954. The State Librarian originally ordered books "of a salacious, vulgar or obscene" character to be taken out of circulation, but later stated that his order "was never intended to result in what has been termed a wholesale withdrawal of books."

Similarly, in 1959, *The Rabbits' Wedding* (Harper & Row), a book for children aged three to seven, was banished to the "reserved" shelf of the

Alabama Public Library Service Division after the Alabama State Senate charged that the book represented a sneaky appeal for racial integration. In it, a black rabbit and a white rabbit get married at a moonlight ceremony in a forest. On the "reserved" shelf, *The Rabbits' Wedding* joined other books considered pro-integration and books considered obscene.

An ugly incident that did not involve banning of books, but rather an attack on a librarian's freedom of opinion, illustrates the fear and repression caused by some congressional investigators. In January 1957, Mrs. Mary Knowles, the librarian of Plymouth Meeting, Pennsylvania, was found guilty of contempt of Congress in refusing to answer political questions put by the Senate's subcommittee on internal security. In 1953 she had invoked the Fifth Amendment to the Constitution and had been discharged from the position she held then as librarian in Norwood, Massachusetts, under pressure from financial supporters of the library.

Obscenity was the charge leveled against *The Arrangement* (Stein & Day; Avon), a novel by Elia Kazan, when it was barred from an Iowa municipal library in 1967. The publisher of the book, which at that time was on top of the nation's best-seller list, countered this action by offering a free copy to every adult head of family in the community of 8,600 residents. This countermeasure called on the town citizens to decide for themselves if their library board was "practicing a form of censorship inconsistent with American tradition." After more than 800 free copies were requested, the publisher said: "If there is a good deal of discussion, pro and con, whether or not the book is obscene, we will have reached our objective. The point is that a library board should not make any book unavailable to the members of a community."

For some time a slang dictionary was the object of controversy in California. Agitation against *A Dictionary of American Slang* (T. Y. Crowell) began in 1963 when Max Rafferty, Superintendent of Public Instruction, suggested that a "little bit of censorship" was necessary to remove the book from school libraries. To document their case that the book was "dirty," supporters of Mr. Rafferty combed through the dictionary's 8,000-odd entries, found the 150 dirtiest and listed them in a mimeographed publication. Although the book was banned in several communities and literally burned in at least one other, most libraries decided to keep the book for restricted use by serious students. Early in 1978, the banning of the *American Heritage Dictionary* was reported from a Missouri town, as cited in the main section of this book.

Zealous groups, believing themselves to be patriotic, bring up strangely mixed complaints. In 1964 a group in Long Beach, California, assailed the public library director's selection of *The American Way of Death* by Jessica Mitford (Simon & Schuster; Crest) as being procommunist and critical of morticians. They attacked Langston Hughes as a leftist poet, and they charged major book reviews—*Library Journal, New York Times*

Book Review, New York Herald Tribune Books, and *Saturday Review*—with "brainwashing" their readers and unduly influencing the purchase of books. The Long Beach group also campaigned for several years against the Greek novelist, Nikos Kazantzakis. (See the note under his name.)

In 1970 another strange attack on libraries came to light. Protests against the Vietnam war were widespread, and authorities worried about bombings. The Internal Revenue Service (IRS) asked permission to look over the circulation records of libraries in order to see who had checked out books that might contain information on explosive devices. The American Library Association (ALA) said libraries should consider their circulation records confidential; the IRS dropped the idea, and returned to the collecting of revenues.

At the ALA's annual midwinter conference in January 1978, reports on censorship indicated that an array of right-of-center groups were making concerted efforts to restrict librarians and educators. Their methods were correct—the use of campaign mailings, letters of protest, petitions, and various forms of legal complaints. Subjects of their concern were listed as including subversion, art, civil rights, defense policies, education, fluoridation, mental health, and the press. Renewed criticism of textbooks was said to be especially strong in Florida, California, and Texas. Among specific books, very frequent targets were reported to be: *Our Bodies, Ourselves* by the Boston Women's Health Collective (Simon & Schuster); *Man, A Course of Study* by the National Science Foundation (Curriculum Development Associates); and *American Heritage Dictionary* (Grosset & Dunlap).

The use of reserved or restricted shelves has been one of several ways in which librarians have attempted to beat censors at their own game. The Fiske Report, *Book Selection and Censorship: A Study of School and Public Libraries in California,* published in 1959, clearly established a do-it-yourself movement among librarians. Of the 90 libraries and 204 librarians sampled in 26 localities, two-thirds of the respondents reported refusals to purchase because of the controversial nature of a book or its author, one-third reported the permanent removal or restriction of controversial materials, and a fifth reported an habitual avoidance of all controversial matter.

On a different level, a strong feeling among children's librarians that L. Frank Baum's *The Wizard of Oz* and related books were somehow unworthy kept those books out of children's libraries for many years. This practice was somewhat reduced after a public uproar over it developed in 1957.

School Textbooks and School Libraries

The question of the censorship of textbooks used in the public schools in recent years has not been so much one of banning as of rejection or disapproval of certain texts as a result of pressure by local or national groups.

In the 1930s and 1940s the charge usually leveled against such texts had been that the books were designed to change the existing social order or to record changes in the American way of life. An outstanding instance was the attack in 1939 by the Advertising Federation of America against Harold O. Rugg's *An Introduction to Problems of American Culture* (Ginn). Professor Rugg, of Teachers College, Columbia University, was the author of many textbooks, of which more than two million copies had been sold within 20 years. In their campaign against Rugg's textbook, the Federation charged the author with "attacking business from every angle" and sneering "at the ideas and traditions of American democracy, making a subtle plea for abolition of our free enterprise system and the introduction of a new social order based on the principles of collectivism. . . ."

In 1940 the National Association of Manufacturers was aroused to action on textbooks and undertook an investigation of some 600 school texts to determine the social viewpoint expressed by the authors. The survey by Ralph West Robey aroused a storm of protest from varied quarters, from the American Historical Association to the Harvard Graduate School of Education. Within 15 years after these violent discussions practically all the books which featured in the controversies were either out of print or not in general use, but this was not necessarily the result of the furor, since books in these fields become outdated by the passage of time. In many cases, however, the new books were more cautiously written.

For several years the New York City Board of Superintendents banned *The Nation* from its list of approved publications for school libraries. The original ban was imposed in June 1948, because of a series of articles on the Roman Catholic Church by Paul Blanshard, subsequently expanded and published as *American Freedom and Catholic Power* (Beacon Press).

During the next two decades, attacks on textbooks were based frequently on the suspicion of subversive material. In 1952 the Texas State Board of Education authorized the Education Commission to request that each publisher submitting books for adoption state whether the authors, illustrators, and editors could qualify under the terms of the state's nonsubversive oath. At a hearing of the State Textbook Commission in 1953, critics asked the commission to bar from the schools the Garden City editions of Chaucer's *Canterbury Tales* and Melville's *Moby Dick* that were illustrated by Rockwell Kent, because of his alleged Communist connections. Some 600 titles were proposed for exclusion, purportedly for the same reason—books by Albert Einstein, Thomas Mann, Louis Untermeyer, Dorothy Canfield Fisher, Allan Lomax, Norbert Wiener, Dorothy Parker, Louis Adamic, Harlow Shapley, and Norman Corwin, among others.

Ten years later the Birch-like Texans for America were successful in dominating the state's textbook adoption hearings and subsequent legislative hearings. Prominent in the objections raised by Texans for America was favorable mention of the income tax, the TVA, Social Security, unemployment compensation, labor unions, racial integration, General of the Armies George C. Marshall and the U.S. Supreme Court. Among 50 textbooks that Texans for America wanted banned from classrooms were: *America: Land of Freedom* (Heath); *A History of the United States* (American Book Co.); *The Story of Our Country* (Allyn & Bacon); *American History* (Ginn); *Living World History* (Scott, Foresman); *Rise of the American Nation* (Harcourt); *Story of America* (Holt, Rinehart & Winston); *This Is Our Nation* (Webster); *The Record of Mankind* (Heath); *United States History* (Heath) (attacked because it failed to mention, among other patriot-statesmen, Davy Crockett); and *The Adventure of the American People* (Rand-McNally).

In 1953 the State Legislature of Alabama adopted an anti-Communist law governing the adoption of textbooks in the state's public schools which was to become effective January 1, 1954. It provided that no textbook "will be adopted . . . without a statement by the publisher or author indicating that the author is or is not a known advocate of Communism or Marxist Socialism." This proved to be a law with which publishers found it impossible to comply, and under the leadership of the American Textbook Publishers Institute, 25 textbook publishers joined in a suit against the Alabama State Board of Education and the State Textbook Commission. On May 10, 1954, the Circuit Court of Montgomery County adjudged the act void, unenforceable and in violation of the Fourteenth Amendment of the Constitution of the United States.

UNESCO and the UN Declaration of Human Rights have also come in for criticism. In 1954 in El Paso, Texas, the school board banned the use of a history textbook which printed without comment the UN Declaration of Human Rights and the Declaration of Independence. The State Board of Education, however, rejected a demand to drop the book from its list.

Frank Magruder's *American Government* (Allyn & Bacon) was often under attack. A campaign against it was led by two strongly right-wing advocates, neither one an accredited educator. One was Allen Zoll, a well-financed pamphleteer. The other was Louise Cardin Crain, who edited the *Educational Reviewer*, a quarterly published by the Conference of American Small Business Organizations. Among the cities where the Magruder book was under fire were Chicago, Houston, Little Rock, and Arlington, Virginia. In Georgia the book was attacked as "unfit for use as a social studies textbook because it advocates strengthening the United Nations Charter."

Publishers' Weekly reported that in 1953, "An Indiana state textbook commissioner achieved international notoriety by urging bans on books about Robin Hood and the Quakers as 'helpful to the Communist policy.'" No action resulted from her efforts.

In 1959 the Daughters of the American Revolution issued their first master list of textbooks, classifying them as "satisfactory" or "unsatisfactory." Only 50 satisfactory books were listed, as opposed to 165 unsatisfactory ones being used in schools at that time. The DAR influence was largely responsible for the 1960 Mississippi legislation which gave Governor Ross Barnett the power to select all of the state's textbooks. Taking up his new responsibilities, the governor urged: "Clean up our textbooks. Our children must be properly informed of the Southern and true American way of life."

As the civil rights movement gained momentum, black studies were instituted in many schools and colleges. Some recent books in this area were realistic works, often including "street language" that was true and appropriate for their settings. In some communities in the late 1960s, these books were banned, even for elective reading, on grounds of vulgarity. In Connecticut, late in 1972, conservatives in Ridgefield objected to Eldridge Cleaver's *Soul on Ice* (McGraw-Hill; Dell); however, all but one of many residents at a school board hearing defended it vigorously.

In the late 1970s an upsurge of militantly fundamentalist Protestantism was reflected in a demand that the "creationist" theory of the development of species—the view of Biblical literalists—be included in schoolbooks. Despite opposition by major religious bodies and by scientists, the California Board of Education voted at the end of 1972 that science textbooks used in the state must be edited along this line and that "scientific dogmatism" must be eliminated.

In 1973, scattered attacks on books and teachers followed the June 21 U.S. Supreme Court decisions making censorship subject to local standards. A teacher in Drake, Iowa, who had assigned *Slaughterhouse-Five* to high school English classes was threatened with dismissal; and for assigning the same book in McBee, South Carolina, a teacher was charged with circulating obscenity.

In 1974, rural fundamentalist parents in Kanawha County, West Virginia, picketed schools and school buses to protest what seemed to them to be "trashy" and "godless" textbooks thrust upon their children. These books were for the most part anthologies of poetry, drama, fiction, and journalistic writing, used mostly in the upper grades and as discretionary, supplementary reading. Coal mines and schools in the area were closed while the picketing was in progress.

Among episodes in 1975, the Butler, Pennsylvania, school board banned a Fawcett anthology, *Contemporary American Short Stories*, because of an excerpt from *Invisible Man* by Ralph Ellison. Toward the end of the same year, in Mississippi, the Catholic and Episcopal dioceses jointly sued the state school authorities for permission to use a Pantheon textbook, *Mississippi: Conflict and Change* by Loewen and Sallis, since the only state history books already authorized ignored the problem of white supremacy.

Selection of books to be used as course material, supplementary reading, or reference had led to various attacks upon school libraries, not only on the books. In Alabama, for instance, in 1959, the state legislature censured the state's public library service division for distributing an issue of the American Library Association's annual list, *Notable Books*, because it named Martin Luther King's *Stride Toward Freedom* (Harper); and the state's Ku Klux Klan cited *Two Is a Team* by Lorraine and Jerrold Beim (Harcourt), among other "pro-integration" books. About ten years later, the school board of a northern town, Roselle, New Jersey, barred the high school librarian from circulating J. K. Galbraith's *The Affluent Society* (Houghton Mifflin, NAL); Robert Lekachman's *The Age of Keynes* (McGraw-Hill); and William Ebenstein's *Today's Isms* (Prentice-Hall). In 1972, a district board in New York City (Borough of Queens) required a junior high school library to remove *Down These Mean Streets* by Piri Thomas (Knopf, NAL).

Early in 1976, Howard County, Maryland, authorities required school media centers to remove, among other books, Tom Wolfe's *The Electric Kool-Aid Acid Test* (Farrar, Straus & Giroux; Bantam), and *Drug Abuse and What We Can Do about It* by Bennett and Demos, from a medical publisher, C. C. Thomas. In 1972 the school board of Strongville, Ohio, forced withdrawal of Joseph Heller's *Catch 22* (Simon & Schuster; Dell) and Kurt Vonnegut, Jr.'s *Cat's Cradle* and *God Bless You, Mr. Rosewater* (Dell) from school libraries; but the faculty's power to use the books was upheld by a circuit court decision in 1976.

In March 1975, the Island Trees School District on Long Island, in New York, gained notoriety by making unavailable, for several months, various Vonnegut titles, *The Naked Ape* by Desmond Morris (McGraw-Hill; Dell); *The Fixer* by Bernard Malamud (Farrar, Straus & Giroux; Dell); and *Black Boy* by Richard Wright (Harper & Row).

That incidents of these kinds were still occurring in 1977 was shown by the Chelsea, Massachusetts, school library banning of the Larrick-Merriam anthology, *Male and Female under 18* (Avon), and by other episodes: the removal of all sex education books from the Brighton, Michigan, school libraries; removal from the Morgantown, West Virginia, high school library of *Our Bodies, Ourselves* by the Boston Women's Health Collective (Simon & Schuster); and a six-county school board ruling in Maine that John Updike's *Rabbit Run* (Knopf, Crest) could be circulated only by parental permission.

Censorship of Mass-Market Paperbound Books

Mass-market paperbacks, because of their easy accessibility through a vast number and diversity of outlets, and their relatively low prices, have had an immense though unmeasured effect upon American culture and in the process have induced cultural shock in many a community. The most popular releases sell high into the hundreds of thousands, sometimes into the millions. They are therefore ubiquitous, inescapable—and, when some groups are offended or troubled by them—vulnerable.

But it is not usually those with the most lurid and obvious covers—a little passé, anyway, by 1978—that invite attempts to censor. More often, objections are raised to books which have had serious critical acclaim, some of which employ the common language, four-letter words and all, and present clearly the realities of sex and society.

As sections of this appendix show, paperbacks used in schools in one way or another are the books most likely to disturb some parents and others. Teachers and librarians have taken much abuse for recommending certain books, and parents have been divided in vehement debate over desirability of making certain paperback editions of modern literature available to young readers.

The attack on paperbacks goes back many years. In 1950, the James Morton News Agency in Des Moines, Iowa, was raided by local authorities for possessing "obscene" books. These turned out to be titles in paperback by John Steinbeck, Mackinlay Kantor, and W. Somerset Maugham, and a volume in the Pocket Books art series, *Old Master Paintings*. A group of local church women had become overheated about paperbacks; politicians overresponded; and the city's press poured ridicule on the whole proceeding.

In the spring of 1961, an Oklahoma City group called Mothers United for Decency hired a trailer, dubbed it a "smutmobile" and set up an interior display of paperbound books they deemed objectionable. The "smutmobile" was pointedly parked in front of the State Legislature building and thrown open to the adult public. Among the paperbacks on view inside were *Lust for Life* (Pocket Books), *Sons and Lovers* (Modern Library), *Tobacco Road* (NAL), *God's Little Acre* (NAL), and *Male and Female* (NAL), by Margaret Mead.

At least four Chicago paperback outlets were involved in a 1962 three-month, one-woman crusade against smut. The deeply religious mother of a grown son and teenage daughter was eventually arrested for gluing shut the pages of dozens of paperbacks she felt should not be opened by children.

In 1963 the Supreme Court made clear the minimum condition under which a state or local censorship committee's or commission's activities can remotely be considered constitutional. The case centered around a Rhode Island statute which three years earlier had created a Commission to Encourage Morality in Youth. The Commission issued lists of publications it considered harmful to youth, with the result that books were removed from sale without adjudication of whether or not they were in fact obscene. Four paperback publishers challenged the Rhode Island system through two rounds in the state courts and into the Supreme Court, which ruled the censorship activities of the Commission unconstitutional in an 8–1 decision. The majority opinion stated: "We are not the first court to look through forms to the substance and recognize that informal censorship may sufficiently inhibit the circulation of publications to warrant injunctive relief. . . . It would be naïve to credit the State's assertion that these blacklists are in the nature of mere legal advice, when they plainly serve as instruments of regulation independent of the laws against obscenity." A commission such as the Rhode Island one, the Court concluded, must at the very least be under direct supervision of the judiciary, and judicial review of such a commission's decisions must be immediately available.

Bawdy satire made accessible through a paperback aroused the anger of some police groups in 1967. The book was *The Sex Life of a Cop* by Oscar Peck, issued by a small publisher, Saber Books, in Los Angeles. News wholesalers who handled it in Grand Rapids, Michigan, were convicted and severely sentenced; the sentences were quashed by the U.S. Supreme Court.

In 1973, one initial reaction to the high court's local-standards decisions was the shredding of the Greenleaf paperback editions of books by Henry Miller. The publisher evidently felt he could no longer sell the books; but other paperback editions remain available.

For other comment on the banning of paperbacks, see the section entitled "School Textbooks and School Libraries" immediately preceding this section.

Censorship in "A Good Cause"

In one sense, virtually all censorship is for "a good cause" in the eyes of the would-be censor, whether it be to maintain purity of religious doctrine or of morals; to protect a nation from subversion, frustrate a military enemy, or preserve civil harmony; or to serve other purposes that are thought to be proper. Yet, as the late attorney Morris L. Ernst pointed out in an earlier edition of this book, all the efforts are the result of fear; and civil libertarians believe that this fear is needless in many cases, exaggerated in most. In this view, there is usually more to be feared from censorship itself than from the things censored.

Whether the civil libertarians are right about this is a subject of heartfelt debate when it comes to writings or other communication that could, conceivably, incite or sustain racial, religious, or ethnic prejudice.

To cite one example in this connection, the constitution of the National Association for the Advancement of Colored People directs local branches to study "material used in the schools and seek to eliminate material therefrom which is racially derogatory." Under this directive, the NAACP has mounted attacks on Stephen Foster songs in music books, sections of history books pertaining to the Civil War, and literature anthologies containing *Huckleberry Finn.*

Like the NAACP, the Anti-Defamation League of B'nai B'rith has sought to eliminate racial stereotypes in school materials. In the past, ADL has opposed school use of *Merchant of Venice* and *Oliver Twist*, containing characterizations often seen as anti-Semitic. On the positive side, the organization has joined with others in urging greater public and in-school education about the mass genocide—the Holocaust—practiced by Nazi Germany against the Jews.

In 1976, an Italian-American group spoke out against Mario Puzo's *The Godfather* (Putnam; Crest) for its use of the term *mafia* in a way that was felt by critics to place Italians generally under this unpleasant label. At about the same time, the Anti-Defamation League criticized *Lansky* by Hank Messick (Putnam), also on grounds of furthering ethnic prejudice.

The women's liberation movement in the 1960s and 1970s was meanwhile raising consciousness of the fact that many schoolbooks and other books for children reinforced traditional gender roles of both girls and boys, roles that tended to set limits on the capacities of each, and preserve an inferior status for girls and women. Similar insensitivity, it was argued, was shown not only in attitudes toward racial and ethnic groups, but also toward age groups, the physically disadvantaged, urban versus rural and suburban ways of life, and so on. During the 1970s, many new titles and new editions of school textbooks and children's books reflected these perceptions. Few if any informed persons regarded the resulting textual changes as censorship.

However, when the Council on Interracial Books for Children (which has played a valuable role in fostering more sensitive attitudes) recommended that certain established books be removed entirely from open shelves, some observers complained that the search for balance was veering over into censorship. Cases in point were some long-beloved books for children. Among those attacked were the folktale about an East Indian child, *Little Black Sambo* by Helen Bannerman (Platt & Munk); the *Doctor Doolittle* books by Hugh Lofting (Lippincott); and *Five Chinese Brothers* by Claire Huchet Bishop (Coward, McCann & Geoghegan).

Racial, sexual, and ethnic interests are not the only ones that demand what others might call censorship. Some business groups have campaigned against textbooks that offended their interpretations of free enterprise or exposed unsavory business practices. In a few cases, people concerned with upholding respect for the police have raised objections. Books supposedly offensive to policemen included, in 1972, *Boss*, Mike Royko's biography of Mayor Daley of Chicago (Dutton; NAL), attacked in Connecticut; *The Inner City Mother Goose* by Eve Meriam (Simon & Schuster), a target in several cities; and, in 1977, William Steig's *Sylvester and the Magic Pebble* (Simon & Schuster; Dutton).

Finally, some prominent individuals and one great university have complained about books that they felt invaded their privacy or cast aspersions upon their reputations or those of their forebears. Several cases of this sort (some are cited in the body of this book) turned up in the midsixties. They involved: a Citadel Press book about Bob Dylan; *Howard Hughes* by John Keats (Random); *Papa Hemingway* by A. E. Hotchner (Random); *The Warren Spahn Story* by Milton J. Shapiro (Messner); material about Henry Clay Frick in a textbook by Sylvester Stevens (Random); *The Death of a President* by William Manchester (Harper & Row); a biography of President Harding by Francis Russell (McGraw-Hill); *Life with Picasso* by Françoise Gilot (McGraw-Hill); and a comic novel about the University of Notre Dame, *John Goldfarb, Please Come Home* by William Peter Blatty (Doubleday). (The university thought Blatty's book and the related movie exploited its name and prestige, but a U.S. Court of Appeals declined to bar distribution.)

APPENDIX 2

Statements on Freedom of the Press

From *Areopagitica*

The Preciousness of a Good Book—I deny not, but that it is of greatest concernment in the Church and Commonwealth, to have a vigilant eye how Bookes demeane themselves as well as men; and thereafter to confine, imprison, and do sharpest justice on them as malefactors: For Books are not absolutely dead things, but doe contain a potencie of life in them to be as active as that soule was whose progeny they are; nay, they do preserve as in a violl the purest efficacie and extraction of that living intellect that bred them. I know they are as lively, and as vigorously productive, as those fabulous Dragons teeth; and being sown up and down, may chance to spring up armed men. And yet on the other hand unlesse warinesse be us'd, as good almost kill a man as kill a good Book; who kills a man kills a reasonable creature, God's Image; but he who destroyes a good Booke, kills reason itselfe, kills the Image of God, as it were in the eye. Many a man lives a burden to the Earth; but a good Booke is the pretious life-blood of a master spirit, imbalm'd and treasur'd up on purpose to a life beyond life. 'Tis true, no age can restore a life, whereof perhaps there is no great losse; and revolutions of ages doe not oft recover the losse of a rejected truth, for the want of which whole Nations fare the worse. We should be wary therefore what persecution we raise against the living labours of publick men, how we spill that season'd life of man preserv'd and stor'd up in Books; since we see a kind of homicide may be thus committed, sometimes a martyrdome; and if it extend to the whole impression, a kinde of massacre, whereof the execution ends not in the slaying of an elementall life, but strikes at that ethereall and fift(h) essence, the breath of reason itselfe, slaies an immortality rather than a life.

A Speech by John Milton for the Liberty of Unlicenced Printing to the Parliament of England, London 1644

From Thomas Jefferson's Writings

I have sworn upon the altar of God eternal hostility against every form of tyranny over the mind of man.

Letter to Benjamin Rush, 1800

Equal and exact justice to all men, of whatever state or persuasion, religious or political; . . . freedom of religion; freedom of the press; freedom of person under the protection of the habeas corpus; and trials by juries impartially selected,—these principles form the bright constellation which has gone before us, and guided our steps through an age of revolution and reformation.

First Inaugural Address, 1801

From *On Liberty*

Who can compute what the world loses in the multitude of promising intellects combined with timid characters, who dare not follow out any bold, vigorous, independent train of thought, lest it should land them in something which would admit of being considered irreligious or immoral? . . . No one can be a great thinker who does not recognize that as a thinker it is his first duty to follow his intellect to whatever conclusions it may lead . . .

By John Stuart Mill, 1859

From Amendments to the Constitution of the United States

Article I

Freedom of religion, of speech, of the press, and right of petition. —Congress shall make no law respecting an establishment of religion, or prohibiting the free exercise thereof; or abridging the freedom of speech, or of the press; or the right of the people peaceably to assemble, and to petition the Government for a redress of grievances.

Article XIV. Section 1

Citizenship defined; privileges of citizens.—All persons born or naturalized in the United States, and subject to the jurisdiction thereof, are citizens of the United States and of the State wherein they reside. No State shall make or enforce any law which shall abridge the privileges or immunities of citizens of the United States; nor shall any State deprive any person of life, liberty, or property, without due process of law; nor deny to any person within its jurisdiction the equal protection of the laws.

Library Bill of Rights

The Council of the American Library Association reaffirms its belief in the following basic policies which should govern the services of all libraries:

1. As a responsibility of library service, books and other library materials selected should be chosen for values of interest, information, and enlightenment of all the people of the community. In no case should library materials be excluded because of the race or nationality or the social, political, or religious views of the authors.

2. Libraries should provide books and other materials presenting all points of view concerning the problems and issues of our times; no library materials should be proscribed or removed from libraries because of partisan or doctrinal disapproval.

3. Censorship should be challenged by libraries in the maintenance of their responsibility to provide public information and enlightenment.

4. Libraries should cooperate with all persons and groups concerned with resisting abridgment of free expression and free access to ideas.

5. The rights of an individual to the use of a library should not be denied or abridged because of age, race, religion, national origins or social or political views.

6. As an institution of education for democratic living, the library should welcome the use of its meeting rooms for socially useful and cultural activities and discussion of current public questions. Such meeting places should be available on equal terms to all groups in the community regardless of the beliefs and affiliations of their members, provided that the meetings be open to the public.

Adopted June 18, 1948, amended February 1, 1961 and June 27, 1967, by the ALA Council. By official action of the council on February 3, 1951, the Library Bill of Rights shall be interpreted to apply to all materials and media of communication used or collected by libraries.

The President's Letter on Intellectual Freedom
to the ALA Meeting in Annual Convention
at Los Angeles, 1953

The White House,
Washington, D.C.
June 24, 1953

Dear Dr. Downs:

Thank you for your letter of June 15. I am glad to know of the annual conference of the American Library Association convening this week, and of the spirit of conscientious citizenship ruling its deliberations.

Our librarians serve the precious liberties of our nation: freedom of inquiry, freedom of the spoken and the written word, freedom of exchange of ideas.

Upon these clear principles, democracy depends for its very life, for they are the great sources of knowledge and enlightenment. And knowledge— full, unfettered knowledge of its own heritage, of freedom's enemies, of the whole world of men and ideas—this knowledge is a free people's surest strength.

The converse is just as surely true. A democracy smugly disdainful of new ideas would be a sick democracy. A democracy chronically fearful of new ideas would be a dying democracy.

For all these reasons, we must in these times be intelligently alert not only to the fanatic cunning of Communist conspiracy—but also to the grave dangers in meeting fanaticism with ignorance. For, in order to fight totalitarians who exploit the ways of freedom to serve their own ends, there are some zealots who—with more wrath than wisdom—would adopt a strangely unintelligent course. They would try to defend freedom by denying freedom's friends the opportunity of studying Communism in its entirety—its plausibilities, its falsities, its weaknesses.

But we know that freedom cannot be served by the devices of the tyrant. As it is an ancient truth that freedom cannot be legislated into existence, so it is no less obvious that freedom cannot be censored into existence. And any who act as if freedom's defenses are to be found in suppression and suspicion and fear confess a doctrine that is alien to America.

The libraries of America are and must ever remain the homes of free, inquiring minds. To them, our citizens—of all ages and races, of all creeds and political persuasions—must ever be able to turn with clear confidence that there they can freely seek the whole truth, unwarped by fashion and uncompromised by expediency. For in such whole and healthy knowledge alone are to be found and understood those majestic truths of man's nature and destiny that prove, to each succeeding generation, the validity of freedom.

Sincerely,
Dwight D. Eisenhower

The Freedom to Read

[Concerned about threats to free communication of ideas, more than 30 librarians, publishers, and others conferred at Rye, N.Y., May 2–3, 1953. Luther Evans was chairman. A committee was appointed to prepare a statement to be made public. This was endorsed officially by the American Library Association Council on June 25, 1953, and subsequently by the American Book Publishers Council (ABPC), American Booksellers Association, Book Manufacturers' Institute, and other national groups. In the light of later developments, a somewhat revised version was prepared after much consultation, and was approved in 1972 by the ALA Council, Association of American Publishers (successor to ABPC and American Educational Publishers Institute), and subsequently by many other book industry, communications, educational, cultural, and public service organizations. (See *Intellectual Freedom Manual*, ALA, 1974 and 1975. The 1972 revision follows.)]

The freedom to read is essential to our democracy. It is continuously under attack. Private groups and public authorities in various parts of the country are working to remove books from sale, to censor textbooks, to label "controversial" books, to distribute lists of "objectionable" books or authors, and to purge libraries. These actions apparently rise from a view that our national tradition of free expression is no longer valid; that censorship and suppression are needed to avoid the subversion of politics and the corruption of morals. We, as citizens devoted to the use of books and as librarians and publishers responsible for disseminating them, wish to assert the public interest in the preservation of the freedom to read.

We are deeply concerned about these attempts at suppression. Most such attempts rest on a denial of the fundamental premise of democracy: that the ordinary citizen, by exercising his critical judgment, will accept the good and reject the bad. The censors, public and private, assume that they should determine what is good and what is bad for their fellow-citizens.

We trust Americans to recognize propaganda, and to reject it. We do not believe they need the help of censors to assist them in this task. We do not believe they are prepared to sacrifice their heritage of a free press in order to be "protected" against what others think may be bad for them. We believe they still favor free enterprise in ideas and expression.

We are aware, of course, that books are not alone in being subjected to efforts at suppression. We are aware that these efforts are related to a larger pattern of pressures being brought against education, the press, films, radio, and television. The problem is not only one of actual censorship. The shadow of fear cast by these pressures leads, we suspect, to an even larger voluntary curtailment of expression by those who seek to avoid controversy.

Such pressure toward conformity is perhaps natural to a time of uneasy change and pervading fear. Especially when so many of our apprehensions are directed against an ideology, the expression of a dissident idea becomes a thing feared in itself, and we tend to move against it as against a hostile deed, with suppression.

And yet suppression is never more dangerous than in such a time of social tension. Freedom has given the United States the elasticity to endure strain. Freedom keeps open the path of novel and creative solutions, and enables change to come by choice. Every silencing of a heresy, every enforcement of an orthodoxy, diminishes the toughness and resilience of our society and leaves it the less able to deal with stress.

Now as always in our history, books are among our greatest instruments of freedom. They are almost the only means for making generally available ideas or manners of expression that can initially command only a small audience. They are the natural medium for the new idea and the untried voice from which come the original contributions to social growth. They are essential to the extended discussion which serious thought requires, and to the accumulation of knowledge and ideas into organized collections.

We believe that free communication is essential to the preservation of a free society and a creative culture. We believe that these pressures towards conformity present the danger of limiting the range and variety of inquiry and expression on which our democracy and our culture depend. We believe that every American community must jealously guard the freedom to publish and to circulate, in order to preserve its own freedom to read. We believe that publishers and librarians have a profound responsibility to give validity to that freedom to read by making it possible for the reader to choose freely from a variety of offerings.

The freedom to read is guaranteed by the Constitution. Those with faith in free men will stand firm on these constitutional guarantees of essential rights and will exercise the responsibilities that accompany these rights.

We therefore affirm these propositions:

1. *It is in the public interest for publishers and librarians to make available the widest diversity of views and expressions, including those which are unorthodox or unpopular with the majority.*

Creative thought is by definition new, and what is new is different. The bearer of every new thought is a rebel until his idea is refined and tested. Totalitarian systems attempt to maintain themselves in power by the ruthless suppression of any concept which challenges the established orthodoxy. The power of a democratic system to adapt to change is vastly strengthened by the freedom of its citizens to choose widely from among conflicting opinions offered freely to them. To stifle every nonconformist idea at birth would mark the end of the democratic process. Furthermore, only through the constant activity of weighing and selecting can the democratic mind attain the strength demanded by times like these. We need to know not only what we believe but why we believe it.

2. *Publishers, librarians, and booksellers do not need to endorse every idea or presentation contained in the books they make available. It would conflict with the public interest for them to establish their own political, moral, or aesthetic views as the sole standard for determining what books should be published or circulated.*

Publishers and librarians serve the educational process by helping to make available knowledge and ideas required for the growth of the mind and the increase of learning. They do not foster education by imposing as mentors the patterns of their own thought. The people should have the freedom to read and consider a broader range of ideas than those that may be held by any single librarian or publisher or government or church. It is wrong that what one man can read should be confined to what another thinks proper.

3. *It is contrary to the public interest for publishers or librarians to determine the acceptability of a book solely on the basis of the personal history or political affiliations of the author.*

A book should be judged as a book. No art or literature can flourish if it is to be measured by the political views or private lives of its creators. No society of free men can flourish which draws up lists of writers to whom it will not listen, whatever they may have to say.

4. *There is no place in our society for extra-legal efforts to coerce the taste of others, to confine adults to the reading matter deemed suitable for adolescents, or to inhibit the efforts of writers to achieve artistic expression.*

To some, much of modern literature is shocking. But is not much of life itself shocking? We cut off literature at the source if we prevent serious artists from dealing with the stuff of life. Parents and teachers have a responsibility to prepare the young to meet the diversity of experiences in life to which they will be exposed, as they have a responsibility to help them learn to think critically for themselves. These are affirmative responsibilities, not discharged simply by preventing them from reading works for which they are not yet prepared. In these matters taste differs, and taste cannot be legislated; nor can machinery be devised which will suit the demands of one group without limiting the freedom of others.

5. *It is not in the public interest to force a reader to accept with any book the prejudgment of a label characterizing the book or author as subversive or dangerous.*

The idea of labelling presupposes the existence of individuals or groups with wisdom to determine by authority what is good or bad for the citizen. It presupposes that each individual must be directed in making up his mind about the ideas he examines. But Americans do not need others to do their thinking for them.

6. *It is the responsibility of publishers and librarians, as guardians of the people's freedom to read, to contest encroachments upon that freedom*

*by individuals or groups seeking to impose their own standards or tastes
upon the community at large.*

It is inevitable in the give and take of the democratic process that the
political, the moral, or the aesthetic concepts of an individual or group will
occasionally collide with those of another individual or group. In a free
society each individual is free to determine for himself what he wishes to
read, and each group is free to determine what it will recommend to its
freely associated members. But no group has the right to take the law into
its own hands, and to impose its own concept of politics or morality upon
other members of a democratic society. Freedom is no freedom if it is
accorded only to the accepted and the inoffensive.

7. *It is the responsibility of publishers and librarians to give full meaning to
   the freedom to read by providing books that enrich the quality of
   thought and expression. By the exercise of this affirmative responsibility, bookmen can demonstrate that the answer to a bad book is a good
   one, the answer to a bad idea is a good one.*

The freedom to read is of little consequence when expended on the
trivial; it is frustrated when the reader cannot obtain matter fit for his
purpose. What is needed is not only the absence of restraint, but the
positive provision of opportunity for the people to read the best that can be
thought and said. Books are the major channel by which the intellectual
inheritance is handed down, and the principal means of its testing and
growth. The defense of their freedom and integrity, and the enlargement of
their service to society, requires of all bookmen the utmost of their
faculties, and deserves of all citizens the fullest of their support.

We state these propositions neither lightly nor as easy generalizations.
We here stake out a lofty claim for the value of books. We do so because we
believe that they are good, possessed of enormous variety and usefulness,
worthy of cherishing and keeping free. We realize that the application of
these propositions may mean the dissemination of ideas and manners of
expression that are repugnant to many persons. We do not state these
propositions in the comfortable belief that what people read is
unimportant. We believe rather that what people read is deeply important;
that ideas can be dangerous; but that the suppression of ideas is fatal to a
democratic society. Freedom itself is a dangerous way of life, but it is ours.

[The members of the 1953 drafting committee and signers of the
statement were Luther Evans, Librarian of Congress; ALA President
Robert Downs, librarian, University of Illinois; Douglas Black, president,
Doubleday & Co.; Arthur Houghton, Jr., president, Steuben Glass;
Harold Lasswell, professor of law and political science, Yale Law School;
John M. Cory, chief, Circulation Department, New York Public Library;
William Dix, chairman, ALA Committee on Intellectual Freedom, and
librarian, Princeton University; and Dan Lacy, managing director, ABPC.

Signers of the statement in addition to those who prepared it were: Bernard Berelson, director, Behavioral Sciences division, Ford Foundation; Mrs. Barry Bingham, Louisville *Courier-Journal*; Paul Bixler, librarian, Antioch College; Charles G. Bolté, executive secretary, ABPC; Cass Canfield, chairman, Harper & Bros., member, ABPC Committee on Reading Development; Robert Carr, professor of law and politics, Dartmouth; David H. Clift, executive secretary, ALA; Harold K. Guinzburg, president, Viking Press, chairman ABPC Committee on Reading Development; Richard Barnes Kennan, secretary, Commission for the Defense of Democracy through Education, National Education Association; Chester Kerr, secretary, Yale University Press, chairman, Committee on Freedom to Publish, Association of American University Presses; Lloyd King, executive secretary, American Textbook Publishers Institute; Donald S. Klopfer, secretary and treasurer, Random House, chairman, ABPC Anti-Censorship Committee; Alfred A. Knopf, president, Alfred A. Knopf, Inc.; David E. Lilienthal, lawyer; Milton Lord, librarian, Boston Public Library; Flora Belle Ludington, librarian, Mt. Holyoke College, newly-installed president, ALA; Horace Manges, counsel, ABPC; Ralph McGill, editor, Atlanta *Constitution*; Robert K. Merton, professor of sociology, Columbia; John O'Connor, president, Grosset & Dunlap, immediate past president, ABPC; Leo Rosten, author; A. Ruth Rutzen, director, Home Reading Services, Detroit Public Library; Francis St. John, librarian, Brooklyn Public Library; Whitney North Seymour, former president, Association of the Bar of the City of New York; Theodore Waller, editorial vice-president, New American Library, former managing director, ABPC; Bethuel M. Webster, Association of the Bar of the City of New York, counsel, the Fund for the Republic; Victor Weybright, chairman and editor, NAL, chairman, ABPC Reprinters Committee; Thomas J. Wilson, director, Harvard University Press, immediate past president, AAUP.]

APPENDIX 3

Excerpts from Important Court Decisions

From the Opinion of Alexander Cockburn, Lord Chief Justice of England

Queen v. *Hicklin and* The Confessional Unmasked, 1868 (Known as the Hicklin Rule on Obscenity)

I think the test of obscenity is this, whether the tendency of the matter charged as obscenity is to deprave and corrupt those whose minds are open to such immoral influences, and into whose hands a publication of this sort may fall.

From the Opinion of Judge Learned Hand, U.S. District Court, Southern District of New York

United States v. *Mitchell Kennerley and* Hagar Revelly, 1913 (Protest against the Hicklin Rule)

. . . I hope it is not improper for me to say that the rule as laid down, however consonant it may be with mid-Victorian morals, (Cockburn opinion) does not seem to me to answer to the understanding and morality of the present time . . . I question whether in the end men will regard that as obscene which is honestly relevant to the adequate expression of innocent ideas, and whether they will not believe that truth and beauty are too precious to society at large to be mutilated in the interests of those most likely to pervert them to base uses. Indeed, it seems hardly likely that we are even to-day so lukewarm in our interest in letters or serious discussion as to be content to reduce our treatment of sex to the standard of a child's library in the supposed interest of a salacious few, or that shame will for long prevent us from adequate portrayal of some of the most serious and beautiful sides of human nature . . .

Yet, if the time is not yet when men think innocent all that which is honestly germane to a pure subject, however little it may mince its words, still I scarcely think that they would forbid all which might corrupt the most corruptible, or that society is prepared to accept for its own limitations those which may perhaps be necessary to the weakest of its members. If there be no abstract definition, such as I have suggested, should not the word "obscene" be allowed to indicate the present critical point in the compromise between candor and shame at which the community may have arrived here and now? . . . To put thought in leash to the average conscience of the time is perhaps tolerable, but to fetter it by the necessities of the lowest and least capable seems a fatal policy.

From the Opinion of Judge John Woolsey, U.S. District Court, Southern District of New York

United States v. Ulysses *and Random House, Inc.,* December 6, 1933

. . . in any case where a book is claimed to be obscene it must first be determined, whether the intent with which it was written was what is called, according to the usual phrase, pornographic,—that is, written for the purpose of exploiting obscenity.

. . . But in *Ulysses*, in spite of its unusual frankness, I do not detect anywhere the leer of the sensualist. I hold, therefore, that it is not pornographic.

. . . although it contains . . . many words usually considered dirty, I have not found anything that I consider to be dirt for dirt's sake.

. . . when such a real artist in words, as Joyce undoubtedly is, seeks to draw a true picture of the lower middle class in a European city, ought it to be impossible for the American public legally to see that picture?

. . . The statute under which the libel is filed only denounces, in so far as we are here concerned, the importation into the United States from any foreign country of "any obscene book."

. . . The meaning of the word "obscene" as legally defined by the Courts is: tending to stir the sex impulses or to lead to sexually impure and lustful thoughts.

. . . Whether a particular book would tend to excite such impulses and thoughts must be tested by the Court's opinion as to its effect on a person with average sex instincts.

. . . It is only with the normal person that the law is concerned.

. . . a book like *Ulysses* . . . is a sincere and serious attempt to devise a new literary method for the observation and description of mankind.

. . . I am quite aware that owing to some of its scenes *Ulysses* is a rather strong draught to ask some sensitive, though normal, persons to take. But my considered opinion, after long reflection, is that whilst in many places the effect of *Ulysses* on the reader undoubtedly is somewhat emetic, no where does it tend to be an aphrodisiac.

Ulysses may, therefore, be admitted into the United States.

From the Opinion of Judge Augustus N. Hand,
New York Circuit Court of Appeals

On an Appeal of the *Ulysses* Case, 1934

While any construction of the statute that will fit all cases is difficult, we believe that the proper test of whether a given book is obscene is its dominant effect. In applying this test, relevancy of the objectionable parts to the theme, the established reputation of the work in the estimation of approved critics, if the book is modern, and the verdict of the past, if it is ancient, are persuasive pieces of evidence; for works of art are not likely to sustain a high position with no better warrant for their existence than their obscene content.

From the Opinion of Judge Curtis Bok,
Court of Quarter Sessions, Philadelphia

State of Pennsylvania v. *Five Booksellers,*
March 18, 1949

. . . I hold that Section 524 may not constitutionally be applied to any writing unless it is sexually impure and pornographic. It may then be applied, as an exercise of the police power, only where there is a reasonable and demonstrable cause to believe that a crime or misdemeanor has been committed or is about to be committed as the perceptible result of the publication and distribution of the writing in question: the opinion of anyone that a tendency thereto exists or that such a result is self-evident is insufficient and irrelevant. The causal connection between the book and the criminal behavior must appear beyond a reasonable doubt.

. . . There is no such proof in the instant case.

. . . Section 524, for all its verbiage, is very bare. The full weight of the legislative prohibition dangles from the word "obscene" and its synonyms. Nowhere are these words defined; nowhere is the danger to be expected of them stated; nowhere is a standard of judgment set forth. I assume that "obscenity" is expected to have a familiar and inherent meaning, both as to what it is and as to what it does.

It is my purpose to show that it has no such inherent meaning; that different meanings given to it at different times are not constant, either historically or legally; and that it is not constitutionally indictable unless it takes the form of sexual impurity, i.e., "dirt for dirt's sake" and can be traced to actual criminal behavior, either actual or demonstrably imminent.

. . . I believe that the consensus of preference today is for disclosure and not stealth, for frankness and not hypocrisy, and for public and not secret distribution. That in itself is a moral code.

It is my opinion that frank disclosure cannot legally be censored, even as an exercise of the police power, unless it is sexually impure and pornographic.

. . . Who can define the clear and present danger to the community that arises from reading a book? If we say it is that the reader is young and inexperienced and incapable of resisting the sexual temptations that the book may present to him, we put the entire reading public at the mercy of the adolescent mind and of those adolescents who do not have the expected advantages of home influence, school training, or religious teaching. Nor can we say into how many such hands the book may come. . . . If the argument be applied to the general public, the situation becomes absurd, for then no publication is safe. . . .

From the Opinion of the U.S. Supreme Court
Roth v. *United States*, June 24, 1957

. . . All ideas having even the slightest redeeming social importance— unorthodox ideas, controversial ideas, even ideas hateful to the prevailing climate of opinion—have the full protection of the guaranties, unless excludable because they encroach upon the limited area of more important interests. But implicit in the history of the First Amendment is the rejection of obscenity as utterly without redeeming social importance. This rejection for that reason is mirrored in the universal judgment that obscenity should be restrained, reflected in the international agreement of over 50 nations, in the obscenity laws of all of the 48 states, and in the 20 obscenity laws enacted by the Congress from 1842 to 1956. . . . We hold that obscenity is not within the area of constitutionally protected speech or press.

. . . However, sex and obscenity are not synonymous. Obscene material is material which deals with sex in a manner appealing to prurient interest. The portrayal of sex, e.g., in art, literature and scientific works, is not itself sufficient reason to deny material the constitutional protection of freedom of speech and press. Sex, a great and mysterious motive force in human life, has indisputably been a subject of absorbing interest to mankind through the ages; it is one of the vital problems of human interest and public concern.

[The test for obscenity is] . . . whether to the average person, applying contemporary community standards, the dominant theme of the material taken as a whole appeals to prurient interest.

From the Opinion of the U.S. Supreme Court
Stanley v. *Georgia*, 1969

. . . If the First Amendment means anything, it means that the State has no business telling a man, sitting alone in his own house, what books he may read or what films he may watch. Our whole constitutional heritage rebels at the thought of giving government the power to control men's minds.

From the Opinion of the U.S. Supreme Court

United States v. *New York Times Company et al.*
United States v. *Washington Post Company et al.*
June 30, 1971

"Any system of prior restraints of expression comes to this Court bearing a heavy presumption against its constitutional validity." *Bantam Books, Inc.* v. *Sullivan*, 372 U.S. 58, 70 (1963); see also *Near* v. *Minnesota*, 283 U.S. 697 (1931). The Government "thus carries a heavy burden of showing justification for the enforcement of such a restraint.". . .

The District Court for the Southern District of New York in the *New York Times* case and the District Court for the District of Columbia and the Court of Appeals for the District of Columbia Circuit in the *Washington Post* case held that the Government had not met that burden. We agree.

Guidelines Stated in the Opinion of the U.S. Supreme Court

Miller v. *California*, June 21, 1973

[Guidelines for the determination of obscenity]

a. whether the average person, applying contemporary community standards, would find that the work, taken as a whole, appeals to the prurient interest . . .

b. whether the work depicts or describes, in a patently offensive way, sexual conduct specifically defined by the applicable state law; and

c. whether the work, taken as a whole, lacks serious literary, artistic, political, or scientific value.

[Also] To require a State to structure obscenity proceedings around evidence of a national "community standard" would be an exercise in futility. . . . people in different states vary in their tastes and attitudes and this diversity is not to be strangled by the absolutism of imposed uniformity.

Commission on Obscenity and Pornography (Excerpts from the Report)

[*Editor's Note:* The excerpts presented here are taken from *The Report of the Commission on Obscenity and Pornography,* an uncopyrighted U.S. government document, as printed in an edition published in 1970 by Random House in hardcover and by Bantam Books in paperback. The Random-Bantam edition includes copyrighted material, primarily a special introduction by Clive Barnes, then of the *New York Times,* which also published the government report.

The full official report (following a letter of transmittal to the President and Congress of the United States, and a list of Commission members and staff) consists of a preface and four parts: an overview of the findings, recommendations by the Commission as a whole, reports of special panels, and separate statements by Commission members—700 pages in all, from which a few highlights are given here.

The Commission consisted of 18 members, a senior staff of three, a professional staff of nine, and a support staff of nine. The various final recommendations were supported by majorities of different sizes, and there were some dissents on specific points; space does not permit their inclusion in these excerpts, nor does it permit selections from the interesting and detailed special reports by the staff.

Three members vehemently opposed the Commission majority report as a whole. Their views were included in the report among the separate statements by members, and are represented in the last section of this appendix.

The entire report deserves close attention by all who have faith in freedom. It is hoped that these selections will lead readers to the complete Random House or Bantam Books edition.—*C.B.G.*]

Preface

Congress, in Public Law 90–100, found the traffic in obscenity and pornography to be "a matter of national concern." The Federal Government was deemed to have a "responsibility to investigate the gravity of this situation and to determine whether such materials are harmful to the public, and particularly to minors, and whether more effective methods should be devised to control the transmission of such materials." To this end, the Congress established an advisory commission whose purpose was "after a thorough study which shall include a study of the causal relationship of such materials to antisocial behavior, to recommend advisable, appropriate, effective, and constitutional means to deal effectively with such traffic in obscenity and pornography."

Congress assigned four specific tasks:

"(1) with the aid of leading constitutional law authorities, to analyze the laws pertaining to the control of obscenity and pornography; and to evaluate and recommend definitions of obscenity and pornography;

"(2) to ascertain the methods employed in the distribution of obscene and pornographic materials and to explore the nature and volume of traffic in such materials;

"(3) to study the effect of obscenity and pornography upon the public, and particularly minors, and its relationship to crime and other antisocial behavior; and

"(4) to recommend such legislative, administrative, or other advisable and appropriate action as the Commission deems necessary to regulate effectively the flow of such traffic, without in any way interfering with constitutional rights."

Public Law 90–100 became law in October, 1967, and the President appointed members to the Commission in January, 1968. Funds were appropriated for the Commission's operation in July, 1968; at the same time the tenure of the Commission was extended to provide it the originally intended two years for its studies.

The Commission elected William B. Lockhart as chairman and Frederick H. Wagman as vice-chairman. The Commission then organized itself into four working panels: (1) Legal; (2) Traffic and Distribution; (3) Effects; and (4) Positive Approaches. It appointed a committee to recommend a director and a general counsel for the Commission's staff. . . .

The Commission fully subscribed from the beginning to the Congressional directive to make recommendations only after thorough study. To implement this approach, it was determined that confidentiality by Commission members should be maintained. This was felt to be necessary to encourage maximum exploration and free discussion of opinions, data and new ideas at meetings of the Commissioners, to enhance open and unbiased investigations in sensitive areas, to avoid public misinterpretations of research data and to prevent premature conclusions. Moreover, the Commissioners felt it was important, in order to avoid confusion as to the activities of the Commission, to have but one spokesman prior to the completion of its Report. Commissioner Charles H. Keating, Jr., a replacement [named by President Nixon] for one of the original Commissioners, did not subscribe to this decision after his appointment.

Because its initial survey of available information relating to the various tasks assigned by Congress amply demonstrated the insufficiency of existing factual evidence as a basis for recommendations, the Commission initiated a program of research designed to provide empirical information relevant to its tasks. The responsibility for the details of the research program was delegated to the four working panels which reported to the Commission on their progress and direction from time to time. The Commission's energies were devoted at the beginning principally to the design and implementation of the research program, at a later point to the assimilation and integration of the results of the research, and finally to the discussion of alternatives and the making of decisions regarding recommendations.

Some members of the Commission suggested that public hearings be held at the beginning of the Commission's life. The Commission concluded, however, that in the first stage of its work public hearings would not be a likely source of accurate data or a wise expenditure of its limited resources. Approximately 100 national organizations were invited to express their views on the problems of obscenity and pornography by submitting written statements, and views were also solicited from those involved in law enforcement, from the legal profession generally, and from constitutional law experts. The Commission left open the possibility of holding public hearings at a later date when it would be possible to invite witnesses to focus on particular issues and proposals as those evolved from the Commission's studies and discussions. Public hearings were held in Los Angeles, California, on May 4 and 5, 1970, and in Washington, D. C. on May 12 and 13, 1970. Fifty-five persons, representing law enforcement agencies, courts, government at many levels, civic organizations, writers, publishers, distributors, film producers, exhibitors, actors, librarians, teachers, youth organizations, parents and other interested groups, were invited to appear before the Commission. Thirty-one of these persons accepted the Commission's invitation. In addition, the Commission heard statements from numerous private citizens who attended the hearings. A broad spectrum of views was presented to the Commission through these hearings. . . .

Material may be deemed "obscene" because of a variety of contents:

religious, political, sexual, scatological, violent, etc. The Commission has limited its concern to sexual obscenity, including sadomasochistic material, because the legislative history indicated this as the focus of congessional concern as reflected by the linking of obscenity with pornography in the Act creating the Commission. The application of obscenity laws has been directed in recent times almost exclusively to sexual obscenity; indeed, court decisions regarding permissible legal definitions of the term "obscene" have appeared in recent years to delimit its application to such sexual obscenity. Thus, the Commission's inquiry was directed toward a wide range of explicit sexual depictions in pictorial and textual media.

Just as obscenity may involve a variety of contents and judgments, so also may "antisocial" behavior and moral character. A declining concern with established religions, new questions as to the wisdom and morality of war, changes in attitudes toward races and minorities, and conflicts regarding the responsibility of th · state to the individual and the individual to the state may all be considered to represent changes in the moral fiber of the nation. To some, these phenomena are considered to be signs of corroding moral decay; to others, signs of change and progress. It was impossible during the brief life of the Commission to obtain significant data on the effects of the exposure to pornography on nonsexual moral attitudes. Consequently, the Commission has focused on that type of antisocial behavior which tends to be more directly related to sex. This includes premarital intercourse, sex crimes, illegitimacy, and similar items.

Discussions of obscenity and pornography in the past have often been devoid of fact. Popular rhetoric has often contained a variety of estimates of the size of the "smut" industry and assertions regarding the consequences of the existence of these materials and exposure to them. Many of these statements, however, have had little anchoring in objective evidence. Within the limits of its time and resources, the Commission has sought, through staff and contract research, to broaden the factual basis for future continued discussion. The Commission is aware that not all issues of concern have been completely researched nor all questions answered. It also recognizes that the interpretations of a set of "facts" in arriving at policy implications may differ even among men of good will. Nevertheless, the Commission is convinced that on most issues regarding obscenity and pornography the discussion can be informed by important and often new facts. It presents its Report, hopeful that it will contribute to this discussion at a new level. Since it may be anticipated that in any controversial area some of the research will be questioned as to method and the validity and reliability of the results, the Commission hopes that responsible scientific organizations will carefully scrutinize these studies and that new and continuing research will result. . . .

Overview of Findings
Law and Law Enforcement*

FEDERAL STATUTES

. . . The cost to the federal government of enforcing the five federal statutes generally prohibiting the distribution of obscene materials appears to be at least $3 to $5 million per year. Enforcement of the Anti-Pandering Act has cost the Post Office about an additional $1 million per year. . . .

ADULT OBSCENITY STATUTES

Although upholding the constitutionality of broad prohibitions upon the dissemination of obscene materials, the Roth decision imposed a narrow standard for defining what is "obscene" under such prohibitions. Subsequent decisions have narrowed the permissible test even further.

The prevailing view today [until June 21, 1973—*Ed.*] in the Supreme Court of the United States, the lower federal courts and the courts of the States is that three criteria must all be met before the distribution of material may be generally prohibited for all persons, including adults, on the ground that it is "obscene." These criteria are: (1) the dominant theme of the material, taken as a whole, must appeal to a "prurient" interest in sex; (2) the material must be "patently offensive" because it affronts "contemporary community standards" regarding the depiction of sexual matters; and (3) the material must lack "redeeming social value." All three criteria must coalesce before material may be deemed "obscene" for adults. . . .

The results of empirical research regarding the application of the three constitutional criteria confirm the difficulties of application as well as their exceedingly narrow scope. Several studies have found that "arousingness" and "offensiveness" are independent dimensions when applied to sexual materials; that is, material that is offensive may or may not be arousing, and material that is arousing may or may not be offensive. Only a very restricted range of material seems to be capable of meeting both of these criteria for most people. Further, there is very little consensus among people regarding either the "arousingness" or the "offensiveness" of a given sexual depiction. . . .

*Other parts of this "Overview" deal with: volume of traffic and patterns of distribution of sexually oriented materials; effects of explicit sexual materials; and positive approaches—sex education, industry self-regulation, and citizens' action groups.

An additional and very significant limiting factor is introduced by the criterion of social value. In the national survey of American public opinion sponsored by the Commission, substantial portions of the population reported effects which might be deemed socially valuable from even the most explicit sexual materials. For example, about 60% of a representative sample of adult American men felt that looking or reading such materials would provide information about sex . . . [Among women] 35%, 24% and 21% reported, respectively, information, entertainment, and improved sexual relations in themselves or someone they personally knew as a result of looking at or reading very explicit sexual materials . . . two experimental studies found that a substantial number of married couples reported more agreeable and enhanced marital communication and an increased willingness to discuss sexual matters with each other after exposure to erotic stimuli.

In pursuit of its mandate from Congress to recommend definitions of obscenity which are consistent with constitutional rights, the Commission considered drafting a more satisfactory definition of "obscene" for inclusion in adult obscenity prohibitions, should such prohibitions appear socially warranted. To be satisfactory from the point of view of its enforcement and application, such a definition would have to describe the material to be proscribed with a high degree of objectivity and specificity, so that those subject to the law could know in advance what materials were prohibited and so that judicial decisions would not be based upon the subjective reactions of particular judges or jurors. In light of the empirical data, described above, showing both the lack of consensus among adults as to what is both arousing and offensive and the values attributed by substantial numbers of adults to even the most explicit sexual materials, the construction of such a definition for adults within constitutional limits would be extremely difficult. In any event, the Commission, as developed in its legislative recommendations set forth later in this Report, does not believe that a sufficient social justification exists for the retention or enactment of broad legislation prohibiting the consensual distribution of sexual materials to adults. . . .

SPECIFIC OBSCENITY STATUTES

. . . The areas of latitude for greater control overlap the areas of greatest public concern. Prosecuting attorneys who reported a serious community concern about obscenity to the Commission attributed this concern primarily to the thrusting of offensive materials upon unwilling recipients and to fear that materials would be distributed to minors. It is in these areas that effective legislative prohibitions may be formulated and enforced. . . .

A national survey of American public opinion sponsored by the Commission shows that a majority of American adults believe that adults should be allowed to read or see any sexual materials they wish. On the other hand, a substantial consensus of American adults favors prohibiting young persons access to some sexual materials. Almost half the population believes that laws against sexual materials are impossible to enforce. Americans also seem to have an inaccurate view of the opinions of others in their communities; the tendency is to believe that others in the community are more restrictive in outlook than they actually are.

Public opinion regarding restrictions on the availability of explicit sexual materials is, however, quite divided in several ways. Principally this split of opinion is related to the characteristics of the person expressing the attitude and the issue of potential harmfulness of the material. . . .

POTENTIALITY OF HARMFUL EFFECTS

When questioned as to whether they favored access of adults or young persons to sexually explicit materials, about 40% of all the respondents on the national survey made their responses contingent on the issue of whether or not such materials cause harm. About two-thirds of the persons who favor no legal restrictions said their views would be changed if it were clearly demonstrated that certain materials have harmful effects. On the other hand, about one-third of the persons who favor some restrictions or extensive restrictions would change their views if it were clearly demonstrated that sexual materials have no harmful effects.

OBSCENITY LAWS IN OTHER COUNTRIES

. . . Advisory commissions in countries other than the United States have, like this Commission, all concluded that consensual exposure of adults to explicit sexual materials causes no demonstrable damaging individual or social effects.

Recommendations of the Commission

Non-Legislative Recommendations

The Commission believes that much of the "problem" regarding materials which depict explicit sexual activity stems from the inability or reluctance of people in our society to be open and direct in dealing with sexual matters. This most often manifests itself in the inhibition of talking openly and directly about sex. Professionals use highly technical language when they discuss sex; others of us escape by using euphemisms—or by not talking about sex at all. Direct and open conversation about sex between parent and child is too rare in our society.

Failure to talk openly and directly about sex has several consequences. It overemphasizes sex, gives it a magical, nonnatural quality, making it more attractive and fascinating. It diverts the expression of sexual interest out of more legitimate channels, into less legitimate channels. Such failure makes teaching children and adolescents to become fully and adequately functioning sexual adults a more difficult task. And it clogs legitimate channels for transmitting sexual information and forces people to use clandestine and unreliable sources.

The Commission believes that interest in sex is normal, healthy, good. Interest in sex begins very early in life and continues throughout the life cycle although the strength of this interest varies from stage to stage. With the onset of puberty, physiological and hormonal changes occur which both quicken interest and make the individual more responsive to sexual interest. The individual needs information about sex in order to understand himself, place his new experiences in a proper context, and cope with his new feelings. . . .

The Commission believes that accurate, appropriate sex information provided openly and directly through legitimate channels and from reliable sources in healthy contexts can compete successfully with potentially distorted, warped, inaccurate, and unreliable information from clandestine, illegitimate sources; and it believes that the attitudes and orientations toward sex produced by the open communication of appropriate sex information from reliable sources through legitimate channels will be normal and healthy, providing a solid foundation for the basic institutions of our society.

The Commission, therefore, presents the following positive approaches to deal with the problem of obscenity and pornography.

1. The Commission recommends that a massive sex education effort be launched. . . .

(a) its purpose should be to contribute to healthy attitudes and orientations to sexual relationships so as to provide a sound foundation for our society's basic institutions of marriage and family;

(b) it should be aimed at achieving an acceptance of sex as a normal and natural part of life and of oneself as a sexual being;

(c) it should not aim for orthodoxy; rather it should be designed to allow for a pluralism of values;

(d) it should be based on facts and encompass not only biological and physiological information but also social, psychological, and religious information;

(e) it should be differentiated so that content can be shaped appropriately for the individual's age, sex, and circumstances;

(f) it should be aimed, as appropriate, to all segments of our society, adults as well as children and adolescents;

(g) it should be a joint function of several institutions of our society: family, school, church, etc.;

(h) special attention should be given to the training of those who will have central places in the legitimate communication channels—parents, teachers, physicians, clergy, social service workers, etc.;

(i) it will require cooperation of private and public organizations at local, regional, and national levels with appropriate funding;

(j) it will be aided by the imaginative utilization of new educational technologies for example, educational television could be used to reach several members of a family in a family context.

The Commission feels that such a sex education program would provide a powerful positive approach to the problems of obscenity and pornography. By providing accurate and reliable sex information through legitimate sources, it would reduce interest in and dependence upon clandestine and less legitimate sources. By providing healthy attitudes and orientations toward sexual relationships, it would provide better protection for the individual against distorted or warped ideas he may encounter regarding sex. By providing greater ease in talking about sexual matters in appropriate contexts, the shock and offensiveness of encounters with sex would be reduced.

2. The Commission recommends continued open discussion, based on factual information, on the issues regarding obscenity and pornography.

Discussion has in the past been carried on with few facts available and the debate has necessarily reflected, to a large extent, prejudices and fears. Congress asked the Commission to secure more factual information before making recommendations. Some of the facts developed by the Commission are contrary to widely held assumptions. These findings provide new perspectives on the issues.

The information developed by the Commission should be given wide distribution, so that it may sharpen the issues and focus the discussion.

3. The Commission recommends that additional factual information be developed.

The Commission's effort to develop information has been limited by time, financial resources, and the paucity of previously existing research. Many of its findings are tentative and many questions remain to be answered. We trust that our modest pioneering work in empirical research into several problem areas will help to open the way for more extensive and long-term research based on more refined methods directed to answering more refined questions. We urge both private and public sources to provide the financial resources necessary. . . .

4. The Commission recommends that citizens organize themselves at

local, regional, and national levels to aid in the implementation of the foregoing recommendations.

The sex education effort recommended by the Commission can be achieved only with broad and active citizen participation. Widespread discussion of the issues regarding the availability of explicit sexual materials implies broad and active citizen participation. A continuing research program aimed at clarifying factual issues regarding the impact of explicit sexual materials on those who encounter them will occur only with the support and cooperation of citizens. . . .

Legislative Recommendations

. . . In general outline, the Commission recommends that federal, state, and local legislation should not seek to interfere with the right of adults who wish to do so to read, obtain, or view explicit sexual materials. On the other hand, we recommend legislative regulations upon the sale of sexual materials to young persons who do not have the consent of their parents, and we also recommend legislation to protect persons from having sexual materials thrust upon them without their consent through the mails or through open public display. . . .

STATUTES RELATING TO ADULTS

The Commission recommends that federal, state, and local legislation prohibiting the sale, exhibition, or distribution of sexual materials to consenting adults should be repealed. Twelve of the 17 participating members of the Commission join in this recommendation. Two additional Commissioners subscribe to the bulk of the Commission's Report, but do not believe that the evidence presented at this time is sufficient to warrant the repeal of all prohibitions upon what adults may obtain. Three Commissioners dissent from the recommendation to repeal adult legis- lation and would retain existing laws prohibiting the dissemination of obscene materials to adults.

The Commission believes that there is no warrant for continued governmental interference with the full freedom of adults to read, obtain or view whatever such material they wish. Our conclusion is based upon the following considerations:

1. Extensive empirical investigation, both by the Commission and by others, provides no evidence that exposure to or use of explicit sexual materials play a significant role in the causation of social or individual harms such as crime, delinquency, sexual or nonsexual deviancy or severe emotional disturbances. This research and its results are described in de- tail in the report of the Effects Panel of the Commission. . . .

In sum, empirical research designed to clarify the question has found no evidence to date that exposure to explicit sexual materials plays a significant role in the causation of delinquent or criminal behavior among youth or adults.

2. On the positive side, explicit sexual materials are sought as a source of entertainment and information by substantial numbers of American adults. At times, these materials also appear to serve to increase and facilitate constructive communication about sexual matters within marriage. The most frequent purchaser of explicit sexual materials is a college-educated, married male, in his thirties or forties, who is of above average socio-economic status. Even where materials are legally available to them, young adults and older adolescents do not constitute an important portion of the purchases of such materials.

3. Society's attempts to legislate for adults in the area of obscenity have not been successful. Present laws prohibiting the consensual sale or distribution of explicit sexual materials to adults are extremely unsatisfactory in their practical application. The Constitution permits material to be deemed "obscene" for adults only if, as a whole, it appeals to the "prurient" interest of the average person, is "patently offensive" in light of "community standards," and lacks "redeeming social value." These vague and highly subjective aesthetic, psychological and moral tests do not provide meaningful guidance for law enforcement officials, juries or courts. As a result, law is inconsistently and sometimes erroneously applied. . . .

4. Public opinion in America does not support the imposition of legal prohibitions upon the right of adults to read or see explicit sexual materials. While a minority of Americans favors such prohibitions, a majority of the American people presently are of the view that adults should be legally able to read or see explicit sexual materials if they wish to do so.

5. The lack of consensus among Americans concerning whether explicit sexual materials should be available to adults in our society, and the significant number of adults who wish to have access to such materials, pose serious problems regarding the enforcement of legal prohibitions upon adults, even aside from the vagueness and subjectivity of present law. Consistent enforcement of even the clearest prohibitions upon consensual adult exposure to explicit sexual materials would require the expenditure of considerable law enforcement resources. In the absence of a persuasive demonstration of damage flowing from consensual exposure to such materials, there seems no justification for thus adding to the overwhelming tasks already placed upon the law enforcement system. . . .

6. The foregoing considerations take on added significance because of the fact that adult obscenity laws deal in the realm of speech and communication. Americans deeply value the right of each individual to determine for himself what books he wishes to read and what pictures or films he wishes to see. Our traditions of free speech and press also value

and protect the right of writers, publishers, and booksellers to serve the diverse interests of the public. The spirit and letter of our Constitution tell us that government should not seek to interfere with these rights unless a clear threat of harm makes that course imperative. Moreover, the possibility of the misuse of general obscenity statutes prohibiting distributions of books and films to adults constitutes a continuing threat to the free communication of ideas among Americans—one of the most important foundations of our liberties.

7. . . . The Commission carefully considered the view that adult legislation should be retained in order to aid in the protection of young persons from exposure to explicit sexual materials. We do not believe that the objective of protecting youth may justifiably be achieved at the expense of denying adults materials of their choice. It seems to us wholly inappropriate to adjust the level of adult communication to that considered suitable for children. Indeed, the Supreme Court has unanimously held that adult legislation premised on this basis is a clearly unconstitutional interference with liberty.

8. There is no reason to suppose that elimination of governmental prohibitions upon the sexual materials which may be made available to adults would adversely affect the availability to the public of other books, magazines, and films. . . .

9. The Commission has also taken cognizance of the concern of many people that the lawful distribution of explicit sexual materials to adults may have a deleterious effect upon the individual morality of American citizens and upon the moral climate in America as a whole. This concern appears to flow from a belief that exposure to explicit materials may cause moral confusion which, in turn, may induce antisocial or criminal behavior. As noted above, the Commission has found no evidence to support such a contention. Nor is there evidence that exposure to explicit sexual materials adversely affects character or moral attitudes regarding sex and sexual conduct.

The concern about the effect of obscenity upon morality is also expressed as a concern about the impact of sexual materials upon American values and standards. Such values and standards are currently in a process of complex change, in both sexual and nonsexual areas. The open availability of increasingly explicit sexual materials is only one of these changes. The current flux in sexual values is related to a number of powerful influences, among which are the ready availability of effective methods of contraception, changes of the role of women in our society, and the increased education and mobility of our citizens. The availability of explicit sexual materials is, the Commission believes, not one of the important influences on sexual morality.

The Commission is of the view that it is exceedingly unwise for government to attempt to legislate individual moral values and standards independent of behavior, especially by restrictions upon consensual communication. . . .

The Commission recognizes and believes that the existence of sound moral standards is of vital importance to individuals and to society. To be effective and meaningful, however, these standards must be based upon deep personal commitment flowing from values instilled in the home, in educational and religious training, and through individual resolutions of personal confrontations with human experience. Governmental regulation of moral choice can deprive the individual of the responsibility for personal decision which is essential to the formation of genuine moral standards. Such regulation would also tend to establish an official moral orthodoxy, contrary to our most fundamental constitutional traditions.

Therefore, the Commission recommends the repeal of existing federal legislation which prohibits or interferes with consensual distribution of "obscene" materials to adults. . . .

STATUTES RELATING TO YOUNG PERSONS

The Commission recommends the adoption by the States of legislation . . . prohibiting the commercial distribution or display for sale of certain sexual materials to young persons. Similar legislation might also be adopted, where appropriate, by local governments and by the federal government for application in areas, such as the District of Columbia, where it has primary jurisdiction over distributional conduct.

The Commission's recommendation of juvenile legislation is joined in by 14 members of the Commission. . . .

A primary basis for the Commission's recommendation for repeal of adult legislation is the fact that extensive empirical investigations do not indicate any causal relationship between exposure to or use of explicit sexual materials and such social or individual harms such as crime, delinquency, sexual or nonsexual deviancy, or severe emotional disturbances. The absence of empirical evidence supporting such a causal relationship also applies to the exposure of children to erotic materials. However, insufficient research is presently available on the effect of the exposure of children to sexually explicit materials to enable us to reach conclusions with the same degree of confidence as for adult exposure. Strong ethical feelings against experimentally exposing children to sexually explicit materials considerably reduced the possibility of gathering the necessary data and information regarding young persons.

In view of the limited amount of information concerning the effects of sexually explicit materials on children, other considerations have assumed primary importance in the Commission's deliberations. The Commission has been influenced, to a considerable degree, by its finding that a large majority of Americans believe that children should not be exposed to certain sexual materials. In addition, the Commission takes the view that parents should be free to make their own conclusions regarding the suitability of explicit sexual materials for their children and that it is appropriate for legislation to aid parents in controlling the access of their children to such materials during their formative years. The Commission recognizes that legislation cannot possibly isolate children from such materials entirely; it also recognizes that exposure of children to sexual materials may not only do no harm but may, in certain instances, actually facilitate much needed communication between parent and child over sexual matters. The Commission is aware, as well, of the considerable danger of creating an unnatural attraction or an enhanced interest in certain materials by making them "forbidden fruit" for young persons. The Commission believes, however, that these considerations can and should be weighed by individual parents in determining their attitudes toward the exposure of their children to sexual materials, and that legislation should aid, rather than undermine, such parental choice.

Taking account of the above considerations, the model juvenile legislation recommended by the Commission applies only to distributions to children made without parental consent. The recommended legislation applies only to commercial distributions and exhibitions; in the very few instances where noncommercial conduct in this area creates a problem, it can be dealt with under existing legal principles for the protection of young persons, such as prohibitions upon contributing to the delinquency of minors. The model legislation also prohibits displaying certain sexual materials for sale in a manner which permits children to view materials which cannot be sold to them. . . .

The Commission, pursuant to Congressional direction, has given close attention to the definitions of prohibited material included in its recommended model legislation for young persons. A paramount consideration in the Commission's deliberations has been that definitions of prohibited materials be as specific and explicit as possible. Such specificity aids law enforcement and facilitates and encourages voluntary adherence to law on the part of retail dealers and exhibitors, while causing as little interference as possible with the proper distribution of materials to children and adults. The Commission's recommended legislation seeks to eliminate subjective definitional criteria insofar as that is possible and goes further in that regard than existing state legislation.

The Commission believes that only pictorial material should fall within prohibitions upon sale or commercial display to young persons. An attempt to define prohibited textual materials for young persons with the same degree of specificity as pictorial materials would, the Commission believes, not be advisable. Many worthwhile textual works, containing considerable value for young persons, treat sex in an explicit manner and are presently available to young persons. There appears to be no satisfactory way to distinguish, through a workable legal definition, between these works and those which may be deemed inappropriate by some persons for commercial distribution to young persons. . . .

The definition recommended by the Commission for inclusion in juvenile legislation covers a range of explicit pictorial and three-dimensional depictions of sexual activity. It does not, however, apply to depictions of nudity alone, unless genital areas are exposed and emphasized. The definition is applicable only if the explicit pictorial material constitutes a dominant part of a work. An exception is provided for works of artistic or anthropological significance.

Seven Commissioners would include verbal materials within the definition of materials prohibited for sale to young persons. They would, however, also include a broad exception for such textual materials when they bear literary, historical, scientific, educational, or other similar social value for young persons.

Because of changing standards as to what material, if any, is inappropriate for sale or display to children, the Commission's model statute contains a provision requiring legislative reconsideration of the need for, and scope of, such legislation at six-year intervals.

The model statute also exempts broadcast or telecast activity from its scope. . . .

The Commission has not fixed upon a precise age limit for inclusion in its recommended juvenile legislation, believing that such a determination is most appropriately made by the States and localities which enact such provisions in light of local standards. All States now fix the age in juvenile obscenity statutes at under 17 or under 18 years. The recommended model statute also excludes married persons, whatever their age, from the category of juveniles protected by the legislation.

The Commission considered the possibility of recommending the enactment of uniform federal legislation requiring a notice or label to be affixed to materials by their publishers, importers or manufacturers, when such materials fall within a definitional provision identical to that included within the recommended state or local model juvenile statute. . . .

Finally, the Commission considered, but does not affirmatively recommend, the enactment by the federal government of juvenile legislation which would prohibit the sale of certain explicit materials to juveniles through the mails. Such federal legislation would, the Commission believes, be virtually unenforceable since the constitutional requirement of proving the defendant's guilty knowledge means that a prosecution could be successful only if proof were available that the vendor knew that the purchaser was a minor. . . .

PUBLIC DISPLAY AND UNSOLICITED MAILING

The Commission recommends enactment of state and local legislation prohibiting public displays of sexually explicit pictorial materials, and approves in principle of the federal legislation, enacted as part of the 1970

Postal Reorganization Act, regarding the mailing of unsolicited advertisements of a sexually explicit nature. The Commission's recommendations in this area are based upon its finding, through its research, that certain explicit sexual materials are capable of causing considerable offense to numerous Americans when thrust upon them without their consent. The Commission believes that these unwanted intrusions upon individual sensibilities warrant legislative regulation and it further believes that such intrusions can be regulated effectively without any significant interference with consensual communication of sexual material among adults.

The Commission's recommendations in the public display area have been formulated into a model state public display statute. . . .

The model statute recommended by the Commission (which would also be suitable for enactment in appropriate instances by local government units and by the federal government for areas where it has general legislative jurisdiction) prohibits the display of certain potentially offensive sexually explicit pictorial materials in places easily visible from public thoroughfares or the property of others. . . . In addition, the fact that there are few, if any, "dirty" words which do not already appear fairly often in conversation among many Americans and in some very widely distributed books and films indicates that such words are no longer capable of causing the very high degree of offense to a large number of persons which would justify legislative interference. Five Commissioners disagree and would include verbal materials in the display prohibition because they believe certain words cause sufficient offense to warrant their inclusion in display prohibitions. . . .

The Commission, with three dissents, also approves of federal legislation to prevent unsolicited advertisements containing potentially offensive sexual material from being communicated through the mails to persons who do not wish to receive such advertisements. The Federal Anti-Pandering Act, which went into effect in 1968, imposes some regulation in this area, but it permits a mail recipient to protect himself against such mail only after he has received at least one such advertisement and it protects him only against mail emanating from that particular source. The Commission believes it more appropriate to permit mail recipients to protect themselves against all such unwanted mail advertisements from any source. . . .

DECLARATORY JUDGMENT LEGISLATION

The Commission recommends the enactment, in all jurisdictions which enact or retain provisions prohibiting the dissemination of sexual materials to adults or young persons, of legislation authorizing prosecutors to obtain declaratory judgments as to whether particular materials fall within existing legal prohibitions and appropriate injunctive relief. A model statute embodying this recommendation is presented in the Drafts of Proposed Statutes. . . .

A declaratory judgment procedure such as the Commission recommends would permit prosecutors to proceed civilly, rather than through the criminal process, against suspected violations of obscenity prohibition. . . .

WITHDRAWAL OF APPELLATE JURISDICTION

The Commission recommends against the adoption of any legislation which would limit or abolish the jurisdiction of the Supreme Court of the United States or of other federal judges and courts in obscenity cases. Two Commissioners favor such legislation; one deems it inappropriate for the Commission to take a position on this issue. . . .

Report of [Three] Commissioners*

Overview

The Commission's majority report is a Magna Carta for the pornographer.

It is slanted and biased in favor of protecting the business of obscenity and pornography, which the Commission was mandated by the Congress to regulate.

The Commission leadership and majority recommend that most existing legal barriers between society and pornography be pulled down. In so doing, the Commission goes far beyond its mandate and assumes the role of counsel for the filth merchant—a role not assigned by the Congress of the United States.

The Commission leadership and majority recommend repeal of obscenity law for "consenting adults." It goes on, then, to recommend legislation for minors, public display and thrusting of pornography on persons through the mails.

The American people should be made aware of the fact that this is precisely the situation as it exists in Denmark today. The Commission, in short, is presumptuously recommending that the United States follow Denmark's lead in giving pornography free rein.

We feel impelled to issue this report in vigorous dissent.

The conclusions and recommendations in the majority report will be found deeply offensive to Congress and to tens of millions of Americans. And what the American people do not know is that the scanty and

*This report is by Morton A. Hill, S. J., Winfrey C. Link, and concurred in by Charles H. Keating, Jr. It is one of eight separate statements filed by Commission members. This one, and two others, denounced the majority recommendations as too permissive. The other five generally approved the majority findings or urged less restrictive recommendations—*Ed.*

manipulated evidence contained within this report is wholly inadequate to support the conclusions and sustain the recommendations. Thus, both conclusions and recommendations are, in our view, fraudulent.

What the American people have here for the two million dollars voted by Congress, and paid by the taxpayer, is a shoddy piece of scholarship that will be quoted ad nauseam by cultural polluters and their attorneys within society. . . .

In sum, the conclusions and recommendations of the Commission majority represent the preconceived views of the Chairman and his appointed counsel that the Commission should arrive at those conclusions most compatible with the viewpoint of the American Civil Liberties Union. Both men singlemindedly steered the Commission to this objective. . . .

Our Position

We stand in agreement with the Congress of the United States: the traffic in obscenity and pornography is a matter of national concern.

We believe that pornography has an eroding effect on society, on public morality, on respect for human worth, on attitudes toward family love, on culture.

We believe it is impossible, and totally unnecessary, to attempt to prove or disprove a cause-effect relationship between pornography and criminal behavior.

Sex education, recommended so strongly by the majority, is the panacea for those who advocate license in media. The report suggests sex education, with a plaint for the dearth of instructors and materials. It notes that three schools have used "hard-core pornography" in training potential instructors. The report does not answer the question that comes to mind immediately: Will these instructors not bring the hard-core pornography into the grammar schools? Many other questions are left unanswered: How assure that the instructor's moral or ethical code (or lack of same) will not be communicated to children? Shouldn't parents, not children, be the recipients of sex education courses?

Children cannot grow in love if they are trained with pornography. . . . And if this Commission majority's recommendations are heeded, there will be a glut of pornography for teachers and children.

In contrast to the Commission report's amazing statement that "public opinion in America does not support the imposition of legal prohibitions upon the consensual distribution" of pornography to adults, we find, as a result of public hearings conducted by two of the undersigned in eight cities throughout the country, that the majority of the American people favor tighter controls. Twenty-six out of twenty-seven witnesses at the hearing in New York City expressed concern and asked for remedial measures. . . .

Recommendations

DEFINITION OF OBSCENITY

A thing is "obscene" if, by contemporary community standards, and considered as a whole, its predominant appeal is to the prurient interest. As a matter of public policy, anything which is obscene by this definition shall be conclusively deemed to be utterly without redeeming social importance. Any slight social value in such obscenity shall be deemed outweighed by the social interest in order and morality.

"Prurient interest" is defined as a shameful or morbid interest in nudity, sex or excretion which goes substantially beyond customary limits of candor in description or representation of such matters. If it appears from the character of the material or the circumstances of its dissemination that the subject matter is designed for, or directed to a specially susceptible audience, the subject matter shall be judged with reference to such audience. When the subject matter is distributed or exhibited to minors who have not attained their 18th birthday, the subject matter shall be judged with reference to an average person in the community of the actual age of the minor to whom such material is distributed or exhibited. In all other cases, the subject matter shall be judged with reference to the average person in the community. . . .

FEDERAL LEGISLATION

. . . We recommend legislation or a Presidential Directive establishing a Division, in the Office of the Attorney General of the United States, under the direction of a Deputy Attorney General, made up of a team of skilled lawyers ready and able to assist District Attorneys throughout the nation in prosecutions against sex exploiters. . . .

We recommend the establishment, by Federal legislation, of a National Crime Research and Reference Library on the Law of Obscenity. The Library will be unique, since the Librarian of Congress has indicated that after diligent search, "no reference to any special law library in this area has been found, and . . . such a library would be unique and unduplicated as a single collection."

The purpose of the library will be to service prosecutors nationwide to expedite preparation of cases. It will be available also to the judiciary, behavioral scientists, clergymen, writers and other professionals who can contribute to stem the flow of obscene material. . . .

STATE LEGISLATION

(a) *Model State Obscenity Statute.*   Attached to this Report . . . is our recommended Model State Obscenity Statute based on the concept of variable obscenity and taking into consideration all U.S. Supreme Court cases. . . .

(b) We also recommend to the States that they establish, by legislation, a Board of Film Review. . . .

(c) In addition, we suggest that some States might desire to permit local ordinances for the establishment of Film Review Boards. . . .

(d) We recommend the employment of the injunctive remedy. . . . This is a most effective weapon sanctioned by the decisions of the U.S. Supreme Court, and will reach all types of obscenity.

(e) We recommend that the Attorney General's Office be required to review for possible prosecution any type of suspected obscenity distributed or about to be distributed, of which he gains knowledge, and which falls into any of the descriptive categories listed below:

[A list of 22 categories is given, including: "paperbacks with themes of homosexuality, sado-masochism, incest, bestiality; hardcover books devoted to homosexuality, sado-masochism, incest"; stag films; commercial x-rated and unrated films and advertising for them; "underground newspapers"; "pseudo-scientific sex publications"; "sensational tabloids"; "lyrics on commercially distributed rock records"; and other items.—*Ed.*]

(f) We advocate the establishment in the office of the Attorney General of each State, a team of one or more skilled attorneys, under the direction of a Deputy Attorney General, to be used to assist in the local prosecutions where intrastate commerce is involved or where federal assistance from the Department of Justice is not readily available.

(g) We advocate the establishment in State Police headquarters of a similar division, working closely with the legal staff just mentioned. The state police have experts in arson, ballistics and other specialties. The formation of a special unit on pornography is long overdue.

(h) We advocate the establishment of [a] permanent State Commission to examine the laws on obscenity, to make recommendations to the legislature, and recommendations for more effective means of enforcement. . . .

(i) We recommend the establishment of a State Commission to review and classify Motion Pictures and printed materials for minors. . . .

(j) As minimum legislation, we advocate elimination of the phrase "utterly without redeeming social value" in any State statute. . . .

LOCAL ORDINANCES

(a) We recommend a review of existing ordinances in the light of our review of U.S. Supreme Court decisions . . . and the modifying or amending of some to comply therewith, including the elimination of the phrase, "utterly without redeeming social value" whenever found.

(b) We recommend the adoption of local ordinances (wherever the State has not adopted a Film Review Statute) to review Motion Pictures. . . .

(c) On an optional basis, or as part of a general ordinance on motion picture review, we recommend a Film Review and Classification Ordinance for minors. . . .

(d) We recommend an ordinance designed to protect minors from being exposed, on the highway or street, to drive-in movie scenes of motion pictures that are unsuitable for children.

(e) We recommend a local ordinance to penalize the showing of obscene motion pictures, and to penalize the licensee found guilty.

PRIVATE ACTION BY THE PUBLIC

(a) We recommend that private citizens join with or form private, non-sectarian, community organizations that take organized, but constitutional action against obscenity.

(b) We recommend citizens bring official legal complaints whenever evidence of obscenity comes to their attention.

(c) We recommend that citizens continually urge their municipal, State and federal officials, to prosecute obscenity cases. Here, again, this is best accomplished in an organized manner, working through an existing community organization.

APPENDIX 5

Selected U.S. Laws and Regulations Compiled by Henry R. Kaufman

Criminal Statutes

18 U.S.C. 552   Officers Aiding Importation of Obscene or Treasonous Books and Articles

Whoever, being an officer, agent, or employee of the United States, knowingly aids or abets any person engaged in any violation of any of the provisions of law prohibiting importing, advertising, dealing in, exhibiting, or sending or receiving by mail obscene or indecent publications or representations, or books, pamphlets, papers, writings, advertisements, circulars, prints, pictures, or drawings containing any matter advocating or urging treason or insurrection against the United States or forcible resistance to any law of the United States, or containing any threat to take the life of or inflict bodily harm upon any person in the United States, or means for procuring abortion, or other articles of indecent or immoral use or tendency, shall be fined not more than $5,000 or imprisoned not more than ten years, or both.

18 U.S.C. 1461   Mailing Obscene or Crime-Inciting Matter

Every obscene, lewd, lascivious, indecent, filthy or vile article, matter, thing, device, or substance; and—

Every article or thing designed, adapted, or intended for preventing conception or producing abortion, or for any indecent or immoral use; and

Every article, instrument, substance, drug, medicine, or thing which is advertised or described in a manner calculated to lead another to use or apply it for preventing conception or producing abortion, or for any indecent or immoral purpose; and

Every written or printed card, letter, circular, book, pamphlet, advertisement, or notice of any kind giving information, directly or indirectly, where, or how, or from whom, or by what means any of such mentioned matters, articles, or things may be obtained or made, or where or by whom any act or operation of any kind for the procuring or producing of abortion will be done or performed, or how or by what means conception may be prevented or abortion produced, whether sealed or unsealed; and

Every letter, packet, or package, or other mail matter containing any filthy, vile, or indecent thing, device, or substance; and

Every paper, writing, advertisement, or representation that any article, instrument, substance, drug, medicine, or thing may, or can, be used or applied for preventing conception or producing abortion, or for any indecent or immoral purpose; and

Every description calculated to induce or incite a person to so use or apply such article, instrument, substance, drug, medicine, or thing—

Is declared to be nonmailable matter and shall not be conveyed in the mails or delivered from any post office by any letter carrier.

Whoever knowingly uses the mails for the mailing, carriage in the mails, or delivery of anything declared by this section to be nonmailable, or knowingly causes to be delivered by mail according to the direction thereon, or at the place at which it is directed to be delivered to the person to whom it is addressed, or knowingly takes any such thing from the mails for the purpose of circulating or disposing thereof; or of aiding in the circulation or disposition thereof, shall be fined not more than $5,000 or imprisoned not more than five years, or both, for the first such offense, and shall be fined not more than $10,000 or imprisoned not more than ten years, or both, for each such offense thereafter.

The term "indecent," as used in this section, includes matter of a character tending to incite arson, murder, or assassination.

18 U.S.C. 1462   Importation or Transportation of Obscene Matters

Whoever brings into the United States, or any place subject to the jurisdiction thereof, or knowingly uses any express company or other common carrier, for carriage in interstate or foreign commerce—

(a) any obscene, lewd, lascivious, or filthy book, pamphlet, picture, motion-picture film, paper, letter, writing, print, or other matter of indecent character; or

(b) any obscene, lewd, lascivious, or filthy phonograph recording, electrical transcription, or other article or thing capable of producing sound; or

(c) any drug, medicine, article, or thing designed, adapted, or intended for producing abortion, or for any indecent or immoral use; or any written or printed card, letter, circular, book, pamphlet, advertisement, or notice of any kind giving information, directly or indirectly, where, how, or of whom, or by what means any of such mentioned articles, matters, or things may be obtained or made; or

Whoever knowingly takes from such express company or other common carrier any matter or thing the carriage of which is herein made unlawful—

Shall be fined not more than $5,000 or imprisoned not more than five years, or both, for the first such offense and shall be fined not more than $10,000 or imprisoned not more than ten years, or both, for each such offense thereafter.

18 U.S.C. 1463   Mailing Indecent Matter on Wrappers or Envelopes

All matter otherwise mailable by law, upon the envelope or outside cover or wrapper of which, and all postal cards upon which, any delineations, epithets, terms, or language of an indecent, lewd, lascivious, or obscene character are written or printed or otherwise impressed or apparent, are nonmailable matter, and shall not be conveyed in the mails nor delivered from any post office nor by any letter carrier, and shall be withdrawn from the mails under such regulations as the Postal Service shall prescribe.

Whoever knowingly deposits for mailing or delivery, anything declared by this section to be nonmailable matter, or knowingly takes the same from the mails for the purpose of circulating or disposing of or aiding in the circulation or disposition of the same, shall be fined not more than $5,000 or imprisoned not more than five years, or both.

18 U.S.C. 1464   Broadcasting Obscene Language

Whoever utters any obscene, indecent, or profane language by means of radio communication shall be fined no more than $10,000 or imprisoned not more than two years, or both.

18 U.S.C. 1465   Transportation of Obscene Matters for Sale or Distribution

Whoever knowingly transports in interstate or foreign commerce for the purpose of sale or distribution any obscene, lewd, lascivious, or filthy book, pamphlet, picture, film, paper, letter, writing, print, silhouette, drawing, figure, image, cast, phonograph recording, electrical transcription or other article capable of producing sound or any other matter of indecent or immoral character, shall be fined not more than $5,000 or imprisoned not more than five years, or both.

The transportation as aforesaid of two or more copies of any publication or two or more of any article of the character described above, or a combined total of five such publications and articles, shall create a presumption that such publications or articles are intended for sale or distribution, but such presumption shall be rebuttable.

When any person is convicted of a violation of this Act, the court in its judgment of conviction may, in addition to the penalty prescribed, order the confiscation and disposal of such items described herein which were found in the possession or under the immediate control of such person at the time of his arrest.

18 U.S.C. 1717   Letters and Writings as Nonmailable; Opening Letters

(a) Every letter, writing, circular, postal card, picture, print, engraving, photograph, newspaper, pamphlet, book, or other publication, matter or thing, in violation of sections 499, 506, 793, 794, 915, 954, 956, 957, 960, 964, 1017, 1542, 1543, 1544 or 2388 of this title or which contains any matter advocating or urging treason, insurrection, or forcible resistance to any law of the United States is nonmailable and shall not be conveyed in the mails or delivered from any post office or by any letter carrier.

(b) Whoever uses or attempts to use the mails or Postal Service for the transmission of any matter declared by this section to be nonmailable, shall be fined not more than $5,000 or imprisoned not more than ten years or both.

As amended Aug. 12, 1970, Pub.L. 91-375, §6(j)(27), 84 Stat. 780.

18 U.S.C. 1718   Libelous Matter on Wrappers or Envelopes

All matters otherwise mailable by law, upon the envelope or outside cover or wrapper of which, or any postal card upon which is written or printed or otherwise impressed or apparent any delineation, epithet, term, or language of libelous, scurrilous, defamatory, or threatening character, or calculated by the terms or manner or style of display and obviously intended to reflect injuriously upon the character or conduct of another, is nonmailable matter, and shall not be conveyed in the mails nor delivered from any post office nor by any letter carrier, and shall be withdrawn from the mails under such regulations as the Postal Service shall prescribe.

Whoever knowingly deposits for mailing or delivery, anything declared by this section to be nonmailable matter, or knowingly takes the same from the mails for the purpose of circulating or disposing of or aiding in the circulation or disposition of the same, shall be fined not more than $1,000 or imprisoned not more than one year, or both.

As amended Aug. 12, 1970, Pub.L. 91-375, §6(j)(27), 84 Stat. 780.

18 U.S.C. 1735   Sexually Oriented Advertisements

(a) Whoever—

(1) willfully used the mails for the mailing, carriage in the mails, or delivery of any sexually oriented advertisement in violation of section 3010 of title 39, or willfully violates any regulations of the Board of Governors issued under such section; or

(2) sells, leases, rents, lends, exchanges, or licenses the use of, or, except for the purpose expressly authorized by section 3010 of title 39, uses a mailing list maintained by the Board of Governors under such section;

shall be fined not more than $5,000 or imprisoned not more than five years, or both, for the first offense, and shall be fined not more than $10,000 or imprisoned not more than ten years, or both, for any second or subsequent offense.

(b) For the purposes of this section, the term "sexually oriented advertisement" shall have the same meaning as given it in section 3010(d) of title 39.

Added Pub.L. 91-375, §6(j)(37)(A), Aug. 12, 1970, 84 Stat. 781.

18 U.S.C. 1737   Manufacturer of Sexually Related Mail Matter

(a) Whoever shall print, reproduce, or manufacture any sexually related mail matter, intending or knowing that such matter will be deposited for mailing or delivery by mail in violation of section 3008 or 3010 of title 39, or in violation of any regulation of the Postal Service issued under such section, shall be fined not more than $5,000 or imprisoned not more than five years, or both, for the first offense, and shall be fined not more than $10,000 or imprisoned not more than ten years, or both, for any second or subsequent offense.

(b) As used in this section, the term "sexually related mail matter" means any matter which is within the scope of section 3008(a) or 3010(d) of title 39.

Added Pub.L. 91-375, §6(j)(37)(A), Aug. 12, 1970, 84 Stat. 781.

18 U.S.C. 1842 *Disseminating Obscene Material**

(a) *Offense.*—A person is guilty of an offense if he:
   (1) disseminates obscene material:
      (A) to a minor; or
      (B) to any person *in a manner affording no immediately effective opportunity to avoid exposure to such material*; or
   (2) commercially disseminates obscene material to any person.
(b) *Definitions.*—As used in this section:
   (1) "commercially disseminate" means to disseminate for profit and shall include nonprofit means of mass communication;
   (2) "community" means the state or local community in which the obscene material is disseminated;
   (3) "disseminate" means:
      (A) to transfer, distribute, dispense, lend, display, exhibit, send, or broadcast, whether for profit or otherwise; or
      (B) to produce, transport, or possess with intent to do any of the foregoing;
   (4) "minor" means an unmarried person less than seventeen years old;
   (5) "obscene material" means material that:
      (A) sets forth in a patently offensive way:
         (i) an explicit representation, or a detailed written or verbal description, of an act of sexual intercourse, including genital-genital, anal-genital, or oral-genital intercourse, whether between human beings or between a human being and an animal; of masturbation; or of flagellation, torture, or other violence indicating a sado-masochistic sexual relationship; or
         (ii) an explicit, close-up representation of a human genital organ;
      (B) taken as a whole, appeals predominantly to the prurient interest of:
         (i) the average person, applying contemporary community standards; or
         (ii) the average person within a sexually deviant class of persons, if such material is designed for dissemination to such class of persons; and
      (C) taken as a whole, lacks serious artistic, scientific, literary, or political value.
(c) *Affirmative Defense.*—It is an affirmative defense to a prosecution under subsection (a) (1) (B) or (a) (2) that dissemination of the material was legal in the political subdivision or locality in which it was disseminated.
(d) *Affirmative Defenses.*—It is an affirmative defense to a prosecution under this section that dissemination of the material was restricted to:
   (1) a person associated with an institution of higher learning, either as a member of the faculty or as an enrolled student, teaching or pursuing a bona fide course of study, or conducting or engaging in a bona fide research program, to which such material is pertinent; or

*Proposed revisions of Title 18, U.S. Code, regarding obscenity, passed by the U.S. Senate in S. 1437, January 30, 1978.

(2) a person whose receipt of such material was authorized in writing by a licensed or certified psychiatrist, psychologist, or medical practitioner.

(e) *Grading.*—An offense described in this section is a Class E felony.

(f) *Jurisdiction.*—There is federal jurisdiction over an offense described in this section if:

(1) the offense is committed within the special jurisdiction of the United States;

(2) the United States mail or a facility of interstate or foreign commerce is used in the commission of the offense; or

(3) the material is moved across a state or United States boundary.

18 U.S.C. 6035   *Mailing, Importing, or Transporting Obscene Matter*

(a) Every article or thing designed, adapted, or intended for producing abortion, or for any indecent or immoral use; and

Every article, instrument, substance, drug, medicine, or thing which is advertised or described in a manner calculated to lead another to use or apply it for producing abortion, or for any indecent or immoral purpose; and

Every written or printed card, letter, circular, book, pamphlet, advertisement, or notice of any kind giving information, directly or indirectly, where, or how, or from whom, or by what means any of such mentioned matters, articles, or things may be obtained or made, or where or by whom any act or operation of any kind for the procuring or producing of abortion will be done or performed, or how or by what means abortion may be produced, whether sealed or unsealed; and

Every paper, writing, advertisement, or representation that any article, instrument, substance, drug, medicine, or thing may, or can, be used or applied for producing abortion, or for any indecent or immoral purpose; and

Every description calculated to induce or incite a person to so use or apply any such article, instrument, substance, drug, medicine, or thing—

Is declared to be nonmailable matter and shall not be conveyed in the mails or delivered from any post office or by any letter carrier.

Whoever knowingly uses the mails for the mailing, carriage in the mails, or delivery of anything declared by this subsection or section 3001 (3) of title 39 to be nonmailable, or knowingly causes to be delivered by mail according to the direction thereon, or at the place at which it is directed to be delivered by the person to whom it is addressed, or knowingly takes any such thing from the mails for the purpose of circulating or disposing thereof, or of aiding in the circulation or disposition thereof, shall be guilty of a Class D felony.

The term "indecent" as used in this subsection includes matter of a character tending to incite arson, murder, or assassination.

(b) Whoever brings into the United States, or any place subject to the jurisdiction thereof, or knowingly uses any express company or other common carrier, for carriage in interstate commerce or foreign commerce any drug, medicine, article, or thing designed, adapted, or intended for producing abortion, or for any indecent or immoral use; or any written or printed card, letter, circular, book, pamphlet, advertisement, or notice of any kind giving information, directly or indirectly, where, how or of whom, or by what means any of such mentioned articles, matters, or things may be obtained or made; or whoever knowingly takes from such express company or other common carrier any matter or thing the carriage of which is herein made unlawful shall be guilty of a Class D felony.

Civil Statutes and Regulations

Postal

39 U.S.C. 3001   Nonmailable Matter

(a) Matter the deposit of which in the mails is punishable under section 1302, 1341, 1342, 1461, 1463, 1714, 1715, 1716, 1717 or 1718 of title 18 is nonmailable.

(b) Except as provided in subsection (c) of this section, nonmailable matter which reaches the office of delivery, or which may be seized or detained for violation of law, shall be disposed of as the Postal Service shall direct.

(c) (1) Matter which—

    (A) exceeds the size and weight limits prescribed for the particular class of mail; or

    (B) is of a character perishable within the period required for transportation and delivery;

is nonmailable.

    (2) Matter made nonmailable by this subsection which reaches the office of destination may be delivered in accordance with its address, if the party addressed furnishes the name and address of the sender.

(d) Matter otherwise legally acceptable in the mails which—

    (1) is in the form of, and reasonably could be interpreted or construed as, a bill, invoice, or statement of account due; but

    (2) constitutes, in fact, a solicitation for the order by the addressee of goods or services, or both;

is nonmailable matter, shall not be carried or delivered by mail, and shall be disposed of as the Postal Service directs, unless such matter bears on its face, in conspicuous and legible type in contrast by typography, layout, or color with other printing on its face, in accordance with regulations which the Postal Service shall prescribe—

    (A) the following notice: "This is a solicitation for the order of goods or services, or both, and not a bill, invoice, or statement of account due. You are under no obligation to make any payments on account of this offer unless you accept this offer."; or

    (B) in lieu thereof, a notice to the same effect in words which the Postal Service may prescribe.

(e) (1) Any matter which is unsolicited by the addressee and which is designed, adapted, or intended for preventing conception (except unsolicited samples thereof mailed to a manufacturer thereof, a dealer therein, a licensed physician or surgeon, or a nurse, pharmacist, druggist, hospital, or clinic) is nonmailable matter, shall not be carried or delivered by mail, and shall be disposed of as the Postal Service directs.

    (2) Any unsolicited advertisement of matter which is designed, adapted, or intended for preventing conception is nonmailable matter, shall not be carried or delivered by mail, and shall be disposed of as the Postal Service directs unless the advertisement—

(A) is mailed to a manufacturer of such matter, a dealer therein, a licensed physician or surgeon, or a nurse, pharmacist, druggist, hospital, or clinic; or

(B) accompanies in the same parcel any unsolicited sample excepted by paragraph (1) of this subsection.

An advertisement shall not be deemed to be unsolicited for the purposes of this paragraph if it is contained in a publication for which the addressee has paid or promised to pay a consideration or which he has otherwise indicated he desires to receive.

(f) Except as otherwise provided by law, proceedings concerning the mailability of matter under this chapter and chapters 71 and 83 of title 18 shall be conducted in accordance with chapters 5 and 7 of title 5.

(g) The district courts, together with the District Court of the Virgin Islands and the District Court of Guam, shall have jurisdiction, upon cause shown, to enjoin violations of section 1716 of title 18.

39 U.S.C. 3006   Unlawful Matter

Upon evidence satisfactory to the Postal Service that a person is obtaining or attempting to obtain remittances of money or property of any kind through the mail for an obscene, lewd, lascivious, indecent, filthy, or vile thing or is depositing or causing to be deposited in the United States mail information as to where, how, or from whom such a thing may be obtained, the Postal Service may—

(1) direct any postmaster at an office at which mail arrives, addressed to such a person or to his representative, to return the mail to the sender marked "Unlawful"; and

(2) forbid the payment by a postmaster to such a person or his representative of any money order or postal note drawn to the order of either and provide for the return to the remitter of the sum named in the money order.

39 U.S.C. 3007   Detention of Mail for Temporary Periods

(a) In preparation for or during the pendency of proceedings under sections 3005 and 3006 of this title, the United States district court in the district in which the defendant receives his mail shall, upon application therefor by the Postal Service and upon a showing of probable cause to believe either section is being violated, enter a temporary restraining order and preliminary injunction pursuant to rule 65 of the Federal Rules of Civil Procedure directing the detention of the defendant's incoming mail by the postmaster pending the conclusion of the statutory proceedings and any appeal therefrom. The district court may provide in the order that the detained mail be open to examination by the defendant and such mail be delivered as is clearly not connected with the alleged unlawful activity. An action taken by a court hereunder does not affect or determine any fact at issue in the statutory proceedings.

(b) This section does not apply to mail addressed to publishers of newspapers and other periodical publications entitled to a periodical publication rate or to mail addressed to the agents of those publishers.

39 U.S.C. 3008   *Prohibition of Pandering Advertisements*

(a) Whoever for himself, or by his agents or assigns, mails or causes to be mailed any pandering advertisement which offers for sale matter which the addressee in his sole discretion believes to be erotically arousing or sexually provocative shall be subject to an order of the Postal Service to refrain from further mailings of such materials to designated addresses thereof.

(b) Upon receipt of notice from an addressee that he has received such mail matter, determined by the addressee in his sole discretion to be of the character described in subsection (a) of this section, the Postal Service shall issue an order, if requested by the addressee, to the sender thereof, directing the sender and his agents or assigns to refrain from further mailing to the named addressees.

(c) The order of the Postal Service shall expressly prohibit the sender and his agents or assigns from making any further mailings to the designated addresses, effective on the thirtieth calendar day after receipt of the order. The order shall also direct the sender and his agents or assigns to delete immediately the names of the designated addressees from all mailing lists owned or controlled by the sender or his agents or assigns and, further, shall prohibit the sender and his agents or assigns from the sale, rental, exchange, or other transaction involving mailing lists bearing the names of the designated addressees.

(d) Whenever the Postal Service believes that the sender or anyone acting on his behalf has violated or is violating the order given under this section, it shall serve upon the sender, by registered or certified mail, a complaint stating the reasons for its belief and request that any response thereto be filed in writing with the Postal Service within 15 days after the date of such service. If the Postal Service, after appropriate hearing if requested by the sender, and without a hearing if such a hearing is not requested, thereafter determines that the order given has been or is being violated, it is authorized to request the Attorney General to make application, and the Attorney General is authorized to make application, to a district court of the United States for an order directing compliance with such notice.

(e) Any district court of the United States within the jurisdiction of which any mail matter shall have been sent or received in violation of the order provided for by this section shall have jurisdiction, upon application by the Attorney General, to issue an order commanding compliance wich such notice. Failure to observe such order may be punishable by the court as contempt thereof.

(f) Receipt of mail matter 30 days or more after the effective date of the order provided for by this section shall create a rebuttable presumption that such mail was sent after such effective date.

(g) Upon request of any addressee, the order of the Postal Service shall include the names of any of his minor children who have not attained their nineteenth birthday, and who reside with the addressee.

(h) The provisions of subchapter II of chapter 5, relating to administrative procedure, and chapter 7, relating to judicial review, of title 5, shall not apply to any provisions of this section.

(i) For purposes of this section—

(1) mail matter, directed to a specific address covered in the order of the

Postal Service, without designation of a specific addressee thereon, shall be considered as addressed to the person named in the Postal Service's order; and

(2) the term "children" includes natural children, stepchildren, adopted children, and children who are wards of or in custody of the addressee or who are living with such addressee in a regular parent-child relationship.

39 U.S.C. 3010   Mailing of Sexually Oriented Advertisements

(a) Any person who mails or causes to be mailed any sexually oriented advertisement shall place on the envelope or cover thereof his name and address as the sender thereof and such mark or notice as the Postal Service may prescribe.

(b) Any person, on his own behalf or on the behalf of any of his children who has not attained the age of 19 years and who resides with him or is under his care, custody, or supervision, may file with the Postal Service a statement, in such form and manner as the Postal Service may prescribe, that he desires to receive no sexually oriented advertisements through the mails. The Postal Service shall maintain and keep current, insofar as practicable, a list of the names and addresses of such persons and shall make the list (including portions thereof or changes therein) available to any person, upon such reasonable terms and conditions as it may prescribe, including the payment of such service charge as it determines to be necessary to defray the cost of compiling and maintaining the list and making it available as provided in this sentence. No person shall mail or cause to be mailed any sexually oriented advertisement to any individual whose name and address has been on the list for more than 30 days.

(c) No person shall sell, lease, lend, exchange, or license the use of, or, except for the purpose expressly authorized by this section, use any mailing list compiled in whole or in part from the list maintained by the Postal Service pursuant to this section.

(d) "Sexually oriented advertisement" means any advertisement that depicts, in actual or simulated form, or explicitly describes, in a predominantly sexual context, human genitalia, any act of natural or unnatural sexual intercourse, any act of sadism or masochism, or any other erotic subject directly related to the foregoing. Material otherwise within the definition of this subsection shall be deemed not to constitute a sexually oriented advertisement if it constitutes only a small and insignificant part of the whole of a single catalog, book, periodical, or other work the remainder of which is not primarily devoted to sexual matters.

39 U.S.C. 3011   Judicial Enforcement

(a) Whenever the Postal Service believes that any person is mailing or causing to be mailed any sexually oriented advertisement in violation of section 3010 of this title, it may request the Attorney General to commence a civil action against such person in a district court of the United States. Upon a finding by the court of a violation of that section, the court may issue an order including one or more of the following provisions as the court deems just under the circumstances:

(1) a direction to the defendant to refrain from mailing any sexually oriented advertisement to a specific addressee, to any group of addressees, or to all persons;

(2) a direction to any postmaster to whom sexually oriented advertisements originating with such defendant are tendered for transmission through the mails to refuse to accept such advertisements for mailing; or

(3) a direction to any postmaster at the office at which registered or certified letters or other letters or mail arrive, addressed to the defendant or his representative, to return the registered or certified letters or other letters or mail to the sender appropriately marked as being in response to mail in violation of section 3010 of this title, after the defendant, or his representative, has been notified and given reasonable opportunity to examine such letters or mail and to obtain delivery of mail which is clearly not connected with activity alleged to be in violation of section 3010 of this title.

(b) The statement that remittances may be made to a person named in a sexually oriented advertisement is prima facie evidence that such named person is the principal, agent, or representative of the mailer for the receipt of remittances on his behalf. The court is not precluded from ascertaining the existence of the agency on the basis of any other evidence.

(c) In preparation for, or during the pendency of, a civil action under subsection (a) of this section, a district court of the United States, upon application therefor by the Attorney General and upon a showing of probable cause to believe the statute is being violated, may enter a temporary restraining order or preliminary injunction containing such terms as the court deems just, including, but not limited to, provisions enjoining the defendant from mailing any sexually oriented advertisement to any person or class of persons, directing any postmaster to refuse to accept such defendant's sexually oriented advertisements for mailing, and directing the detention of the defendant's incoming mail by any postmaster pending the conclusion of the judicial proceedings. Any action taken by a court under this subsection does not affect or determine any fact at issue in any other proceeding under this section.

(d) A civil action under this section may be brought in the judicial district in which the defendant resides, or has his principal place of business, or in any judicial district in which any sexually oriented advertisement mailed in violation of section 3010 has been delivered by mail according to the direction thereon.

(e) Nothing in this section or in section 3010 shall be construed as amending, preempting, limiting, modifying, or otherwise in any way affecting section 1461 or 1463 of title 18 or section 3006, 3007, or 3008 of this title.

P.S.M. 123.5.   Sexually Oriented Advertisements*

.51   General

.511   Section 3010 of title 39, United States Code, provides a means by which a member of the public can act to protect himself and his minor children from receiving unsolicited sexually oriented advertisements through the mails. This section permits any person who is served by the U.S. Postal Service to file with the Postal Service a statement that he does not desire to receive any sexually oriented advertisements through the mails. Any mailer who sends that person an unsolicited

*Postal Service Manual, 2-7-75, Issue 97.

sexually oriented advertisement more than 30 days after the date on which the Postal Service adds his name to its reference List of those who desire this protection, may be subject to both civil and criminal sanctions, as provided in 39 U.S.C. 3011 and in 18 U.S.C. 1735–37.

.512   39 U.S.C. 3010 (d) defines a "sexually oriented advertisement" as "any advertisement that depicts, in actual or simulated form, or explicitly describes, in a predominantly sexual context, human genitalia, any act of natural or unnatural sexual intercourse, any act of sadism or masochism, or any other erotic subject directly related to the foregoing." It further provides that "material otherwise within the definition of this subsection shall be deemed not to constitute a sexually oriented advertisement if it constitutes only a small and insignificant part of the whole of a single catalog, book, periodical or other work the remainder of which is not primarily devoted to sexual matters."

.513   The responsibility for ensuring that no unsolicited sexually oriented advertisement is sent through the mails to any person in violation of section 3010 is placed by that section on the mailers of sexually oriented advertisements. No provision of Postal Service regulations may be used to place this responsibility upon the Postal Service. For example, the privilege of a sender to recall a piece of mail provided by section 153.5 may not be so used, although it may be used in good faith to request the recall of a specific piece of mail inadvertently deposited in the mails addressed to a person on the List.

.52   Application for Listing

.521   A person may invoke the protection of section 3010 by completing and filing, with any postmaster or other designated Postal Service representative, Part II of Application for Listing Pursuant to 39 U.S.C. 3010, Form 2201, which may be obtained at any post office. Form 2201 bears a preprinted identifying number in two places: On the instruction portion (part I) and on the application portion (part II). After filing the application portion the customer should retain the instruction portion and should use the identifying number in any subsequent communication with the Postal Service concerning his application.

.522   A person may file on his own behalf and on behalf of any of his children under the age of 19 years who reside with him or are under his care, custody or supervision. An authorized officer, agent, fiduciary, surviving spouse or other representative, may file in behalf of a corporation, firm, association, estate, or deceased or incompetent addressee.

.523   Each postmaster shall transmit all applications received at his post office to the Office of ADP Services, Management Information Systems Department, U.S. Postal Service, Box 677, Washington DC 20044 on a daily basis. The applications shall be packaged so that they will not be subject to folding, bending or other mutilation or damage.

.524   The Office of Mail Classification, Rates and Classification Department, as soon as practical after receipt of a Form 2201, shall place the customer's name and address, the names and addresses of his minor children if any are included on the application, on the Postal Service's List (hereafter, "List") of persons desiring not to receive sexually oriented advertising. This information will be processed during the month, and at the end of each month a revised or supplemental list will be prepared. The List will be dated the 10th day of the month following the month in which the Forms 2201 were processed. The 30-day period provided by section 3010(b) starts on the effective date of the List on which the person's name first appears.

.525 A person's name and address will be retained on the List for a period of 5 years, unless a request for revocation is sooner filed by that person. A person must file a new application at the end of the 5-year period if he desires to continue his name on the List. The names and addresses of minor children will be automatically removed from the List when they attain 19 years of age. A minor must file an original application in his own behalf if he desires to continue his name on the List after reaching 19 years of age.

Customs

19 U.S.C. 1305   Immoral Articles; Prohibition of Importation

(a) All persons are prohibited from importing into the United States from any foreign country any book, pamphlet, paper, writing, advertisement, circular, print, picture, or drawing containing any matter advocating or urging treason or insurrection against the United States, or forcible resistance to any law of the United States, or containing any threat to take the life of or inflict bodily harm upon any person in the United States, or any obscene book, pamphlet, paper, writing, advertisement, circular, print, picture, drawing, or other representation, figure, or image on or of paper or other material, or any cast, instrument, or other article which is obscene or immoral, or any drug or medicine or any article whatever for causing unlawful abortion, or any lottery ticket, or any printed paper that may be used as a lottery ticket, or any advertisement of any lottery. No such articles whether imported separately or contained in packages with other goods entitled to entry, shall be admitted to entry; and all such articles and, unless it appears to the satisfaction of the appropriate customs officer that the obscene or other prohibited articles contained in the package were inclosed therein without the knowledge or consent of the importer, owner, agent, or consignee, the entire contents of the package in which such articles are contained, shall be subject to seizure and forfeiture as hereinafter provided: *Provided,* That the drugs hereinbefore mentioned, when imported in bulk and not put up for any of the purposes hereinbefore specified, are excepted from the operation of this subdivision: *Provided further,* That the Secretary of the Treasury may, in his discretion, admit the so-called classics or books of recognized and established literary or scientific merit, but may, in his discretion, admit such classics or books only when imported for noncommercial purposes.

Upon the appearance of any such book or matter at any customs office, the same shall be seized and held by the appropriate customs officer to await the judgment of the district court as hereinafter provided; and no protest shall be taken to the United States Customs Court from the decision of such customs officer. Upon the seizure of such book or matter such customs officer shall transmit information thereof to the district attorney of the district in which is situated the office at which such seizure has taken place, who shall institute proceedings in the district court for the forfeiture, confiscation, and destruction of the book or matter seized. Upon the adjudication that such book or matter thus seized is of the character the entry of which is by this section prohibited, it shall be ordered destroyed and shall be destroyed. Upon adjudication that such book or matter thus seized is not of the character the entry of which is by this section prohibited, it shall not be excluded from entry under the provisions of this section.

In any such proceeding any party in interest may upon demand have the facts at issue determined by a jury and any party may have an appeal or the right of review as in the case of ordinary actions or suits.

22 U.S.C. 611 (j)   Definitions

As used in and for the purpose of this subchapter

(j) The term "political propaganda" includes any oral, visual, graphic, written, pictorial, or other communication or expression by any person (1) which is reasonably adapted to, or which the person disseminating the same believes will, or which he intends to, prevail upon, i idoctrinate, convert, induce, or in any other way influence a recipient or any section of the public within the United States with reference to the political or public interests, policies, or relations of a government of a foreign country or a foreign political party or with reference to the foreign policies of the United States or promote in the United States racial, religious, or social dissensions, or (2) which advocates, advises, instigates, or promotes any racial, social, political, or religious disorder, civil riot, or other conflict involving the use of force or violence in any other American republic or the overthrow of any government or political subdivision of any other American republic by any means involving the use of force or violence. As used in this subsection the term "disseminating" includes transmitting or causing to be transmitted in the United States mails or by any means or instrumentality of interstate or foreign commerce or offering or causing to be offered in the United States mails.

22 U.S.C. 614   Filing and Labeling of Political Propaganda

(a) Every person within the United States who is an agent of a foreign principal and required to register under the provisions of this subchapter and who transmits or causes to be transmitted in the United States mails or by any means or instrumentality of interstate or foreign commerce any political propaganda for or in the interests of such foreign principal (i) in the form of prints, or (ii) in any other form which is reasonably adapted to being, or which he believes will be, or which he intends to be, disseminated or circulated among two or more persons shall, not later than forty-eight hours after the beginning of the transmittal thereof, file with the Attorney General two copies thereof and a statement, duly signed by or on behalf of such agent, setting forth full information as to the places, times, and extent of such transmittal.

(b) It shall be unlawful for any person within the United States who is an agent of a foreign principal and required to register under the provisions of this subchapter to transmit or cause to be transmitted in the United States mails or by any means or instrumentality of interstate or foreign commerce any political propaganda for or in the interests of such foreign principal (i) in the form of prints, or (ii) in any other form which is reasonably adapted to being, or which he believes will be or which he intends to be, disseminated or circulated among two or more persons, unless such political propaganda is conspicuously marked at its beginning with, or prefaced or accompanied by, a true and accurate statement, in the language or languages used in such political propaganda, setting forth the relationship or connection between the person transmitting the political propaganda or causing it to be transmitted and such propaganda; that the person transmitting such political propaganda or causing it to be transmitted is registered under this subchapter with the Department of Justice, Washington, District of Columbia, as an agent of a foreign principal, together with the name and address of such agent of a foreign principal and of such foreign principal; that, as required by this subchapter, his registration statement is available for inspection at and copies of such political propaganda are being filed with the Department of Justice; and that registration of agents of foreign principals required by the subchapter does not indicate approval by the United States Government of the contents of their political propaganda. The Attorney General, having due regard for the national security and the public interest, may by regulation prescribe the language or languages and the manner and form in which such statement shall be made and require the inclusion of such other information contained in the registration statement identifying such agent of a foreign principal and such political propaganda and its sources as may be appropriate.

(c) The copies of political propaganda required by this subchapter to be filed with the Attorney General shall be available for public inspection under such regulations as he may prescribe.

(d) For purposes of the Library of Congress, other than for public distribution, the Secretary of the Treasury and the Postmaster General are authorized, upon the request of the Librarian of Congress, to forward to the Library of Congress fifty copies, or as many fewer thereof as are available, of all foreign prints determined to be prohibited entry under the provisions of section 1305 of Title 19 and of all foreign prints excluded from the mails under authority of section 343 of Title 18.

Notwithstanding the provisions of section 1305 of Title 19 and of section 343 of Title 18, the Secretary of the Treasury is authorized to permit the entry and the Postmaster General is authorized to permit the transmittal in the mails of foreign prints imported for governmental purposes by authority or for the use of the United States or for the use of the Library of Congress.

(e) It shall be unlawful for any person within the United States who is an agent of a foreign principal required to register under the provisions of this subchapter to transmit, convey, or otherwise furnish to any agency or official of the Government (including a Member or committee of either House of Congress) for or in the interests of such foreign principal any political propaganda or to request from any such agency or official for or in the interests of such foreign principal any information or advice with respect to any matter pertaining to the political or public interests, policies or relations of a foreign country or of a political party or pertaining to the foreign or domestic policies of the United States unless the propaganda or the request is prefaced or accompanied by a true and accurate statement to the effect that such person is registered as an agent of such foreign principal under this subchapter.

(f) Whenever any agent of a foreign principal required to register under this subchapter appears before any committee of Congress to testify for or in the interests of such foreign principal, he shall, at the time of such appearance, furnish the committee with a copy of his most recent registration statement filed with the

Department of Justice as an agent of such foreign principal for inclusion in the records of the committee as part of his testimony. As amended July 4, 1966, Pub.L 89-486, §4, 80 Stat. 246.

22 U.S.C. 618 (d)   Nonmailable matter

(d) The Postmaster General may declare to be nonmailable any communication or expression falling within clause (2) of section 611(j) of this title in the form of prints or in any other form reasonably adapted to, or reasonably appearing to be intended for, dissemination or circulation among two or more persons, which is offered or caused to be offered for transmittal in the United States mails to any person or persons in any other American republic by any agent of a foreign principal, if the Postmaster General is informed in writing by the Secretary of State that the duly accredited diplomatic representative of such American republic has made written representation to the Department of State that the admission or circulation of such communication or expression in such American republic is prohibited by the laws thereof and has requested in writing that its transmittal thereto be stopped.

19 C.F.R. 12.40   Immoral Articles: Seizure; Disposition of Seized Articles; Reports to U.S. Attorney*

(a) Any book, pamphlet, paper, writing, advertisement, circular, print, picture, or drawing containing any matter advocating or urging treason or insurrection against the United States or forcible resistance to any law of the United States, or containing any threat to take the life of or inflict bodily harm upon any person in the United States, seized under section 305, Tariff Act of 1930, shall be transmitted to the United States attorney for his consideration and action.

(b) Upon the seizure of articles or matter prohibited entry by section 305, Tariff Act of 1930 (with the exception of the matter described in paragraph (a) of this section), a notice of the seizure of such articles or matter shall be sent to the consignee or addressee.

(c) When articles of the class covered by paragraph (b) of this section are of small value and no criminal intent is apparent, a blank assent to forfeiture, Customs Form 4607, shall be sent with the notice of seizure. Upon receipt of the assent to forfeiture duly executed, the articles shall be destroyed if not needed for official use and the case closed.

(d) In the case of a repeated offender or when the facts indicate that the importation was made deliberately with intent to evade the law, the facts and evidence shall be submitted to the United States attorney for consideration of prosecution of the offender as well as an action in rem under section 305 for condemnation of the articles.

(e) If the importer declines to execute an assent to forfeiture of the articles other than those mentioned in paragraph (a) of this section and fails to submit, within 30 days after being notified of his privilege so to do, a petition under section 618, Tariff

*Customs Federal Regulations.

Act of 1930, for the remission of the forfeiture and permission to export the seized merchandise, information concerning the seizure shall be submitted to the United States attorney in accordance with the provisions of the second paragraph of section 305 (a), Tariff Act of 1930, for the institution of condemnation proceedings.

(f) If seizure is made of books or other articles which do not contain obscene matter but contain information or advertisements relative to means of causing abortion, the procedure outlined in paragraphs (b), (c), (d), and (e) of this section shall be followed.

(g) In any case when a book is seized as being obscene and the importer declines to execute an assent to forfeiture on the ground that the book is a classic, or of recognized and established literary or scientific merit, a petition addressed to the Secretary of the Treasury with evidence to support the claim may be filed by the importer for release of the book. Mere unsupported statements or allegations will not be considered. If the ruling is favorable, release of such book shall be made only to the ultimate consignee.

(h) Whenever it clearly appears from information, instructions, advertisements enclosed with or appearing on any drug or medicine or its immediate or other container, or otherwise that such drug or medicine is intended for inducing abortion, such drug or medicine shall be detained or seized.

(Secs. 305, 624, 46 Stat. 688, as amended, 759; 19 U.S.C. 1305, 1624) [28 F.R. 14710, Dec. 31, 1963, as amended by T.D. 71-165, S6 F.R. 12209, June 29, 1971; T.D. 76-261, 41 FR 39022, Sept. 14, 1976]

19 C.F.R. 12.41   Prohibited Films

(a) Importers of films, shall certify on Customs Form 3291 that the imported films contain no obscene or immoral matter, nor any matter advocating or urging treason or insurrection against the United States or forcible resistance to any law of the United States, nor any threat to take the life or inflict bodily harm upon any person in the United States. When imported films are claimed to be free of duty as American goods returned, this certification may be made on Customs Form 3311 in the space designated "Remarks" in lieu of on Form 3291.

(b) Films exposed abroad by a foreign concern or individual shall be previewed by a qualified employee of the Customs Service before release. In case such films are imported as undeveloped negatives exposed abroad, the approximate number of feet shall be ascertained by weighing before they are allowed to be developed and printed and such film shall be previewed by a qualified employee of the Customs Service after having been developed and printed.

(c) Any objectionable film shall be detained pending instructions from Headquarters, U.S. Customs Service or a decision of the court as to its final disposition.

(Sec. 305, 46 Stat. 688, as amended: 19 U.S.C. 1305)

Selected Readings and References

The following list of periodicals, books, and pamphlets represents a mere sample of the vast literature concerning censorship. Emphasis here is on U.S. publications that are in print or easily available as this edition of *Banned Books* goes to press. Many additional, older sources will be found in the bibliography of the 1970 edition. Those titles that were especially helpful in preparing this revised edition are marked with an asterisk (*).

Periodicals

American Libraries. Chicago: American Library Association.

*Library Journal. New York: Bowker.

*Newsletter on Intellectual Freedom. Chicago: American Library Association.

*Publishers Weekly. New York: Bowker.

*School Library Journal. New York: Bowker.

Books and Pamphlets

Adams, Michael. *Censorship: The Irish Experience.* University, Ala.: University of Alabama Press, 1968.

Alpert, Hollis et al. *Censorship For and Against.* New York: Hart Publishing Co., 1971.

American Library Association, Intellectual Freedom Committee. *Freedom of Inquiry: Supporting the Library Bill of Rights: Proceedings of the Conference on Intellectual Freedom, January 23–24, 1965. Washington, D.C.* Chicago: American Library Association, 1965.

Berninghausen, David K. *The Flight from Reason: Essays on Intellectual Freedom in the Academy, the Press, and the Library.* Chicago: American Library Association, 1975.

*Blanshard, Paul. *The Right to Read: The Battle against Censorship.* Boston: Beacon Press, 1955.

Bradbury, Ray. *Fahrenheit 451.* New York: Simon and Schuster, 1967; Ballantine, 1976.

Busha, Charles H., ed. *An Intellectual Freedom Primer*. Littleton, Colo.: Libraries Unlimited, 1977.

Chafee, Zechariah. *Free Speech in the United States*. Cambridge, Mass.: Harvard University Press, 1941; New York: Atheneum, 1969.

Clor, Harry M. *Obscenity and Public Morality: Censorship in a Liberal Society*. Chicago: University of Chicago Press, 1969 and 1971.

*Craig, Alec. *The Banned Books of England and Other Countries*. London: George Allen & Unwin, 1962. Published in the United States as *Suppressed Books*. Foreword by Morris L. Ernst. Cleveland: World Publishing Co., 1963.

*Daily, Jay E. *The Anatomy of Censorship*. New York: Marcel Dekker, 1973.

DeGrazia, Edward, comp. *Censorship Landmarks*. New York: Bowker, 1969.

Downs, Robert B., ed. *The First Freedom: Liberty and Justice in the World of Books and Reading*. Chicago: American Library Association, 1960.

Ernst, Morris L., and Lindey, Alexander. *The Censor Marches On*. New York: Doubleday, 1940; New York: DaCapo, 1971.

Ernst, Morris L., and Schwartz, Alan U. *Censorship: The Search for the Obscene*. New York: Macmillan, 1964.

Ernst, Morris L., and Seagle, William. *To the Pure: A Study of Obscenity and the Censor*. New York: Viking Press, 1928.

Fiske, Marjorie. *Book Selection and Censorship: A Study of School and Public Libraries in California*. Berkeley: University of California Press, 1968.

Franklin, Benjamin. *An Apology for Printers* (1731). Various editions, e.g., Randolph Goodman, ed. Washington, D.C.: Acropolis Books, 1975.

Gallagher, Neil. *How to Stop the Pornography Plague*. Minneapolis: Bethany Fellowship, 1977.

Gardner, Harold C., S.J. *Catholic Viewpoint on Censorship*. Garden City, N.Y.: Hanover House, 1958.

Haney, R. W. *Comstockery in America: Patterns of Censorship and Control*. Boston: Beacon Press, 1960; New York: DaCapo, 1974.

Hohenberg, John. *Free Press, Free People: The Best Cause*. New York: Columbia University Press, 1971; Glencoe, Ill.: Free Press, 1973.

Holbrook, David, ed. *The Case against Pornography*. LaSalle, Ill.: Open Court, 1973.

Hughes, Douglas A., ed. *Perspective on Pornography*. New York: St. Martin's Press, 1970.

Jennison, Peter S. *Freedom to Read* (Public Affairs Pamphlet No. 344). New York: Public Affairs Committee, 1963.

Kilpatrick, James J. *The Smut Peddlers*. New York: Doubleday, 1960.

Kronhausen, Eberhard, and Kronhausen, Phyllis. *Pornography and the Law*. New York: Ballantine Books, 1960.

Levy, Leonard W., ed. *Freedom of the Press from Zenger to Jefferson: Early American Libertarian Theories*. Indianapolis: Bobbs-Merrill, 1966.

Loth, David. *The Erotic in Literature*. New York: Messner, 1961; New York: Macfadden, 1962.

* McClellan, Grant S., ed. *Censorship in the United States.* New York: Wilson, 1967.

*McCormick, John, and MacInnes, Mairi, eds. *Versions of Censorship: An Anthology.* Garden City, N.Y.: Doubleday (Anchor Books), 1962.

McCoy, Ralph E. *Freedom of the Press: An Annotated Bibliography.* Urbana, Ill.: University of Illinois Press, 1968.

McKeon, Richard. "Censorship." In *The New Encyclopaedia Britannica: Macropaedia,* vol. 3, 15th ed. Chicago: Encyclopaedia Britannica, Inc., 1974, pp. 1083–1090.

Marnell, William H. *The Right to Know: Media and the Common Good.* New York: Seabury Press, 1973.

Milton, John. *Areopagitica: A Speech for the Liberty of Unlicenc'd Printing, to the Parliament of England* (1644). Various editions, e.g., K. M. Leo, ed. London and New York: Oxford University Press, 1973.

Moon, Eric, ed. *Book Selection and Censorship in the Sixties.* New York: Bowker, 1969.

Nelson, H. L., ed. *Freedom of the Press from Hamilton to the Warren Court.* Indianapolis, Ind.: Bobbs-Merrill, 1963.

Nelson, Jack, and Roberts, Gene, Jr. *The Censors and the Schools.* Boston: Little, Brown, 1963.

Oboler, Eli. *The Fear of the Word: Censorship and Sex.* Metuchen, N.J.: Scarecrow Press, 1974.

Office for Intellectual Freedom, American Library Association, comp. *Intellectual Freedom Manual.* Chicago: ALA, 1974, 1975.

Orwell, George. *1984.* New York: Harcourt, 1949; NAL, 1961.

*Paul, James C. N., and Schwartz, Murray L. *Federal Censorship: Obscenity in the Mail.* New York: Free Press of Glencoe, 1971.

Perrin, Noel. *Dr. Bowdler's Legacy.* New York: Atheneum, 1969.

*Pilpel, Harriet F. *Obscenity and the Constitution.* R. R. Bowker Memorial Lectures, New Series No. 1. New York: Bowker, 1973.

*Rembar, Charles. *The End of Obscenity: The Trials of Lady Chatterley, Tropic of Cancer, and Fanny Hill.* New York, Random House, 1968; Bantam Books, 1969; rev. ed., Simon and Schuster, 1970.

* *The Report of the Commission on Obscenity and Pornography,* William B. Lockhart, chmn. Washington, D.C.: U.S. Government Printing Office, 1970; New York: Random House, 1970; Bantam Books, 1970.

Rist, Ray C. *The Pornography Controversy: Changing Standards in American Life.* New Brunswick, N.J.: Transaction Books (Rutgers, The State University), 1974.

Rutherford, Livingston. *John Peter Zenger: His Press, His Trial, and a Bibliography of Zenger Imprints.* Various editions; e.g., New York: Arno, 1970.

Schroeder, Theodore A. *A Free Speech Bibliography.* New York: Burt Franklin, 1969.

Shapiro, Morton, ed. *The Pentagon Papers and the Courts.* San Francisco: Chandler Publishing Co., 1974.

Solzhenitsyn, Aleksandr. *A Documentary Record, with the Nobel Prize Lecture.* Bloomington, Ind.: University of Indiana Press, 1973.

Spicer, George W. *The Supreme Court and Fundamental Freedoms*, 2nd ed. New York: Appleton Century Crofts, 1967.

Stanek, Lou Willett. *Censorship: A Guide for Teachers, Librarians, and Others Concerned with Intellectual Freedom.* New York: Dell, 1976.

*Sunderland, Lane V. *Obscenity, the Court, the Congress, and the President's Commission.* Washington, D.C.: American Enterprise Institute for Public Policy Research, 1974.

Swayze, Harold. *Political Control of Literature in the USSR, 1946–1959.* Cambridge, Mass.: Harvard University Press, 1962.

*Thomas, Donald. *A Long Time Burning: The History of Literary Censorship in England.* New York: Praeger, 1969.

Wicker, Tom. *On Press.* New York: Viking, 1978.

Index